The Economic Civil Rights Movement

Economic inequalities have been perhaps the most enduring problem facing African Americans since the civil rights movement, despite the attention they have received from activists. Although the civil rights movement dealt successfully with injustices like disenfranchisement and segregated public accommodations, economic disparities between blacks and whites remain sharp, and the wealth gap between the two groups has widened in the twenty-first century.

The Economic Civil Rights Movement is a collection of thirteen original essays that analyze the significance of economic power to the black freedom struggle by exploring how African Americans fought for increased economic autonomy in an attempt to improve the quality of their lives. It covers a wide range of campaigns ranging from the World War II era through the civil rights and black power movements and beyond. The unfinished business of the civil rights movement primarily is economic. This book turns back in time to examine the ways African Americans have engaged this continuing challenge.

Michael Ezra is a Professor in the American Multicultural Studies Department at Sonoma State University, USA.

Routledge Studies in African American History

1 **The Economic Civil Rights Movement**
African Americans and the Struggle for Economic Power
Edited by Michael Ezra

The Economic Civil Rights Movement

African Americans and the Struggle for Economic Power

Edited by Michael Ezra

LONDON AND NEW YORK

First published 2013
by Routledge
711 Third Avenue, New York, NY 10017

Simultaneously published in the UK
by Routledge
2 Park Square, Milton Park, Abingdon, Oxfordshire OX14 4RN

Routledge is an imprint of the Taylor and Francis Group, an informa business

First issued in paperback 2015

Library of Congress Cataloging-in-Publication Data

The economic civil rights movement : African Americans and the struggle for economic power / edited by Michael Ezra.
pages cm. — (Routledge studies in African American history ; 1)
Includes bibliographical references and index.
1. African Americans—Economic conditions. 2. Equality—Economic aspects—United States. 3. Income distribution—United States. 4. African Americans—Civil rights. 5. Civil rights movements—United States. I. Ezra, Michael, 1972–
E185.8.E33 2013
323.1196'073—dc23
2012051038

ISBN 978-0-415-53736-0 (hbk)
ISBN 978-1-138-95248-5 (pbk)
ISBN 978-0-203-11047-8 (ebk)

Typeset in Sabon
by IBT Global.

Contents

Introduction: The Economic Dimensions of the Black Freedom Struggle 1
MICHAEL EZRA

PART I
African American Campaigns for Economic Power Before the Civil Rights Movement, 1925–1954

1 A. Philip Randolph, Early Pioneer: The Brotherhood of Sleeping Car Porters, National Negro Congress, and the March on Washington Movement 9
RHONDA JONES

2 Mary McLeod Bethune, the National Council of Negro Women, and the Prewar Push for Equal Opportunity in Defense Projects 22
GLORIA-YVONNE

3 The Brooklyn Urban League and Equal Employment Opportunity in New York's War Industries 35
CARLA J. DUBOSE

4 Early Economic Civil Rights in Washington, DC: The New Negro Alliance, Howard University, and the Interracial Workshop 46
DEREK CHARLES CATSAM

5 The Moral Economy of Postwar Radical Interracial Summer Camping 58
ORION A. TEAL

6 The NAACP Boycott of the *Amos 'n' Andy* Show 75
JUSTIN T. LORTS

PART II

African American Campaigns for Economic Power During the Civil Rights Era and Beyond

7 Economic Civil Rights Activism in Pensacola, Florida 91
J. MICHAEL BUTLER

8 Muhammad Ali's Main Bout: African American Economic Power and the World Heavyweight Title 104
MICHAEL EZRA

9 Operation Breadbasket in Chicago: Between Civil Rights and Black Capitalism 125
ENRICO BELTRAMINI

10 Progress Plaza: Leon Sullivan, Zion Investment Associates, and Black Power in a Philadelphia Shopping Center 137
STEPHANIE DYER

11 Black Power on the Factory Floor 154
KIERAN W. TAYLOR

12 Acquiring "A Piece of the Action": The Rise and Fall of the Black Capitalism Movement 172
IBRAM H. ROGERS

13 Soul City, North Carolina and the Business of Black Power 188
CHRISTOPHER B. STRAIN

Contributors 205
Index 209

Introduction

The Economic Dimensions of the Black Freedom Struggle

Michael Ezra

The Economic Civil Rights Movement explores the significance of economic power in the black freedom struggle. It chronicles how African Americans from the World War II era through the 1970s, a period often referred to as "the long civil rights movement," challenged economic discrimination in order to improve the quality of their lives. The book is divided into two sections. The first concentrates on black economic freedom campaigns prior to the Supreme Court's 1954 *Brown v. Board of Education* decision, because this watershed frequently is used to mark the onset of what scholars have referred to as the "classical" or "traditional" phase of the civil rights movement. The second highlights black activism after *Brown*.

By definition a civil rights movement measures citizenry by laws and liberties, but the black freedom struggle has always had a significant economic component, and economic concerns have guided its direction. Economic power helped African Americans defend the gains they made via the courts and politics. The Montgomery Bus Boycott, which used the collective strength of black buying power as a weapon, is a good example. In desegregating Montgomery's buses, the city's leaders made a rational financial decision. Montgomery's African American community demonstrated to them that whites could no longer afford the economic cost of segregated buses. But the boycott was more than that. African Americans didn't simply want to ride buses alongside whites; they also wanted to drive buses and own bus companies. Desegregation was merely a starting point for achieving economic equality. Whereas sit-ins ostensibly tested laws segregating public accommodations, they were never defined entirely by desegregation. Southern blacks didn't want merely to eat at cafés and luncheonettes. They wanted to work at them and own them, too. *The Economic Civil Rights Movement* gives voice to this perspective and illustrates how battles for economic freedom have always accompanied the legal and political campaigns highlighted in most accounts of the civil rights movement.

A common misconception is that the traditional civil rights movement, prior to the late 1960s, did not reckon with factors like discriminatory trade unions, high unemployment rates, inadequate housing and health care for the poor, and educational disparities. Martin Luther King, Jr.'s failed 1966 Chicago campaign, so the story goes, allegedly proved the movement's inability to tackle these inequalities and as a result the movement took a decisive turn as black power advocates deemphasized political and judicial battles to instead focus on building up African American economic power.

Although many black activists stressed such issues by the end of the 1960s, it is incorrect to assert that civil rights leaders during the 1950s and early 1960s did not have their eyes on the economic prize. King's 1963 "I Have a Dream" speech took place at the March on Washington for Jobs and Freedom, a demonstration first envisioned by African American trade union pioneer A. Philip Randolph a generation earlier. The Student Nonviolent Coordinating Committee's John Lewis told the gathering there, "We march today for jobs and freedom, but we have nothing to be proud of, for hundreds and thousands of our brothers are not here. They have no money for their transportation, for they are receiving starvation wages or no wages at all. While we stand here, there are sharecroppers on the Delta of Mississippi who are out in the fields working for less than three dollars a day for twelve hours of work."

Although activists have always focused on economic issues, income and wealth inequalities have been perhaps the most enduring problem facing African Americans since the civil rights movement. There are many injustices that the civil rights movement dealt with like disenfranchisement, segregated public accommodations, and restrictive housing covenants, that have been significantly weakened or even eliminated as a result of the black freedom struggle. But economic disparities between blacks and whites remain significant. African American per capita household wealth, for example, is about one-twentieth that of whites, a gulf that has widened in the twenty-first century. The unfinished agenda of the civil rights movement primarily is economic. Thus this book turns back in time to examine the ways African Americans have engaged this continuing challenge.

Chapter 1, by Rhonda Jones, "A. Philip Randolph, Early Pioneer: The Brotherhood of Sleeping Car Porters, National Negro Congress, and the March on Washington Movement," positions A. Philip Randolph at the center of the pre-World War II black struggle for economic empowerment. From his organizing the Brotherhood of Sleeping Car Porters in 1925, the first major African American trade union, to successfully lobbying President Franklin Roosevelt to end employment discrimination in war industries, Randolph played an unparalleled role in laying the groundwork for the decades of activism that would develop in the years following World War II.

Chapter 2, by gloria-yvonne, "Mary McLeod Bethune, the National Council of Negro Women, and the Prewar Push for Equal Opportunity in Defense Projects," establishes the significance of women in the drive for equal employment on the eve of World War II. Both as individuals with connections to very highest levels of government, like presidential advisor Mary McLeod Bethune, and through organizations like the National

Council of Negro Women, women played indispensable roles in setting the tone for the postwar movement.

Chapter 3, by Carla J. DuBose, "The Brooklyn Urban League and Equal Employment Opportunity in New York's War Industries," chronicles partnerships between the federal government, state anti-discrimination agencies, and local chapters of national organizations like the Urban League, National Negro Congress, and the National Association for the Advancement of Colored People (NAACP). Working with black elected officials and the African American press, these forces desegregated large segments of New York's war industries during the early 1940s. Of particular note was the coalition's successful campaign at the Brooklyn Navy Yard, the largest wartime employer of African Americans.

Chapter 4, by Derek Charles Catsam, "Early Economic Civil Rights in Washington, DC: The New Negro Alliance, Howard University, and the Interracial Workshop," explains how both before and after World War II, the nation's capital was an important site where the black freedom struggle anticipated what would become the classical phase of the civil rights movement. Student-led sit-ins and boycotts of segregated businesses, for example, took place in Washington more than a decade prior to their widespread deployment across the South during the early 1960s.

Chapter 5, by Orion A. Teal, "The Moral Economy of Postwar Radical Interracial Summer Camping," examines interracial summer camps that were run by leftwing white allies of the black freedom struggle. A fierce commitment to interracialism helped some of these camps to survive in the face of the Red Scare, whereas others were unable to navigate their relationships with the local communities that hosted them. The business model of the camps was an ideological one; the product they were selling was an integrated space where youngsters would form antiracist sensibilities.

Chapter 6, by Justin T. Lorts, "The NAACP Boycott of *The Amos 'n' Andy Show*," explores the failed attempt by the NAACP to run *Amos 'n' Andy* off television shortly after its screen debut in the 1950s following decades of success on the radio. It was not white resistance that stymied the NAACP's attempt to get it banned but rather its inability to convince rank-and-file African Americans that the campaign was worth fighting. To the surprise of boycott leaders, black viewers didn't find the show particularly offensive.

Chapter 7, by J. Michael Butler, "Economic Civil Rights Activism in Pensacola, Florida," looks at the desegregation of the city's downtown resulting from a 1962 campaign headed by local ministers. The victory came about despite determined white resistance that included litigation, biased media coverage, and illegal violence. The success in Pensacola came from a winning formula that combined charismatic leadership, an awareness of black consumer strength, the organizational and inspirational power of the black church, and the vigorous participation of young people.

Chapter 8, by Michael Ezra, "Muhammad Ali's Main Bout: African American Economic Power and the World Heavyweight Title," tells the story of Main Bout, Inc., which Muhammad Ali formed in 1966 to control the promotional rights to his title fights and put control of the most lucrative prize in professional sports into the hands of African Americans. From its earliest days, Main Bout faced white resistance, at first from the media and then from politicians and government officials. A national boycott of Main Bout portended its being run out of business once Ali was banned from boxing for draft evasion.

Chapter 9, by Enrico Beltramini, "Operation Breadbasket in Chicago: Between Civil Rights and Black Capitalism," focuses on the economic arm of the Southern Christian Leadership Conference known as Operation Breadbasket. Under the leadership of Jesse Jackson during the early 1970s, it represented the transformation of the black freedom struggle into one where many activists redefined progress in terms of economic power, entrepreneurship, and profit. An essential dilemma for the movement became balancing community empowerment against the difficulties of succeeding in business, the increasing conservatism of the federal government, and an economic recession.

Chapter 10, by Stephanie Dyer, "Progress Plaza: Leon Sullivan, Zion Investment Associates, and Black Power in a Philadelphia Shopping Center," recounts the rise of Progress Plaza, the first African American-owned and -operated shopping center. Progress Plaza's investors and directors initially were dedicated to principles of community empowerment but eventually profits became their primary concern. In order to survive, Progress Plaza had to cater to chain stores run by national corporations. Progress Plaza became, ironically, a vehicle for dollars to flow away from the neighborhood it was created to empower economically.

Chapter 11, by Kieran W. Taylor, "Black Power on the Factory Floor," highlights the importance of organized labor to the African American struggle for economic equality. Black activists infiltrated factories in an effort to mobilize workers, resulting in an unprecedented number of strikes during the prosperous early days of the 1970s. As the country fell into recession, however, radicals miscalculated the willingness of workers to risk their jobs in times of economic uncertainty. Although the contemporary labor movement failed to reach a critical mass, working-class activism remains one of the most vital legacies of the civil rights movement.

Chapter 12, by Ibram H. Rogers, "Acquiring 'A Piece of the Action': The Rise and Fall of the Black Capitalism Movement," investigates the national black capitalism movement from 1965–74 that was galvanized by grassroots activism and federal government support, primarily from the Nixon Administration. Proponents asserted that it put unprecedented autonomy into the hands of African American entrepreneurs and the communities they empowered, but critics warned that black capitalism was a cooptation of the black power values that had given it rise in the first place. The withdrawal of federal support and the recession of the 1970s undermined the black capitalism movement.

Chapter 13, by Christopher B. Strain, "Soul City, North Carolina and the Business of Black Power," explains how former Congress of Racial Equality National Director Floyd McKissick led the movement to create Soul City, the first sustainable black community built from scratch in the twentieth century, assisted by the federal government. Soul City's failure to meet expectations was not necessarily a result of the project's lack of viability. Hostile politicians and a skeptical media targeted Soul City, while the federal government, whose backing was both promised and vital to the project's development, abandoned it. Thus Soul City stagnated and never fulfilled its potential.

Part I

African American Campaigns for Economic Power Before the Civil Rights Movement, 1925–1954

1 A. Philip Randolph, Early Pioneer

The Brotherhood of Sleeping Car Porters, National Negro Congress, and the March on Washington Movement

Rhonda Jones

As one of the key links between the black protest movement of the early twentieth century and the classical 1960s phase of the civil rights movement, A. Philip Randolph's five-decade tenure as an organizer inspired countless African Americans to pursue freedom through economic empowerment. Although battles for political recognition have always been important, Randolph's emphasis on the workplace opened up a battleground that would become central to the movement. Randolph was not only concerned with the black rank-and-file gaining their share of the pie; he also knew that the very survival of the black freedom struggle depended on adequate funding for the direct-action campaigns that drove it. Even the smallest tasks associated with petitioning for fair and equitable wages, civil inclusion, enfranchisement, and equal protection required financial backing and manpower. Randolph's pursuit of "freedom dollars" came primary from black constituents, although occasionally circumstances caused him to pursue external donations.

Randolph's activism began when in 1925 he organized the Brotherhood of Sleeping Car Porters (BSCP) in New York. The Pullman Company had employed the porters, who labored in an environment akin to sharecropping, since the late 1890s. They worked twenty-one-hour shifts, earning about eighteen cents per hour while traveling approximately 11,000 miles monthly. Their uniforms, food, shoe polish, and other necessities were deducted from their pay. Randolph and the BSCP won a major victory in 1937, finally securing a labor contract and collective bargaining rights from Pullman. But with unionization came expenses. The BSCP lacked manpower, funding, and adequate facilities. Seeking $50,000 in start-up costs, Randolph orchestrated a two-pronged fundraising campaign. BSCP representatives traversed Pullman's routes, soliciting appeals for initiation fees and membership dues from workmen. The organization also requested aid from the general public, through individual appeals to wealthy sympathizers and via small grants from the Garland Fund, otherwise known as the American Fund for Public Service. This approach would characterize Randolph's early leadership. Get as much money from blacks as possible and retain as much self-sufficiency as you can before soliciting support from outsiders.

At the heart of BSCP activity were Women's Economic Councils (WEC) made up primarily of porter wives, mothers, daughters, and widows. These auxiliaries collected dues, secured meeting halls, and distributed propaganda for BSCP locals. WECs also took part in direct action. Members walked picket lines and educated trade unionists about the advantages of cooperative buying, thrift, and responsible consumerism. There was also important behind-the-scenes work to be done. Committees generated thousands of dollars for the fledging union through raffles, dances, parties, picnics, flea markets, and card tournaments where they charged admission and sold refreshments. WECs also coordinated events with businesses. A series of 1928 benefits in New York and Philadelphia, for example, netted nearly $6,000 for the BSCP. WECs would remain significant to the BSCP even after the BSCP secured its labor contract in 1937 and existing WECs were reorganized into forty-four Ladies' Auxiliary chapters. Concentrating on fundraising in order to ensure the BSCP's financial stability, Ladies' Auxiliaries collected membership dues and held social events that raised thousands of dollars.[1]

As non-employees, WEC members were somewhat insulated from Pullman's threats and other anti-union forces, although they were not completely shielded. The husband of the St. Louis WEC chapter president was furloughed when an informant reported her affiliation. The family's insurance was also revoked. A St. Paul BSCP member was terminated because his wife was the recording secretary of the local WEC. At times BSCP loyalty splintered households and pitted husbands against wives. Pullman maid Mary Frances Albrier asserted, "A lot of black women didn't understand that the union was fighting for porter families to have a more abundant life. Some of the men would pay and some of the wives would be very upset because they were afraid. . . . They were naturally frightened because their families would suffer, and they didn't feel it was worth fighting and exposing themselves."[2]

The BSCP relied on its members for funding, but it also responded reciprocally to their requests for aid and support in times of need. The union sponsored soup kitchens and rent parties for workers laid off during the Great Depression or fired because of their union activities. Such action not only sustained aggrieved individuals, but also bolstered community morale. The BSCP's annual ball regularly assisted vulnerable locals. Its headquarters, located in Harlem, served as a community center. It offered classes four days a week and every Saturday afternoon provided an attorney whose *pro bono* legal advice allowed the BSCP to secure more than 1,631 cases of relief and 147 old-age security pensions on behalf of Harlem residents.[3]

NATIONAL NEGRO CONGRESS

The union was politically active throughout the Depression, including a key role in the National Negro Congress (NNC). The BSCP identified and publicized racial inequities in New Deal economic recovery programs. The economic aspects of social justice campaigns was the theme of a 1933 conference of academics and intellectuals that resulted in a condemnation of the National Association for the Advancement of Colored People (NAACP) for its limited stance on economic issues and a call for a new organization that would forge alliances between the African American middle and laboring classes. Spurred by this, BSCP President Randolph and 250 other prominent individuals, including John P. Davis, Executive Secretary of the Joint Committee of National Recovery, political scientist Dr. Ralph Bunche, and the Urban League's Lester Granger, formed the NNC in 1935.[4]

The NNC was an umbrella organization that sought not to replicate the function of the several hundred existing groups that were defenders of civil liberties but instead to federate them and identify their common directions. Randolph was appointed NNC President. Davis became its executive secretary. Ella Baker, whose own legendary organizing career paralleled Randolph's, was named director of publicity. The NNC petitioned for anti-lynching legislation, sought patronage for black businesses, addressed the plight of oppressed people abroad, drummed up support for Ethiopia, and strategized about trade unions and black labor. Although its founders emphasized that African Americans would sustain the organization, they also sought patronage from white organizations that provided entry into the corridors of power.[5]

The planning of the NNC's first convention provided a potential template for future fundraising efforts by cultivating grassroots black support without ignoring more significant sums that might come from sympathetic whites. The gathering was held in Chicago in 1936 and would cost $10,000, including $125 to rent the Eighth Regiment Armory for five days; nearly $5,000 for supplies and employees; and $1,000 for travel. The NNC spent $1,200 on printing. There were pamphlets, postcards, stationary, placards, posters, and pre-convention newsletters. On top of this was $1,000 more for postage and handling charges. In Harlem, Roi Ottley of the *New York Amsterdam News* and Reverend Adam Clayton Powell of Abyssinian Baptist Church organized a finance committee. Teams of African American churches, lodges, businesses, labor unions, fraternities, sororities, and women's clubs were organized in Richmond, Detroit, Pittsburgh, Baltimore, Washington, and Chicago. Davis also applied for a $5,000 grant from the American Fund for Public Service. The NNC hoped that these sources, in addition to proceeds from five-, ten-, and twenty-five-cent stamps, sales of the pamphlet "Let Us Build a National Negro Congress," and donations and collections from individuals and local groups would cover the convention's expenses.[6]

Randolph's and the BSCP's belief in trade unionism's centrality to African American emancipation characterized convention rhetoric. In his presidential address, Randolph explained how the struggle for freedom was enmeshed with worker dignity, fair wages, and the right to organize.

Economic self-determination was the key, he believed. The delegation must never put "their problems for solution down at the feet of their white sympathetic allies which has been and is the common fashion of old school Negro leadership, for in the final analysis, salvation of the Negro, like the workers, must come from within."[7]

More than 5,000 people attended the opening session. There were 817 participants representing 585 organizations. Conventioneers came from nearly thirty states and included laborers, black nationalists, Republicans, New Dealers, Social Democrats, housewives, clubwomen, trade unionists, fraternal organizations, lodge groups, Garveyites, communists, and representatives from international organizations. Randolph's message resonated with conventioneers, who were charged with making the organization a national voice for civil rights politics. Randolph returned afterward to his responsibilities with the BSCP and in 1937 the Pullman Company agreed to the Brotherhood's union contract. Wages rose, workplace conditions improved, and job security increased.[8]

The NNC carried great momentum out of its first convention and into the field. Members organized labor committees in seventy cities, including New York, Cleveland, and San Francisco. They stumped steel towns and tobacco fields both soliciting help from and providing help to local black communities. Newspaper editorials and press releases reported on the effectiveness of NNC direct-action protest campaigns, contrasting them with the less-aggressive techniques of groups like the NAACP. The NNC developed surveys on labor conditions, which it gave to workers. They proved to be a valuable tool used to analyze community leadership. The NNC utilized the data it gathered from them to pressure ministers, clubs, and organizations to sponsor mass meetings and support black workers who wished to unionize.[9]

The NNC provided a wide range of programs for African Americans. Its organizers cultivated relationships with local leaders and arranged meetings with workers at plants, their homes, and lodge halls. The NNC coordinated parties, picnics, and games for workers' wives and children. It launched campaigns for better housing conditions, led employment drives, and organized rent strikes in Chicago, where it partnered with the International Ladies Garment Workers Union to assist African American women in the clothing industry. It surveyed public parks and recreational facilities and led a ban against offensive and derogatory public school textbooks in Boston. It called for federal investigations of the enslavement of southern blacks that were forced to pick cotton. NNC councils in Richmond helped organize tobacco workers. In several large cities, including Los Angeles, Philadelphia, New York, and Washington, DC, the NNC organized domestic workers and provided free employment services and adult education classes. The NNC carried its program throughout 1937, which culminated in its second annual convention in October in Philadelphia.[10]

The decline of the NNC over the next two years indicated just how important Randolph was to the organization's success. As he turned his attention back to the BSCP, the NNC was unable to sustain what it had initially built. The organization went two-and-a-half years before hosting its third convention in 1940. Internal documents reveal that the NNC was chronically short of funds and financially unstable during this period as its leaders frantically planned the convention. Although the gathering opened with much fanfare, as Washington NNC Chairman Arthur Gray called the meeting to order using a gavel carved from a piece of wood from one of the last slave ships to touch American shores, especially made for the occasion by Hampton Institute students, it would be the organization's last great moment. The convention featured panels on economic security and citizenship. More than 1,200 delegates from twenty states made the trip to Washington, DC.[11]

As ceremonious as the opening of the third convention may have been, all momentum was lost when Randolph announced his official resignation from the NNC, which he felt had become the tool of white communists. From its inception Randolph had exhorted the NNC to remain "essentially a Negro organization and not to become part and parcel of any labor or political group of policy," but now he worried that NNC support of the non-aggression pact between Hitler and Stalin represented the group's take-over by communists. Randolph was also displeased by what he believed to be NNC overreliance on white support. Organizational records show that the NNC depended on funding by trade unions like the Congress of Industrial Organizations to stay afloat. Randolph insisted that the NNC "must depend upon the resources supplied by Negro people alone. . . . [W]here you get your money, you get your ideas and control. When outsiders come in, they dictate the policy of the organization." Convinced that the NNC no longer represented the will of its black constituents, Randolph left:

> I quit the Congress because I saw the Communists were firmly in the saddle . . . I quit because it was not truly a Negro Congress. Of 1,200 delegates 300 were white, which made the Congress look like a joke. It is unthinkable that the Jewish Congress would have Gentiles in it or Catholics would have Protestants or the famous all-Indian Congress would have members native of Africa. Our people cannot afford to add to the handicap of being black, the handicap of being labeled "red."[12]

Ordinary delegates followed Randolph's lead and the organization was soon finished. Rank-and-file members like Pullman maid Frances Mary Albrier, a longtime Randolph disciple who had followed him into the NNC, recalled, "When the radical element came in like they always do . . . they gradually work themselves up into offices. And when you know it, they have taken over your organization. When that happened Randolph sent a message to all of us to withdraw. And we did." With its membership declining, the NNC's programmatic directives of addressing racial inequality and the exploitation of workers succumbed under the weight of the administrative challenges of establishing local councils, sending out charters, generating publicity, distributing leaflets, writing speeches, and fundraising. The death blow was when the House Un-American Activities Committee alleged that the NNC was a red front that was taking donations from the Communist Party.[13]

The harsh realities of the Great Depression had tinged the black freedom struggle with an undeniably economic bent, but as the military conflict in Europe reframed American values, African Americans put aside much of the watchdog consumerism, cooperative buying, and labor campaigns that had characterized the 1930s for legal cases against segregation and voter registration campaigns in the 1940s. Inspired by America's intervention into World War II, many African American activists seized upon the rhetoric of the era to challenge discrimination, injustice, and socioeconomic inequalities in the name of patriotism. Alarmed by the possibility of a military draft, civil rights organizations with Washington connections began to lobby the Roosevelt administration and its "Negro Cabinet" of black advisors about desegregating the military. On September 27, 1940 President Franklin D. Roosevelt met with a group of influential African Americans to discuss the issue of discrimination in the U.S. Armed Forces.[14]

MARCH ON WASHINGTON MOVEMENT

Randolph's blueprint for a national civil rights movement, once envisioned through the NNC, now took the form of mass protests in the nation's capital. As president of one of the most successful and influential African American trade unions, Randolph hoped that positive changes in race relations would materialize through the grassroots efforts of working-class blacks. But trade unions did not have the political reach that a national protest movement would. Frustrated with the Roosevelt Administration's resistance to confronting racism in the Armed Forces, in January 1941 Randolph and the Brotherhood of Sleeping Car Porters announced a proposal to lead 10,000 blacks to the nation's capital to protest Jim Crow in the military and racial discrimination in defense employment. The demonstration would be set for July 1.[15]

The idea quickly gained the support of other civil rights leaders, most notably NAACP Executive Director Walter White. Massive demonstrations in the nation's capital, claimed White, were the best way to "get the whole question of national defense and the Negro probed by the Senate." White threw NAACP backing behind the movement, organizing a day of "National Defense" that involved protest meetings in twenty-three states. Randolph formed a March on Washington Committee in cooperation with the BSCP. Over the first few months of the year, the BSCP organized March offices in New York, Detroit, Los Angeles, and Chicago. Members of the black press and clergy promoted the march while articles in the *Black Worker* kept people abreast of the details. Plans were made to charter 50,000 people to Washington, DC by train and bus.[16]

Randolph enlisted the help of the black press and the NAACP to keep the connections between economic power and equal treatment primary in the minds of rank-and-file African Americans. Disappointed by Roosevelt's continued foot dragging, in March he placed an op-ed piece in the *Afro-American* chain of newspapers headlined, "March of 10,000 Workers on Capital Called Way to Get Jobs." From the march's Harlem headquarters, Randolph coordinated the effort while the NAACP contributed funding and pushed local branches to organize marchers, distribute buttons, and disseminate publicity. He wrote press releases and built momentum for the massive demonstration by providing updates about its tactical plans. Organizers hired Bayard Rustin to galvanize support for the demonstration. Living day-by-day and soliciting funds so he could make it to the next city either by train or hitchhiking, Rustin traveled the country drumming up publicity for the March on Washington. He piggybacked meetings onto NAACP, Urban League, and church gatherings, developing his organizing talents that would become so vital to the classical phase of the civil rights movement during the 1960s.[17]

As the summer approached, Randolph and his allies within civil rights organizations and the black press stepped up their efforts to mobilize support for the demonstration. African American civic and religious leaders pledged their backing; Young Men's Christian Associations (YMCA), fraternal orders, college, youth, and women's clubs, social service agencies, and labor groups all pledged to contribute marchers. Randolph toured southern cities Atlanta, Savannah, Jacksonville, Tampa, and Richmond, bringing his message of economic self-sufficiency. "Negroes can no longer depend on outside agencies as the philanthropic foundation for solving our economic problems," he said. "The future of the Negro depends entirely upon . . . action and one individual cannot act alone. This period calls for mass action, and from mass action there is power."[18]

Organizations and individuals increased their efforts as the demonstration date approached. The over 150 dailies and weeklies that constituted the black press and had a readership base of nearly four million people published bulletins explaining the main objectives of the march. Local committees placed posters in beauty parlors, pool halls, churches, and stores. Magazines and newspapers announced the formation of local committees in eighteen cities including Richmond, Philadelphia, Trenton, Jersey City, Newark, Jacksonville, Atlanta, Chicago, Kansas City, Cleveland, Memphis, St. Louis, Trenton, Baltimore, and Washington, DC. Over 50,000 buttons were sold for ten cents each in New York City to help defray expenses, as every Saturday leading up to the event was set aside as "button day." The publicity campaign took on a national scope. BSCP organizers used union dues to arrange activities, make announcements, and sponsor speaking tours. They held rallies and placed leaflets in taverns, barber shops, grocery stores, and other retail outlets. Alabama organizer E.D. Nixon arranged transportation for locals who would not otherwise be able to get to Washington. Oakland Pullman porters canvassed their community for support. An article in the *New York Amsterdam Star-News* reported that "more than one hundred ministers urged their congregants to join the fight," and that "hundreds of letters from Negro citizens in all walks of life voiced their complete accord with the program and volunteered to do their best to promote the drive." Financial records of the March on Washington Movement New York Committee indicate thousands of small donations to this burgeoning grassroots movement.[19]

There were some who argued that the march would alienate sympathetic Washington allies. A *Pittsburgh Courier* columnist criticized Randolph's "crackpot proposal" because, "Marches on Washington have always failed of their purpose because Congress has regarded them as merely nuisances organized by publicity hounds, job-hunters . . . and consisting of the mob-minded and misguided." Randolph's plan, he argued, to bring perhaps 100,000 people to Washington in the scorching July heat would only create hardships and potential bloodshed for protestors who would be angered by Jim Crow restrictions that would deny them places to eat and sleep. President Roosevelt opposed the march and sent his wife Eleanor to persuade Randolph that the demonstration in Washington could erupt in violence. Randolph vowed that this would not happen, but agreed to meet with the president to discuss a possible settlement.[20]

On June 18, Randolph and Walter White met President Roosevelt at the White House and reached a compromise. The demonstration would be called off, but Roosevelt would sign Executive Order (EO) 8802 on June 25 banning racial discrimination in government defense industries and creating an executive committee to enforce the law. Randolph addressed the NAACP's annual convention that week in Houston to talk about what many called a Pyrrhic victory. Although the order did not address segregation in the Armed Forces, the president's establishment of the Fair Employment Practices Commission (FEPC) ensured a measure of economic citizenship for black workers and firms. By establishing a formal federal commitment to racial economic equality, EO 8802 accomplished one of Randolph's key goals since his early days of unionizing on the behalf of the Brotherhood.[21]

On June 28, via a live national radio broadcast, Randolph announced that the march would be called off. March on Washington Committee members including Walter White, Lester Granger, Rayford Logan, and Adam Clayton Powell, Jr., quickly seconded the decision. Although it could have done more to end widespread discrimination, EO 8802 was first executive order issued by a president on behalf of African Americans since the Emancipation Proclamation, and was thus regarded as a victory in the battle to end unfair employment practices. Randolph disagreed with critics who claimed that he settled for less because the order set a precedent for federal recognition of labor conditions being under the broad purview of civil rights. It affirmed what Randolph had been saying all along, that workers' rights would be at the heart of any successful, broad-based African American freedom movement. Randolph's coalition did not simply dissolve in the wake of Roosevelt's order. It officially named itself the March on Washington Movement (MOWM) and took on a watchdog function to monitor EO 8802 compliance. Randolph warned that federal failure to ensure the enforcement of the order would result in the immediate remobilization of the march. MOWM was rightfully concerned with what seemed to be FEPC's lack of enforcement power.[22]

Meanwhile, Randolph attempted to build the MOWM from a committee into a movement. In late 1941 he began recruiting activists via neighborhood-block-based coalitions. He told reporters that MOWM was short on funds and the only way to staff the organization was on a volunteer basis. Membership would be free. In the last three months of the year, Randolph traveled the nation addressing audiences in Seattle, Spokane, Portland, Oakland, Los Angeles, Salt Lake City, Denver, Omaha, Kansas City, St. Louis, and Chicago. He helped organize local MOWM chapters and explained the MOWM guidelines for organization and structure. Although Randolph had been burned by the NNC, he recognized even while his new coalition was still a committee that it possessed elements of a potentially successful mass movement.[23]

With neither a platform nor any data to determine whether the FEPC was achieving its objectives, MOWM struggled to justify its existence. The *Pittsburgh Courier* again proved hostile: "All we have so far are ear-splitting generalities and blowsy platitudes. We do not have a program. Nor does there exist any machinery for carrying out a program if there was one." Activist Pauli Murray was also critical, writing Randolph a letter in March 1942. "Somewhere between [the] mass meetings of last summer and today," she wrote, "the MOWM has lost ground rather than gained it . . . I get the impression from reading the press that you are a leader without a movement . . . [MOWM is plagued by] internal dissensions, lack of direction, defeatism, inability to carry forward with a sense of crusading for freedom."[24]

Knowing that the organization needed to do something big in order to be taken more seriously, Randolph announced in April a series of MOWM summer protest meetings in prestigious venues like New York's Madison Square Garden, Chicago Stadium, and St. Louis's City Auditorium. This was no bluff, said Randolph, because "substantial sums of money were paid out for rentals and dates were committed for meeting plans." Probably smarting from the stinging public debacle of the National Negro Congress's succumbing to communist influence, Randolph insisted that this grassroots coalition be limited only to African American participants. Randolph's black nationalism and self-reliance was neither separatist nor anti-white but rather the only way to ensure political independence.[25]

Carrying out this vision in which white allies and external contributors were to be excluded required Randolph to mobilize mass black support. Requesting promotional coverage from local newspapers, Randolph estimated that the MOWM would need to spend $3,500 to lease the Garden and $6,000 to cover expenses for Chicago Stadium. Through twenty-five-cent ticket sales, individuals and organizations were encouraged to forward their contributions in advance. Volunteers were recruited "to share in the fight for their freedom" and were encouraged to register at Harlem's Theresa Hotel if they were able "to serve as speakers, typists, ushers, distributors of circulars and to participate in torch light parades." MOWM's New York committee set an important example when it put down a $700 deposit to reserve Madison Square Garden for Tuesday, June 16. MOWM drummed up support through street-corner rallies; slogans like "Mobilize Now! Manhood, Courage, Guts, Determination!" widely appealed to the masses. The adoption of street-corner speakers better suited the needs of working people whose schedules did not always allow for meetings and also promoted the sense of militancy and urgency required to transform talk into action that meetings did not.[26]

Randolph and the MOWM coordinated a massive publicity campaign and a call for volunteers. *The Black Worker* devoted its entire June issue to the event at Madison Square Garden. The rally was set to coincide with a two-hour blackout of Harlem, in order to dramatize mass support. Keeping Harlem "dark, dry, and silent" as a way to convey unity and focus, the blackout symbolized "the economic and political blackout through which our people still stumble and fall in their too-slow progress toward the light in half-free America." MOWM barraged the streets with leaflets, stickers, and signage. Advertisements blared: "Let Us Stop Hitler in Europe and Hitlerism Here in America," "Hear the Greatest Program in History for Negro Rights," "It's Now or Never: Fight for the Right to Live, Work and Be Free," "Admission 25c, Buy Tickets Today. Contribute your might from a penny up to fight the dangerous monster of Jim-Crowism in America." It would be difficult for a local resident to be oblivious to the rally. Although his apparent success enabled him to elicit volunteers for committee planning, fundraising, publicity, logistics, and administrative support, Randolph knew that manpower alone would not be enough to transform these large gatherings into dramatic and forceful protest mobilizations. He needed money. Fundraising, therefore, was even more crucial during this time. BSCP locals sold stamps that proclaimed, "We Are Americans." The NAACP, Urban League, Harlem YMCA, African American unions, fraternal organizations, and other groups pledged support. Black newspapers published long lists of individuals who contributed.[27]

The rally at the Garden on June 16, 1942 and the follow-up event ten days later at Chicago Stadium drew large crowds that indicated strong community support, but MOWM had trouble sustaining the energy these events generated. The 18,000 attendees in New York heard Randolph talk about segregation, employment discrimination, and other offenses against African Americans. The audience was asked "to remember Sikeston, Missouri, the scene of lynching that struck the race more dastardly than treachery by Nippon on Pearl Harbor." Advertising banners for the Chicago rally read, "Fight or Be Slaves!" Businesses were encouraged to participate in a blackout. A squad of 100 civilians wearing arm bands would visit business owners and encourage them to place signs in store windows, close their doors, and turn off the lights out of respect and in solidarity with the black freedom struggle. Non-participatory proprietors would be blacklisted, boycotted, and picketed as enemies to the cause. Twelve thousand people attended the Chicago rally. MOWM tried to use the momentum from these two events to launch a series of local activities in conjunction with BSCP chapters over the next few months. By the end of the summer, however, the organizers who just a few weeks earlier had sold out major arenas now barely drew a crowd. Plans to gather at a ballpark in Washington, DC collapsed and the St. Louis event was canceled.[28]

These failures and President Roosevelt's transference of FEPC oversight to Congress called into question the entire MOWM. Although the organization might have been able to effectively lobby the White House by threatening mass action, it would have a more difficult time influencing Congress. To address its purpose and future, the MOWM scheduled a conference in Detroit in late September 1942. Randolph held firmly that the organization should remain all-black to "insure against whites dominating it in an unhealthy way. We don't want any white people in the MOWM. In fact we're not going to have any. . . . [C]ollective organization among black Americans must come from within to be effective." But Randolph's black nationalism came into conflict with the credos of his most powerful allies, including the NAACP and Urban League. Without their help, the MOWM was little more than a collective of BSCP members. It lasted a few more years, but never regained the promise of those two large rallies in New York and Chicago.[29]

For several decades, the socioeconomic political campaigns of A. Philip Randolph represented a tremendous struggle on behalf of African Americans at a time when the obstacles of Jim Crow segregation, lynching, and white supremacy were near their height. A wide range of sources illustrate how the Brotherhood of Sleeping Car Porters and its Ladies' Auxiliaries, the National Negro Congress, and the March on Washington Movement galvanized a large and faithful following of (mostly) all-black coalitions of progressive-minded organizations, intellectuals, grassroots workers, and others who believed that unionization and protest could be used to ensure racial equality. As the tidal wave of political activity increased, Randolph's affiliate organizations implemented skillful public relations techniques that were used to publicize their cause and solicit funds. Despite geographical boundaries, the revenue raised through button sales, pamphlets, individual memberships, newspaper ads, direct-mail appeals, mass meetings, rallies, special events, and demonstrations generated support for civil rights campaigns. Fostering symbolic affiliations among friends, co-workers, and neighbors, raising funds for Randolph's campaigns not only legitimized the cause, but also eventually transformed solicitation requests from "begging" ventures into skilled business enterprises. Such hard-earned lessons would serve future civil rights trailblazers well. Although the 1940s would end with Randolph's efforts seemingly stalled, they inspired a new generation of activists. Randolph's influence would culminate in 1963, when Martin Luther King, Jr. gave his "I Have a Dream" speech at the Randolph-led March on Washington two decades after it was originally conceived.

NOTES

1. "Thanks from the Brotherhood," *New York Amsterdam News*, April 3, 1929; "Local Theater Managers Eager to Help Pullman Porters' Brotherhood," *New York Amsterdam News*, July 11, 1928; Deborah Gray White, *Too Heavy a Load: Black Women in Defense of Themselves, 1894–1994* (New York: W.W. Norton & Company, 1999), 91.
2. Melinda Chateauvert, *Marching Together: Women of the Brotherhood of Sleeping Car Porters* (Urbana: University of Illinois, 1998); Online Archive of California, Inventory of the Malca Chall Research Collection, "Determined Advocate for Racial Equality, Mary Frances Albrier" interview, 1977–78, http://www.oac.cdlib.org/view?docId=hb696nb3ht;NAAN=13030&doc.view=frames&chunk.id=div00145&toc.id=div00013&brand=oac4 [accessed June 28, 2012].
3. William Harris, *Keeping the Faith: A. Phillip Randolph, Milton P. Webster, and the Brotherhood of Sleeping Car Porters, 1925–1937* (Urbana: University of Illinois Press, 1977), 175; "Porters Will Sponsor Ball," *New York Amsterdam News*, December 1, 1934.
4. Thomas J. Sugrue, *Sweet Land of Liberty: The Forgotten Struggle for Civil Rights in the North* (New York: Random House, 2008), 33.
5. Sugrue, *Sweet Land of Liberty*, 33.
6. John P. Davis to Roger Baldwin, "American Fund for Public Service," November 11, 1935, Papers of National Negro Congress (hereafter cited as "NNC Papers"), Part 1, Box 19, microfilm reels (Frederick, MD: University Publications of America, 1988); "Negro Congress Plans Advanced," *New York Amsterdam News*, December 28, 1935; "Seek Funds for Negro Congress," *New York Amsterdam News*, January 18, 1936.
7. Randolph quoted in Lawrence S. Wittner, "The National Negro Congress: A Reassessment," *American Quarterly* 22:4 (Winter 1970): 886.
8. Wittner, "National Negro Congress," 886.
9. Wittner, "National Negro Congress," 892–93.
10. Wittner, "National Negro Congress," 886; "National Negro Congress Demands Probe of Peonage," *Chicago Defender*, September 27, 1937.
11. "Third National Negro Congress, Statement of Income and Expenses," NNC Papers, Part 1, Box 19, microfilm reels (Frederick, MD: University Publications of America, 1988); "National Negro Congress Convenes Friday," *Chicago Defender*, April 27, 1940; Earl Brown, "Call Negro Congress 'Red': Randolph is Out," *New York Amsterdam News*, May 4, 1940.
12. Beth Tompkins Bates, *Pullman Porters and the Rise of Protest Politics in Black America, 1925–1945* (Chapel Hill: University of North Carolina

Press, 2001), 145; Randolph quoted in Brown, "Call Negro Congress 'Red'"; "Third National Negro Congress"; Randolph quoted in "Randolph Quits National Negro Congress," *Atlanta Daily World*, May 1, 1940; Randolph quoted in "Randolph Tells Why He Would Not Run Again," *Baltimore Afro-American*, May 11, 1940.

13. "Determined Advocate for Racial Equality" Albrier interview; "Charges Reds Gave $100 a Month to the Group," *New York Amsterdam News*, May 11, 1940.
14. Sugrue, *Sweet Land of Liberty*, 46.
15. "10,000 Should March on D.C. Says Randolph," *Baltimore Afro-American*, January 25, 1941.
16. White quoted in Patricia Sullivan, *Lift Every Voice and Sing: The NAACP and the Making of the Modern Civil Rights Movement* (New York: New Press, 2009), 254; Tompkins Bates, *Pullman Porters*, 154.
17. Tompkins Bates, *Pullman Porters*, 156; Daniel Levine, *Bayard Rustin and the Civil Rights Movement* (New Brunswick: Rutgers University Press, 2000), 23.
18. Randolph quoted in "100,000 in March to Capital," *New York Amsterdam Star-News*, May 31, 1941.
19. "100,000 in March to Capital"; Sugrue, *Sweet Land of Liberty*, 47, 55; "Organization of Local 'March on Washington' Committee is Announced," *New York Amsterdam Star-News*, May 24, 1941; Herbert Garfinkel, *When Negroes March: The March on Washington Movement in the Organizational Politics for FEPC* (New York, Free Press, 1959); "March on Washington Drive Draws Nationwide Response," *New York Amsterdam Star-News*, June 7, 1941; "Calling 50,000 Negroes to Storm Madison Square Garden," *New York Amsterdam Star-News*, June 13, 1941.
20. "That March on Washington," *Pittsburgh Courier*, June 14, 1941.
21. "That March on Washington"; Tompkins Bates, *Pullman Porters*, 19, 158–60.
22. A. Philip Randolph, "Randolph Explains Postponement of 'March on Washington,'" *Cleveland Call and Post*, July 12, 1941. For a full treatment of the scope of the MOWM see Garfinkel, *When Negroes March*, 84.
23. A. Philip Randolph, "March on Washington Commish to Organize a Million Negroes," *New York Amsterdam Star-News*, September 13, 1941; Tompkins Bates, *Pullman Porters*, 163.
24. Murray and *Pittsburgh Courier* quoted in Garfinkel, *When Negroes March*, 114, 142–43.
25. Randolph quoted in Garfinkel, *When Negroes March*, 83.
26. J. Robert Smith, "March to Washington Committee Plans Mammoth Mass Meeting," *New York Amsterdam Star-News*, April 18, 1942.
27. Smith, "March to Washington Committee"; Garfinkel, *When Negroes March*, 85–87.
28. Randolph quoted in Garfinkel, *When Negroes March*, 88–90, 112.
29. Randolph quoted in Garfinkel, *When Negroes March*, 88–90, 112; Tompkins Bates, *Pullman Porters*, 168–69.

2 Mary McLeod Bethune, the National Council of Negro Women, and the Prewar Push for Equal Opportunity in Defense Projects

gloria-yvonne

In response to Adolf Hitler's military campaign of the late 1930s, President Franklin D. Roosevelt mobilized American industry and its workforce. He instituted a peacetime draft and acquired funding from Congress to build up the U.S. Army and Navy. Defense preparation meant an increase in government jobs, both civilian and military. African Americans seized upon wartime rhetoric and ideology to highlight the linkages between the black freedom struggle at home and America's preserving of democratic values abroad. The National Council of Negro Women (NCNW), under the leadership of Mary McLeod Bethune, became a significant organization that challenged racial discrimination in the defense industries and U.S. Armed Forces. The NCNW time and again emphasized that the economic and political fates of African Americans were intertwined. Although the organization has been criticized by historians for being top-down and elitist, it anchored several important coalitions across race and class lines. By the onset of American intervention into World War II, the NCNW was near the center of contemporary civil rights efforts, with Bethune as formidable a political insider as any of her black contemporaries.

Mary McLeod Bethune became an influential public figure during the New Deal. A seasoned southern activist-educator, she had founded Bethune-Cookman College in Florida and was president of the National Association of Colored Women (NACW) from 1924–28. By 1935, Bethune had become disillusioned with the NACW as a result of its middle-class conservatism, and that year she founded the National Council of Negro Women, believing that the race should be referred to as Negro rather than colored. An umbrella organization of non-partisan groups—educational, sororities, businesses, and professional societies—Bethune estimated the NCNW's membership in the 1940s to be 800,000 black women. The NCNW established networks called Metropolitan Councils in major cities throughout the country, which linked the organization's local and national strategies and campaigns. In 1936, Bethune took on a new set of challenges when Roosevelt named her as head of the National Youth Administration's (NYA) Division of Negro Affairs. As the first black woman appointed to a top federal position, Bethune was an important symbol to the African

American community. She was the leader of the *ad hoc* "black cabinet," an advisory group of black federal appointees who served in various New Deal agencies; many of them were also affiliated with prominent black organizations. Black cabinet was a term coined by the media; it was not President Roosevelt's idea but rather emerged as a result of pressure by black activists and the black press. The group strived to increase black representation in government positions and to influence policymaking, and Bethune's political alliance with First Lady Eleanor Roosevelt strengthened the position of the black cabinet. Her practical knowledge as a coalition builder made her particularly valuable to the civil rights activism of the period.

Bethune headquartered the NCNW in Washington, DC, where she issued calls for support that rallied black women nationwide against racial discrimination in defense industries, within the military, and in civilian life. During the prewar national defense buildup of 1940–41, Bethune and the NCNW also pressured President Roosevelt to recognize the presence of talented blacks ready to serve the country in leadership positions. This chapter chronicles the NCNW's activism prior to U.S. entry into World War II. At the center of the organization's reformist agenda was the push for labor equality. Bethune and the NCNW lobbied for new federal policies and built coalitions in an effort to facilitate the goals of full black employment and increased economic stability for the African American community.

ORGANIZED RESISTANCE TO DISCRIMINATION IN THE DEFENSE INDUSTRIES

On June 22, 1940 Bethune appealed to Roosevelt that the "Negro womanhood of America" was available to serve the national program to defend democratic values. She arranged for Representative Louis Ludlow to read on the House floor a statement she had written urging the president to "Use our qualified Negro women among the active forces who are working toward the protection of our democratic stronghold." Tying the fight against racism to World War II, Bethune argued that "the basic principles of democracy are being challenged at home and abroad" and demanded a government response on both fronts. She also felt that black participation in the war effort was necessary "to insure the perpetuation of the principles of democracy." The president had at his disposal "a vast army of Negro women who recognize that we must face the dangers that confront us with a united patriotism." Submitting the letter through a congressional representative was efficient and expedient, and put her appeal on the map.[1]

In its annual conference that October, the NCNW reiterated its determination to push the Roosevelt Administration to train and use blacks for all aspects of military service. It passed a resolution calling for an affirmative action policy that would recruit blacks until "full participation" in the U.S. Armed Forces was achieved. In particular, the demands were "admission and training of Negro volunteers and draftees in all branches of the armed services . . . calling up of all Negro reserve officers fit for duty and not engaged in indispensable services; [a]ssurance that the R.O.T.C. units in Negro colleges will be trained in field artillery, aviation, etc., as well as for the infantry." NCNW also "pledged and firmly resolved to uphold, to work and live for those democratic ideals and principles, the retention of which more than one-half of the world has been forcibly denied and which we in America engage in a great struggle to preserve." The organization "condemn[ed] every manifestation of separation of the races, segregation and differentials in treatment whether it emanates from the federal, state or local governments or any other source" and that such discrimination would have to end in order to maintain national security. This powerful rhetoric especially targeted a recent War Department policy "not to intermingle colored and white enlisted personnel in the same regimental organizations" and to limit "the strength of negro personnel of the Army" to the "proportion of the negro population of the country."[2]

Black activists nationwide were outraged by President Roosevelt's unexpected approval of the War Department's initiative. Brotherhood of Sleeping Car Porters founder A. Philip Randolph, National Association for the Advancement of Colored People head Walter White, and National Urban League leader T. Arnold Hill met with Roosevelt in late September to discuss segregation and discrimination in the U.S. Armed Forces. Randolph, White, and Hill represented three major aspects of the black freedom struggle: labor, social, and urban. Secretary of the Navy Frank Knox and Assistant Secretary of War Robert P. Patterson also attended the meeting, where Roosevelt denied the problem. "We're putting them right in, proportionately, into the combat issues," said the president. Although the three black leaders demanded that the U.S. Armed Forces be integrated, both military leaders were adamantly opposed to what they regarded as a revolutionary change. They were particularly against integrating the Navy because of what they deemed to be the "insurmountable difficulties of mixing blacks and whites in close quarters aboard a ship." One cannot overstate the staunch opposition these military officials had to integrating U.S. servicemen. When Roosevelt merely suggested that a black liaison be appointed for the Army and Navy, they took umbrage. Randolph, White, and Hill went home empty-handed, but called for additional meetings to solidify their demands and give the Roosevelt Administration specific recommendations for full (not proportionate) integration of blacks into the military, including the use of black officers and enlisted men throughout the U.S. Armed Forces and the elimination of segregated units. In the meantime, these leaders, like their counterparts in the NCNW, would shift their focus to equal employment opportunity in the defense industries including a federal anti-discrimination policy.[3]

The NCNW developed a list of demands in a brazen attempt to extend further pressure on Roosevelt to ensure equal opportunity in war-industries hiring. Among the requests was black representation on the National Defense Board including its publicity division, job opportunities as clerical workers and in other white-collar positions, and for the federal government to have the power to intervene in cases of job discrimination. The Council distributed its proposal to President Roosevelt and Sidney Hillman, head of the Defense Board. The NCNW was also concerned with segregation's effects on black support for the war effort. The organization's press organ the *Aframerican Woman's Journal* acknowledged that the "spiritual morale of the people" was "at low ebb," and characterized the time as one of "uncertainty and social unrest."[4]

At first the Roosevelt Administration refused to budge, but a series of efforts by black activists and organizations including Bethune and the NCNW gained concessions, at first minor and then more significant. Bethune used her access to the president to send him a January 1940 memorandum pointing out the need for a black appointee as assistant to the Secretary of War, and for "an appreciable percentage of Negroes, by Executive Order, to [be enrolled at] West Point and Annapolis." The memo also requested the promotion of a senior black military officer. In light of these demands and in an effort to assuage black voters, Roosevelt made these symbolic appointments. William Hastie was named assistant to the Secretary of War and Campbell C. Johnson became the executive assistant to the director of the Selective Service. Roosevelt also promoted Colonel Benjamin O. Davis to brigadier general, an important action that superseded the infamous War Department policy by putting white officers under Davis's command.[5]

By the end of 1940 and beginning of 1941, the Roosevelt Administration was making constructive changes with the appointment of Robert Weaver to oversee the hiring of blacks into defense projects. There was also the inclusion of "age, sex, race, or color" into fair-hiring instructions for defense contractors and the development of a national "Negro Employment and Training Branch." Without federal enforcement authority, however, such changes would not mean as much, but it was undeniable that the movement for a well-defined government anti-discrimination policy was underway. It would become the central focus of the era's black activism. Its dire importance was encapsulated by Bethune in February 1941:

> These are perilous and dangerous times, perilous, because in the struggle to maintain our democracy there is always that danger, that the freedom for minority and economically insignificant groups will be suppressed, or even entirely emasculated in the excitement and fear that possesses people when they fear that their safety is being threatened, and dangerous, because in a defense economy, the problems which are ever present with us, are in danger of being ignored or completely overlooked.[6]

BETHUNE AND THE NCNW: COALITION BUILDING IN THE PREWAR PERIOD

In the first six months of 1941, the NCNW strategically moved to build coalitions with other organizations, particularly women's groups, in an effort to combat anti-black discrimination in the war industries. NCNW worked with women across race, class, and cultural boundaries. The first such effort was actually at the end of 1940, when in December the NCNW participated in a two-day "Conference of National Defense" at Vassar College. The conference brought together fifty women who were experienced in civic and political activity, including government officials, heads of national private agencies, and executives from national women's organizations. The NCNW sent representatives, according to its *Aframerican Woman's Journal*, "to take advantage of the general interest in National Defense and to discuss a working program . . . to make each community strong for defense and strong in time of peace."[7]

The delegates were an influential group, and the conference placed the NCNW squarely in the middle of the conversation about how blacks would be used in the inevitable war effort. The NCNW sent as one of its delegates Sue Thurman, editor of the *Aframerican Woman's Journal*. Also at the conference were representatives from the American Nurses Association, National Social Work Council, American National Red Cross, and the American Home Economics Association; governmental representatives came from the Advisory Committee to the National Defense Council (ACNDC), Federal Works Agency, NYA, Social Security Board, U.S. Department of Labor Women's Bureau, and U.S. Employment Service; there were also executives from the Young Women's Christian Association, the National Council of Women, the National Society of Daughters of the American Revolution, the Associated Women of the American Farm Bureau Federation, the Young Women's Hebrew Association, and the Women's Overseas Service League.[8]

The presence of the ACNDC suggests that the conference gave participants the chance to influence federal defense policy. This opportunity would have lasting effects on the NCNW. History professor and political activist Caroline Ware, a white woman who represented the ACNDC at the conference, would go on to have a longstanding partnership with the NCNW. Ware would participate in a 1944 NCNW conference as chair of a panel on fair employment legislation, while U.S. Secretary of Labor Francis Perkins and Eleanor Roosevelt would also attend. Between Bethune's connections and the NCNW's energetic membership, the organization was able to make itself heard by important decision makers who would have an influence on wartime policies and practices.[9]

The conference spawned several NCNW relationships with key women's organizations. At Vassar, the NCNW effectively used its organizational literature, exchanging more than 200 copies of the *Aframerican Woman's*

Journal with attendees who sent their organizational papers in return. This group included the National League of Women Voters, which one historian called the "most prominent women's organization in the public affairs field." The National Council of Jewish Women (NCJW) worked with the NCNW under the "belief that it is necessary to eliminate all forms of discrimination if Jewish rights are to be maintained." Another NCJW statement read: "Negro women have been quietly proving to their fellow citizens that they are an important and integral part of our democracy." The two groups would later work together on a "National Planning Conference on Building Better Race Relationships." The NCNW also joined forces with the National Women's Trade Union League (WTUL), whose president Rose Schneiderman attended the conference. It worked closely with the WTUL in advocating for a permanent Fair Employment Practices Commission. The two organizations submitted a joint statement to the press, speaking out against racial discrimination and the lack of equal opportunity. Joining forces with the National Women's Trade Union League, a blue-collar organization, assisted the NCNW's efforts to educate black women on union policy and labor rights. In addition, the NCNW also built a strong working relationship with the politically influential Alpha Kappa Alpha sorority, one of its affiliates. The NCNW and the sorority hosted a well-attended conference on "The Negro Woman and National Defense" in 1941, which linked the coalition's shared interests in citizenship advocacy, anti-discrimination, and labor equality.[10]

The political influence that the NCNW began to accumulate during this period is best reflected by the Roosevelt Administration's growing regard for the organization. In January 1941, Roosevelt created a women's advisory committee consisting of representatives from women's organizations and labor groups that were considered relevant to the defense program. Neither the NCNW nor any other black women's organization was invited to attend. In a *Chicago Defender* piece, NCNW activist Rebecca Stiles Taylor questioned the president's decision: "Why were the names of the National Association of Colored Women and the National Council of Negro Women omitted? Whose fault is it—the organizations themselves or the Bureau of Labor? How can these omissions be rectified? What are the leaders of these organizations saying?" Bethune also put pressure on the Roosevelt Administration by issuing a statement in the *Chicago Defender*. The campaign by the NCNW to be heard by the White House seems to have paid off, because in April the organization was invited to participate in the "Planning Program of Inter-American Relations," called by Nelson Rockefeller, head of the Office of Inter-American Affairs in the Department of Commerce. Bethune, Thurman, and NCNW International Committee Chair Mary Jackson McCrorey attended the meeting that included representatives from twenty-five other women's organizations. Perhaps key to NCNW inclusion was its transnational advocacy for black equality, as illustrated by its inviting Haiti's Minister Elie Lescot and his wife to its

1940 annual conference, its International Committee building networks with women in Latin America and the Caribbean, and its members traveling to Cuba for a friendship tour.[11]

Just one week after the Rockefeller conference, Bethune pressed the Roosevelt Administration to integrate the national defense program on the government level. She wrote a memorandum to Eleanor Roosevelt to press for "programs of action, pertinent to the needs of the hour," that called for "[i]nclusion of Negroes in the thinking and organization of new agencies set up for defense," including Rockefeller's. Bethune also called for "increased Negro personnel in the regular government agencies that have a large Negro constituency," and were "pertinent to defense efforts," including the departments of Agriculture, Labor, and the "United States Public Health Service." She outlined some of her demands with specific suggestions, such as the "[n]eed for further integration of Negro personnel into the judicial system of the country, by the appointment of one federal judge who is a Negro. New York can take this."[12]

By the middle of 1941 the NCNW had increased its pressure on the Roosevelt Administration, reflecting the urgency of the moment. As A. Philip Randolph's call for a mass March on Washington loomed, Bethune and the NCNW fueled the momentum by hosting a summer conference on "The Negro Woman in National Defense." While the March on Washington was designed to convince Roosevelt to move decisively toward equal opportunity legislation and enforcement in the war industries, Bethune reinforced that challenge in the black press. In her call for participation in the NCNW conference, Bethune announced, "The hour has come for thought and action on the part of the womanhood of our country to the end that the Negro may participate fully in all phases of the National Defense program." The conference would stimulate the "mobilization of women to study the defense program and urge the acceptance of Negroes in it." A conference resolution further emphasized her position that, "This is our hour to proclaim anew our allegiance to America and its democratic ideals by protesting the exclusion of any minority group from a national program in which all citizens should serve and serve alike." She argued that, "[T]he very test of Democracy is the integration of the Negro in all activities in which our government is engaged."[13]

The NCNW was an important outlet for black Americans who were growing increasingly aware of how the fight against racism dovetailed with the goals of America's inevitable war effort. Its rhetoric became more assertive as the inevitability of the war increased. The *Aframerican Woman's Journal* pointed out, "Never has it been so clear that the Negro people are endangered by Hitlerism at home and abroad. To Negro Americans, Hitlerism means the lynch mob, the denial of jobs, and the right to vote and serve on juries. American Hitlerism means the whole systematic curtailment of rights and liberties." Although some blacks were isolationists who urged the United States to turn its moral compass inward, the NCNW never took this position. Bethune and other NCNW members believed in the possibility of a working and viable democracy that included the full integration of black Americans. Four-hundred-fifty NCNW delegates met with Eleanor Roosevelt in 1940 for an annual tea at the White House, a seven-fold increase since a 1938 gathering organized by Bethune which sixty-five delegates attended. The whopping turnout speaks not only to the magnitude of the organizational structure of the NCNW, which at that time included seventeen national organizations as affiliates, but also of its expanded influence during this period.[14]

Bethune's leadership and the NCNW's coalition-building skills and sheer size made the organization an important part of the contemporary civil rights scene. Bethune's strident rhetoric during the period denoted the organization's potency. For example, Bethune's June 1940 open letter to Roosevelt was strongly worded in that it referred to the NCNW as a "vast army." Additionally, her May 1941 appeal for NCNW conference participants called for mass meetings nationwide in order to put pressure on President Roosevelt. Speaking as NCNW president, Bethune called for strategic local and national grassroots action:

> I am hereby requesting all members to participate in this conference—if not in Washington, by setting up smaller conferences during these three days in every section of our country, thereby pressing our claims as American citizens for just participation of the Negro group in every branch and unit of national defense.

Bethune's calls for mass action at this time cohered with Randolph's use of the threat of a March on Washington to influence Roosevelt. The brinkmanship worked and Roosevelt issued Executive Order 8802 in June 1941 that banned discriminatory hiring practices in industries with government war contracts and established what would come to be known as the Fair Employment Practices Commission to investigate discrimination complaints and redress grievances. Most historical interpretations fail to mention the NCNW as backers of Randolph's movement or as an influential force pressing for social change, although there are some exceptions. Bettye Collier-Thomas, for example, positions NCNW activism as critical to spreading word of the March on Washington, as members "sent out letters and information to hundreds of women's groups to obtain their participation."[15]

Bethune's influence as a political insider on a par with Randolph, White, Hill, and the National Urban League's Lester Granger was undoubtedly critical to the NCNW's influence. The organization's 1941 annual conference brought together representatives from more than forty national women's organizations. It was Bethune who met with Sidney Hillman and then broke the news in May to Walter White, Lester Granger, and others that Roosevelt was unwilling to sign an executive order ensuring equal employment opportunity. Bethune's endorsement lent key legitimacy and support to the March on Washington, sending a vital signal to black women, not to mention President Roosevelt. It was Bethune who kept the president and first lady informed about the March on Washington's progress. Her reports clearly had an impact on Roosevelt's understanding of the gravity and legitimacy of Randolph's proposed march and the president's ultimately signing the executive order to eliminate discrimination in defense jobs and create the Fair Employment Practices Commission. Bethune's July speech to the NACW hailed the executive order as historic and praised Roosevelt for "the first proclamation of its kind issued from the President in behalf of the Negro since Lincoln's Emancipation Proclamation."[16]

With Roosevelt's executive order at their backs, activists from around the country arrived in Washington, DC for a three-day "The Negro Woman in National Defense" conference at Howard University in June 1941. Bethune had stressed in her call that the three goals of the conference were to mobilize black women through study of the government's defense program, to maintain democracy through active citizenship, and to proclaim allegiance to America. Living up to those objectives, the conference drew women from government, academia, and forty-three national organizations; men were also invited as guest speakers. Most of the panels concentrated on how black life could be improved through participation in the defense program. Their titles reflected these concerns: "Training and Employment in Defense Industries," "Negro Women in Organized Labor," "In Defense of Civil Liberties," and "Role of the Home, Church and School in National Defense." There were also panels on other issues including "Health, Housing, Recreation," "Farm Security," "Consumer Education and Nutrition," and "Youth Problems." The panels reflected the era's growing belief that economic and political inequalities were inextricably linked. Ruth Whaley of the National Women Lawyers Association emphasized, "The greatest enemy of democracy is unemployment. Following it are racial discrimination, employment unrest in industries, and the threat of war." The delegation agreed to "call upon all Trade Unions, and their Women's Auxiliaries, practicing discrimination against women, particularly Negro women, to eliminate this un-American practice and join with all progressive organized labor in supporting the nation-wide appeal for jobs for Negro women in National Defense." The conference was opened to the public on its second evening for a mass meeting.[17]

The NCNW came out of the conference more determined than ever to impact the defense industries specifically and the problem of black economic instability in general. Bethune outlined a goal for NCNW Metropolitan Councils to study "local problems of domestic employees—and in rural areas, the agricultural worker, to the end that the Council may give all of its resources to securing for these two groups the benefits of Social Security." The NCNW reprinted transcripts from conference panels on "Employment and Job Placement in Defense Industries," "Work Opportunities for Negro Women in the National Defense Program," and "Negro

Women and Organized Labor." In its *Aframerican Woman's Journal*, the organization ran guest articles explaining the political significance of the conference and the historical and contemporary roles of black women as union organizers. Despite characterizations of the NCNW as middle-class, these pieces illuminated how economic and political issues that were critical to the survival of working-class women were central to the organization's agenda. In fact, a piece in the *Journal* called "The Negro Woman Worker" is still used by historians who study the period.[18]

Secretary of War Henry Stimson and the Defense Board continually refused the advice of Bethune and the NCNW although they were at the center of the era's civil rights activism. When a 1941 meeting on women and defense called by the Roosevelt Administration excluded the NCNW, Bethune wrote a protest letter to Stimson, copied Eleanor Roosevelt and other influential people, and sent it to the press. The letter described the systematic marginalization of the NCNW from discussions about defense policy. "We cannot accept any excuse that the exclusion of Negro representation was an oversight," wrote Bethune. "We are anxious for you to know that we want to be, and insist upon being considered a part of our American democracy, not something apart from it." Bethune's indignation and the NCNW's persistence eventually paid off; they gained formal access on Capitol Hill to participate in the conversation about defense and military projects. Bethune accepted an invitation to serve on the War Department's Public Relations Advisory Committee for Women's Interests. Including over thirty presidents of national women's organizations, the committee worked with NCNW Metropolitan Councils to dispense information on defense-related issues.[19]

The NCNW seized upon this momentum by sending delegates to a November 1941 civilian defense conference in Washington, DC alongside representatives from sixty-seven women's groups. The conference returned to the principles of the Vassar gathering by emphasizing how women's participation in the wartime defense industries was vital to the practice of democracy. The organizations focused on strengthening homeland voluntarism, adult education, consumer protection, labor rights, emergency protection, civil rights, fair treatment in education, and equal access to vocational training and jobs. The NCNW reflected the rhetoric of the era by clearly positioning the black freedom struggle as a vital reflection of the American democratic mission. Thus conference participants compared their concerns for the welfare of African Americans to their faith and devotion to democracy.[20]

In America's final prewar moments, the NCNW fittingly shaped its political activism to address labor issues in addition to civil rights. Through sophisticated methods of political communication and coalition building the NCNW gained access to defense policymaking on Capitol Hill. From Mary McLeod Bethune's initial proclamation to President Roosevelt in June 1940 to her public denouncement of his administration's exclusionary policies in the fall of 1941, NCNW activism took on various degrees of militancy. Armed with strategies to be heard through the black press, its own *Journal*, and coalition conferences, the NCNW fought successfully against marginalization. The organization's bold and innovative acts took place when Bethune had a lot to lose as a college president and director of a New Deal agency. Her governmental position and reputation provided political leverage for the NCNW's political communication—letters, memoranda, and reports—to the president, his administration, and his wife. Throughout the war years, the NCNW maintained national recognition and an active voice on Capitol Hill in defense and military policies affecting labor, economic welfare, and society at large. The organization's strategies proved effective in empowering it to become a part of the political discussion on defense planning for American intervention into World War II.

NOTES

1. Representative Louis Ludlow, "Mrs. Mary McLeod Bethune Tenders Services of the Negro Women of America to the President," *Congressional Record* 86:19 (June 22, 1940): 4191.
2. Ludlow, "Mrs. Mary McLeod Bethune Tenders Services of the Negro Women," 4191; *Aframerican Woman's Journal* 1 (Conference Issue 1941): 12, Records of the National Council of Negro Women, Mary McLeod Bethune Council House National Historical Site, Washington, DC (hereafter cited as "NCNW Records"), Series 13, Box 1, Folder 7; Nancy J. Weiss, *Farewell to the Party of Lincoln: Black Politics in the Age of FDR* (Princeton: Princeton University Press, 1983), 277.
3. Weiss, *Farewell to the Party*, 275–77; Merl E. Reed, *Seedtime for the Modern Civil Rights Movement: The President's Committee on Fair Employment Practice: 1941–1946* (Baton Rouge: Louisiana State University Press, 1991), 12; Benjamin Quarles, *Black Mosaic: Essays in Afro-American History and Historiography* (Amherst: University of Massachusetts Press, 1988), 151–79; Charles Johnson, *To Stem This Tide, A Survey of Racial Tension Areas in the United States* (New York: AMS Press, [1943] 1969), 2; Celeste Michelle Condit and John Louis Lucaites, *Crafting Equality: America's Anglo-African World* (Chicago: University of Chicago Press, 1993), 169–70; Lee Finkle, "The Conservative Aims of Militant Rhetoric: Black Protest during World War II," *Journal of American History* 60:3 (December 1973): 698–99. The difference between "full" (which Randolph, White, and Hill wanted) and "proportionate" (Roosevelt's proposal) representation was significant. Black unemployment and underemployment, in a time when nationwide full employment was possible due to wartime productivity, was disproportionately high. Military quotas under proportionate representation capped black employment without regard to need or efficiency.
4. *Aframerican Woman's Journal* 2 (Winter 1941–1942): 6, NCNW Records, Series 13, Box 1, Folder 9; "Findings of the National Council of Negro Women in Meeting Thursday, October 25, 1940," NCNW Records, Series 13, Box 1, Folder 7.
5. Mary McLeod Bethune to the President, "Some of the Things Negroes Desire," January 12, 1940, Bethune Foundation Collection (hereafter cited as "BFC"), microfilm reel 2; Weiss, *Farewell to the Party*, 278–79; Reed, *Seedtime for the Modern*, 12.

6. Louis C. Kesselman, "The Fair Employment Practice Commission Movement in Perspective," *Journal of Negro History* 31:1 (January 1946): 36–37; Harvard Sitkoff, "Review of *From Direct Action to Affirmative Action: Fair Employment Law and Policy in America, 1933–1972* by Paul D. Moreno," *Journal of American History* 84:4 (March 1998): 1559; Bethune quoted in Rebecca Stiles Taylor, "Activities of National Women's Organizations—National Council of Negro Women," *Chicago Defender*, February 8, 1941, NCNW Records, Series 13, Box 1, Folder 8.
7. Linda Gordon, "Black and White Visions of Welfare: Women's Welfare Activism, 1890–1945," in Darlene Clark Hine, Wilma King, and Linda Reed, eds., *We Specialize in the Wholly Impossible: A Reader in Black Women's History* (Brooklyn: Carlson Publishing, [1991] 1995), 449–85; *Aframerican Woman's Journal* 1 (Conference Issue 1941): 29–31.
8. *Aframerican Woman's Journal* 1 (Conference Issue 1941): 29–31.
9. For brief coverage of the 1944 conference, see "Notables Discuss the Problems of the Day in Annual Workshop of National Council," *Pittsburgh Courier*, n.d., news clipping, BFC, microfilm reel 9.
10. Louis Kesselman, *The Social Politics of FEPC: A Study in Reform Pressure Movements* (Chapel Hill: University of North Carolina Press, 1948), 106, 123; "Women Facing New Frontiers," *Aframerican Woman's Journal* 1 (Conference Issue 1941): 7, 11; Susan M. Hartmann, *The Front and Beyond: American Women in the 1940s* (Boston: Twayne Publishers, 1982), 147; *Aframerican Woman's Journal* 3 (Summer Issue 1943): table of contents page, NCNW Records, Series 13, Box 1, Folder 11; "From the National Planning Conference on Building Better Race Relations," *Aframerican Woman's Journal* 3 (Voters Education and Citizenship Issue): 4, NCNW Records, Series 13, Box 1, Folder 13; *Aframerican Woman's Journal* 2 (National Defense Issue 1941): 2–5.
11. Rebecca Stiles Taylor, "Activities of National Women's Organizations—Are Negro Women Participating in Defense Program?," *Chicago Defender*, February 1, 1941; Rebecca Stiles Taylor, "Activities of National Women's Organizations—Contemporary Topics," *Public Administrative Review* 1 (Autumn 1941): 505–11; *Aframerican Woman's Journal* 1 (Conference Issue, 1941): 7, 29; Annual Conference Program, NCNW Records, Series 2, Conventions, Reports, Program 1940.
12. "Mary McLeod Bethune to Eleanor Roosevelt," April 8, 1941, Eleanor Roosevelt Papers, Franklin D. Roosevelt Presidential Library and Museum, Hyde Park, NY. Also see Rebecca Stiles Taylor, "Activities of National Women's Organizations" and "Women's Organizations Called by Rockefeller to Cooperate on Inter-American Defense Acts," both in *Chicago Defender*, April 19, 1941.
13. "Announcing a Nation-Wide Call to Negro Women of America," June 28–30, 1941, National Archives and Records, Washington, DC (hereafter cited as "NA"), Meetings, E120, Box 6. See also "Mrs. Bethune Calls Confab of Negro Women in June," *Chicago Bee*, May 18, 1941, BFC, microfilm reel 9.
14. Richard M. Dalfiume, "The 'Forgotten Years' of the Negro Revolution," in Bernard Sternsher, ed., *The Negro in Depression and War: Prelude to Revolution, 1930–1945* (Chicago: Quadrangle Books, 1969), 302–303; Audley Moore, "Conference Impressions," *Aframerican Woman's Journal* 2 (National Defense Issue 1941): 16; Condit and Lucaites, *Crafting Equality*, 170; Johnson, *To Stem This Tide*, ix; *Aframerican Woman's Journal* 1 (Conference Issue 1941): 6–8.
15. "Mrs. Bethune Calls Confab of Negro Women in June," *Chicago Bee*, May 18, 1941; Dalfiume "'Forgotten Years,'" 305; Elaine Smith, "Politics and

Public Issues," in Audrey Thomas McCluskey and Elaine Smith, *Mary McLeod Bethune: Building a Better World: Essays and Selected Documents* (Bloomington: Indiana University Press, 2001), 205; Kesselman, *The Social Politics of FEPC*, 13; Bettye Collier-Thomas, "For the Race in General and Black Women in Particular: The Civil Rights Activities of African American Women's Organizations: 1915–1950," in Bettye Collier-Thomas and V.P. Franklin, eds., *Sisters in the Struggle: African American Women in the Civil Rights-Black Power Movement* (New York: New York University Press, 2001), 35.

16. Charles V. Hamilton, *The Dual Agenda: Race and Social Welfare Policies of Civil Rights* (New York: Columbia University Press, 1997), 46; Kesselman, *The Social Politics of FEPC*, 100; David Kryder, *Divided Arsenal: Race and the American State During World War II* (New York: Cambridge University Press, 2000), 58; Lucy G. Barber, *Marching On Washington: The Forging of an American Political Tradition* (Berkeley: University of California Press, 2002), 121. For additional information on NCNW activism, see S.J. Kleinberg, *Votes for Women: Women in the United States, 1830–1945* (New Brunswick: Rutgers University Press, 1999); Hartmann, *The Home Front and Beyond*; Mary McLeod Bethune, "Negro Women Facing Tomorrow," National Association of Colored Women, Oklahoma City, Oklahoma, July 27, 1941, BFC, microfilm reel 2; Moore, "Conference Impressions," 16.
17. For conference transcripts see pamphlet and program for "The Negro Woman in National Defense" conference, June 28, 29, 30, 1941, NA, Meetings, E120, Box 6. Also see Annabel Sawyer, "The Negro Woman in National Defense: Summary of Conference Held at Howard University, June 28 to 30, 1941," *Aframerican Woman's Journal* 2 (National Defense 1941): 2, 14–16.
18. "The Council in Action," *Aframerican Woman's Journal* 2 (Winter 1941–1942): 13; Sabina Martinez, "Negro Woman in Organization—Labor," *Aframerican Woman's Journal* 2 (National Defense Issue 1941): 17; Susan Hartmann, *The Home Front and Beyond*; Deborah Gray White, *Too Heavy a Load: Black Women in Defense of Themselves 1894–1994* (New York: W. W. Norton & Company, 1999); Dora Jones, "A Self-Help Program of Household Employees," *Aframerican Woman's Journal* 2 (National Defense Issue 1941): 26–27; Jean Collier Brown, "The Negro Woman Worker," *Aframerican Woman's Journal* 2 (National Defense Issue 1941): 18–25.
19. Bethune quoted in Elaine Smith, "Mary McLeod Bethune and the National Youth Administration," in Mabel E. Deutrich and Virginia C. Purdy, eds., *Clio Was a Woman: Studies in the History of American Women* (Washington, DC: Howard University Press, 1980), 159; "Mary McLeod Bethune to Emily Blair," December 27, 1941, NCNW Records, Series 4, Box 2, Folder 24, Correspondence 1941; Dorothy Height, "Negro Women in Civilian Defense Work," *Aframerican Woman's Journal* 2 (Winter 1941–1942): 9, 12.
20. Height, "Negro Women in Civilian Defense Work," 9, 12.

3 The Brooklyn Urban League and Equal Employment Opportunity in New York's War Industries

Carla J. DuBose

World War II catalyzed black activism and increased the militancy of African American consciousness. Black Americans linked the country's battles against fascism and Nazism with their own against racism in what was popularly known as the "Double V" campaign for democracy at home and abroad. Hatched by the widely read black newspaper the *Pittsburgh Courier* in 1942 while the country was at war, the campaign's effectiveness depended upon its framing the black freedom struggle and its calls for equal rights as patriotic endeavors that complemented the spirit of the times. The "Double V" campaign galvanized local struggles that had been going on since the turn of the decade, as African Americans demanded equal access to the opportunities that government contracts in the war industries provided.

Black activism for economic rights did not begin during the war. Many of the tactics that African American organizations and activists engaged in during the 1940s had been pioneered in the previous decade in the fight for employment opportunities during the Great Depression. Even before the Depression hit, most blacks had low-paying unskilled jobs and little possibility of upward social mobility; therefore housing, healthcare, and crime had always been concerns. The Depression exacerbated these conditions and pushed blacks further into poverty. African Americans were generally the first to be fired from their jobs and usually had the highest unemployment rate of any minority group in a given area. Public agencies and philanthropic organizations responded too slowly to the needs of African Americans in the early years of the Depression, therefore black churches expanded existing services to the community. African American organizations began to advocate for economic opportunities. The most famous protest was the "Don't Buy Where You Can't Work" campaign for employment of black clerks in white-owned department stores, where activists used mass protests and boycotts as the most effective weapons.[1]

One of the most significant campaigns for economic power in the 1940s took place in New York, where black politicians, newspapers, and rights groups launched a series of efforts that focused on equal employment opportunity. New York activists, both on the grassroots level and through local branches of national organizations like the National Association for the Advancement of Colored People (NAACP), the National Negro Congress (NNC), and the National Urban League (NUL), pressured state and federal government agencies to establish and enforce fair employment legislation. They held press conferences and wrote editorials, lobbied politicians, staged protests, and worked with government agencies to pursue equal employment opportunity and fair employment practices for African American workers on federally funded contracts.

Although the wartime mobilization at first created few new jobs in New York, the city's blacks believed that they were not getting their fair share of the work that had become available. In a series of 1940 and 1941 articles, the *New York Amsterdam News* lamented the lack of job opportunities for African Americans in defense industries. The newspaper argued that the shortages of civil, electrical, and mechanical engineers and industrial workers that defense contractors faced would abate if they would just hire skilled African Americans from one of many fine training grounds, such as Hampton Institute, Tuskegee University, or the National Technical Association. The newspaper criticized contractors for perpetuating this labor shortage in a key defense area that needed to be staffed for the sake of national security. Without blacks, *New York Amsterdam News* editors stressed, defense industries were unable to efficiently produce goods and therefore would hamper wartime production. Racism could undermine America's efforts to protect worldwide freedom and democracy.[2]

THE NAACP PUSH FOR ECONOMIC INCLUSION

New York's black activist community initially targeted the aircraft industry, which refused to hire African Americans to work on production lines and offered only janitorial jobs. A *New York Amsterdam News* cartoon depicted the manager of an aircraft production company telling a black mechanic that although there is a need for manpower in the airplane industry, he will not hire Negroes. The NAACP took up the case of Edmond Van Osten, a black tinsmith with nine years of experience whom management of Brewster Airplane Company in Long Island City had rejected as under-qualified for a vacant position. The NAACP brought Van Osten's case to the New York Employment Service (NYES) because Brewster had hired white candidates with only two years of experience for the same position that Van Osten was deemed under-qualified. When an NYES official confirmed Van Osten's qualifications the NAACP reported the results to the press and Brewster responded to the bad publicity by hiring four black workers in August 1941. Although small in number these hires were large in significance because the aeronautic industry was one of the toughest for blacks to penetrate. The Brewster campaign highlighted the effectiveness of linking the black freedom struggle to the war effort. Van Osten was more experienced than the whites that were hired instead of him. His expertise was a matter of national security. Harlem's African American leaders argued that by rejecting Van Osten and other skilled blacks, Brewster was undermining America's efforts to protect worldwide freedom and democracy.[3]

The NAACP quickly expanded the scope of its push for equal economic opportunities for African Americans in war industries. Walter White, the organization's executive secretary, held a community meeting in Brooklyn to discuss the place of blacks in the nation's defense industries and suggest ways to fight for increased minority employment in that borough. The New York NAACP branch declared January 26, 1941 to be National Defense Day. It used media and public gatherings to highlight the discrimination African Americans faced. Ministers, civic leaders, and prominent black New Yorkers emphasized their race's patriotism and the failure of the national defense program to fully include African Americans in military service or war-related jobs. The NAACP began a letter-writing campaign to President Franklin Roosevelt, his cabinet, and members of Congress to protest discrimination in defense industries. It also lobbied for a Congressional investigation into the status and treatment of black workers in the defense program. The organization hoped not only to bring attention to unfair hiring practices but just as importantly to motivate rank-and-file African Americans to support and participate in a movement for equal employment access.[4]

At a town hall meeting in Harlem led by city council candidate Adam Clayton Powell, Jr. called the People's Court of Inquiry, New York's black community directed its concerns toward government officials in attendance about a number of issues including job discrimination. Locals testified about their deplorable living conditions and lack of employment opportunities. One witness was a migrant single mother who left the South in "pursuit of life, liberty, and happiness for herself and her children," but instead found "unemployment, poverty, and public officials who had consistently attempted to deprive her of a miserly relief." The meeting brought the problems of black New Yorkers to the direct attention of city leaders. It also gave Powell the opportunity to call upon African Americans and Puerto Ricans to band together to leverage jobs.[5]

Brooklyn became the center of the campaign for equal employment access because it was where many of the available war industries jobs were located and because the discrimination there was prevalent. New York State War Council Committee on Discrimination (COD) Executive Secretary Robert Washburn called Brooklyn the "capital of discrimination," claiming that job discrimination there against blacks, Jews, and Italians went unchecked and that less progress had been made in Brooklyn than any other defense industry center in the state. Although he acknowledged some exceptions, like the Navy Yard, which was the city's largest employer of black workers, Washburn accused plant and factory owners of systematically excluding African Americans. He felt, however, that discrimination could "not be solved by legislation, but by public opinion operating on employers and labor alike."[6]

This was the path that the Brooklyn NAACP took when it called a January 1941 mass meeting about African American participation in the war industries that was attended by 900 people. Walter White addressed the gathering and urged unity against racial discrimination in the Army, Navy, and Air Corps. White agreed at the meeting to lead a delegation to the Sperry Gyroscope Corporation in Brooklyn, one of the city's largest wartime employers, in an effort to secure jobs for African Americans. The *New York Amsterdam News* covered the story. When Sperry turned away White's delegation, NAACP Branch Coordinator E. Frederic Morrow asked Brooklyn NAACP President Fred Turner if the local chapter would help in the Sperry campaign. Turner was asked to investigate whether African Americans were being employed at Sperry and how they were being used. This information was used in press releases and to lobby politicians. Sperry was repeatedly targeted for negative publicity until it hired its first black workers later that year.[7]

Just as the Depression era saw growth in the scope of African American activism beyond traditional institutions like black churches and the NAACP to the community at large, so did 1940s black activists expand their focus to the political arena in a push for equal economic opportunity in the nation's war industries. Black politicians played a major role in these efforts. They not only pressured industry and commerce to end discrimination, but also pushed their colleagues in government to pass legislation. Harlem-based State Assemblymen William Andrews, Daniel Burrows, and Hulan Jack introduced fifteen bills in March 1941 aimed at eradicating all forms of job discrimination. These proposals focused on banning discrimination by companies that held government contracts, strictly punishing violators, and rewriting state law to define job discrimination as a civil rights violation. Although these bills were not passed, they made an impact. That month Governor Herbert Lehman established the COD to deal with complaints of hiring bias. The following month the New York State Assembly passed the Mahoney Act which allowed the COD to prosecute firms that had discriminatory employment practices. A year later, in the spring of 1942, the Schwartzwald Act amended the Mahoney Law by giving the State Industrial Commissioner the power to enforce anti-discrimination laws and to require corporations to cooperate with COD investigations. These laws marked the start of New York State's process of making equal employment opportunity a right for all its citizens.[8]

What was happening in New York mirrored what was happening nationally. A group of black leaders—National Urban League Executive Secretary Lester Granger, NAACP Executive Secretary Walter White, Channing Tobias of the Young Men's Christian Association, Mary McLeod Bethune of the National Youth Administration, and A. Philip Randolph, founder of the Brotherhood of Sleeping Car Porters—asked President Roosevelt in

April 1941 to desegregate the U.S. Armed Forces and ban discrimination in defense industries. When Roosevelt failed to take meaningful action, Randolph announced plans for an "all-out march" to Washington, DC to demand an executive order ending racial discrimination in defense industries. It was his hope that 10,000 blacks would participate. The pressure exerted by the March on Washington campaign pushed Roosevelt to issue Executive Order 8802 in June 1941 that banned discriminatory hiring practices in industries with government war contracts and established what would come to be known as the Fair Employment Practices Commission (FEPC) to investigate discrimination complaints and redress grievances. Black New Yorkers used regional FEPC offices to report violations and secure employment. The NAACP, NUL, and NNC also made sure that the COD and FEPC heard their constituents' complaints.[9]

BROOKLYN URBAN LEAGUE COOPERATION WITH THE FEPC

The Brooklyn Urban League (BKUL) was particularly effective in getting government agencies to open new areas of employment to black workers. It had a specific department, the Industrial Department, which advised victims on how to refer their cases to the COD and FEPC. It also fed these examples to the press, which often publicized the offenses. In a joint 1942 statement to the *New York Times*, the NYUL and BKUL reported that several industrial companies with war contracts discriminated against African Americans, charging that management obeyed "the letter but not the spirit" of Executive Order 8802 by hiring a few token black workers for unskilled jobs in plants with hundreds of men. They also alleged that war industries often demanded higher qualifications from African American applicants and frequently never even reviewed their applications. The BKUL also conducted independent investigations and upon finding evidence of discrimination would forward its discoveries to COD and FEPC offices for corrective action.[10]

The NUL's history and purpose positioned it perfectly to work with government agencies to alleviate job discrimination. From its inception, one of the organization's primary objectives had been to broaden economic opportunities and break barriers to black employment. It had a job placement service that the COD called the most important for blacks in New York and Brooklyn. When the COD wanted to steer workers to war industries for job placement or to test whether companies fairly hired minorities, it often asked the BKUL to provide qualified black applicants. A major factor in the close relationship between the BKUL and COD was that COD Executive Director Charles Berkley was the former Industrial Secretary of the BKUL. Berkley worked closely with new BKUL Industrial Secretary Lorenzo Davis, who sent him detailed letters about BKUL negotiations with companies that held war contracts. Whenever Davis felt that the BKUL could not move a corporation on its own, he referred the case to the COD. The COD also provided information that aided BKUL campaigns against job discrimination. For example, when the Bulova Watch Company rejected six of seven qualified black female applicants for an advertised position, the BKUL asked the COD to get information on how many black women were employed by the firm in comparison to whites. The BKUL used this information in its reports and public statements which pressed for black employment. Such requests also continually prompted COD officials to review the hiring policies of companies accused of discrimination.[11]

Although challenges remained, black workers made great strides integrating the war industries in 1943 as factories in urban areas received more contracts. Plants producing chemicals, electrical equipment, machinery, ships, and scientific instruments increased their hiring of African Americans. The BKUL played an important role in the placement of these workers. Although the BKUL's employment program still placed about 60 percent of its clients in unskilled positions where blacks traditionally worked, a large minority were able to get high-paying skilled and semi-skilled jobs never before attainable, such as machinist and ship fitter. The BKUL also placed women in semi-skilled clerical positions as well as on the shop floor as power machine operators, dial painters, assemblers, welders, and drill press operators. Such occupations were not open to blacks at all before the war, and the placement of African Americans in these jobs constituted a definite and significant change in employment trends. The activities of African American organizations like the BKUL were integral in the successful placement of black workers in more prestigious, better paying positions not previously available to them.[12]

Getting jobs was only the first step in a process, however, because African American employees often faced discrimination after they were hired. The BKUL's strong relationship with the FEPC was pivotal in countering this on-the-job bias and bettering working conditions for blacks employed in war industries. BKUL officers cooperated with the FEPC to investigate allegations of discrimination against African Americans at the Brooklyn Navy Yard in 1944 and 1945. The Brooklyn Navy Yard had 6,250 blacks on the payroll, making it the largest such employer in New York. Many complaints came from workers who were abused, intimidated, or otherwise received unsatisfactory treatment from peers or superiors. The most common charges came from skilled or semi-skilled employees who claimed they were denied requests for upgrades and promotions because of racial discrimination. When African American women at the Yard filed discrimination complaints alleging that they were forced to labor under conditions detrimental to their health and assigned menial work that was beneath their job classifications and abilities, they were given low efficiency ratings and assigned to even worse jobs. Rear Admiral Monroe R. Kelly, the Commandant of the Brooklyn Navy Yard, categorically denied the existence of any racial discrimination.[13]

The BKUL joined forces with the NNC to get black employee complaints at the Brooklyn Navy Yard registered with the FEPC. The organizations documented worker testimonies and forwarded them to the FEPC; Lorenzo Davis also filed a brief on behalf of the Citizens' Anti-Discrimination Committee on the Brooklyn Navy Yard, which he chaired. The FEPC responded by conducting an intensive series of investigations. Of the twenty-two cases brought before the FEPC in 1944 and 1945 claiming denials of promotions or upgrades, eleven of the plaintiffs won promotions. The BKUL/NNC campaign was not, however, a total victory. The FEPC dismissed all of the complaints about unfair firings and suspensions and all but one of the complaints about discriminatory hiring practices. Nevertheless, the relationships that the BKUL had formed with the NNC and the FEPC had a significant role in helping African American workers achieve higher status and pay and better working conditions at an important place of employment.[14]

While the Brooklyn Urban League cooperated with government agencies to end discrimination against black workers, organizations like the Negro Labor Victory Committee (NLVC), a subsidiary organization of the NNC founded in June 1942, worked with unions to expand job opportunities for New York's African Americans. The purpose of the NLVC was to open the doors of industry to everyone and to encourage black workers to join trade unions. The NLVC focused on increasing black union membership as a route to more hiring and better training of black workers. The NLVC also wanted to make the fight for equality for blacks and other minorities a core focus of the organized labor movement. It began as a coalition of fifty-seven American Federation of Labor (AFL)- and Congress of Industrial Organizations (CIO)-affiliated locals with a combined membership of over 200,000. Its leaders were all trade unionists—Ferdinand Smith of the Maritime Union, Dorothy Funn of the Teachers Union, and the most active member Charles Collins of the Hotel and Club Employees Union. By 1944 the number of unions affiliated with the NLVC increased to 107 with a membership exceeding 300,000. It would later expand into Newark, Buffalo, Baltimore, Philadelphia, St. Louis, and Washington, DC. The Committee petitioned the government to establish training programs for 100,000 black workers and a placement service so that these workers could get jobs in the war industries. It also called upon the federal War Production Board to immediately place trained African American workers in war-industries jobs, asked for additional war contracts for New York City, and urged that African Americans be appointed to policymaking boards and commissions. The organization also tried to convince union locals to alter discriminatory practices and influence nationals to enforce existing non-discrimination policies. In some AFL- and CIO-affiliated locals like the Fur Dressers and Dyers Union and the National Maritime Union, the NLVC received authorization to set up its own anti-discrimination committees. Although its influence was rather small, the NLVC actively pushed labor unions to open their doors to black workers and for black workers to walk through them.[15]

As the war came to a close, concerns about the displacement of black workers became paramount. When American GIs returned and wartime production slowed, African Americans would face massive layoffs and soaring unemployment rates that could lead to major disturbances in urban centers. Black leaders around the country worried that the same events that led to a wave of race riots after World War I would reoccur after World War II. African American organizations shifted their attention from job discrimination to job preservation, but they could not prevent job loss from happening. Many of the advances that black workers made during wartime were eroded when the conflict ended. Black veterans and craftsmen in the building trades faced particular discrimination. Skilled and semi-skilled work dried up as the labor market tightened.

The Urban League of Greater New York responded to these changing conditions by launching a Vocational Opportunity Campaign to train youths for the trades while maintaining its job placement program for people seeking employment. It struggled against difficult contemporary conditions, however, and could only place its applicants at a disheartening 25 percent rate. Its greatest successes were not in the trades, where job discrimination was once again prevalent, but in the clerical and sales sectors of the city's service industry. It placed people with companies that had never before hired African Americans, including Bell Telegraph Laboratories, Dry Dock Savings Bank, Franklin Simon & Co., the Fresh Air Fund, the *New York Herald Tribune*, Johns Manville, National Screen Service, and the New York City Parole Board. The Urban League of Greater New York trained blacks for civil service jobs and provided preparatory classes for civil service exams. Courses were taught by instructors from other social agencies, government offices, and the United Public Workers of America, an organization affiliated with the CIO.[16]

The NLVC and NNC worked during this period to minimize the loss of black industrial positions. The NLVC expanded its education programs to foster racial tolerance among union members. Both organizations called for unions to adjust their seniority policies to avoid the complete layoff of newly hired black workers and a return to exclusionary pre-war labor practices. NLVC Field Secretary M. Moran Weston urged organized labor in the fall of 1944 to implement a program for reconversion. He reported that both the AFL and CIO had broadly accepted the Committee's aims to protect the gains of black workers. The NLVC Executive Board designed a plan to protect the jobs of black workers during peacetime reconversion. The proposal urged unions to ensure maximum employment for African Americans during large-scale layoffs. The NLVC plan accepted seniority rules, but implemented special formulae and procedures to avoid the firing of recently hired black workers. The Committee also called for blacks to have access to all of the union's relocation, training, and settlement programs and compensation packages. The measures would essentially prevent black workers from being relegated to service and unskilled employment, which would have effectively turned back the advances they had made during the war.[17]

For many African Americans, World War II offered opportunities for economic advancement. As defense production increased, blacks around the country looked to get better paying industrial jobs. Black activists in New York City mobilized around the idea of equal employment opportunity to push government to protect what they viewed as a civil right. African American leaders and organizations like the NAACP, the National Negro Congress, and the National Urban League embarked on press campaigns and public protests to pressure war industries to hire black workers. Of the many organizations advocating an end to discrimination in New York's war industries, the Urban League, especially the Industrial Department of the Brooklyn Urban League, played a unique and important role. The Brooklyn Urban League cultivated a close collaborative relationship with government anti-discrimination offices. By directing qualified black workers to interviews at defense industries, sharing information about industry hiring practices with government agencies, and referring discrimination cases to local FEPC and COD offices, the Brooklyn Urban League became part of the fair employment enforcement infrastructure. Its activities ultimately expanded and improved the types of jobs available to black workers in New York's war industries—the major goal for the period's civil rights activists. Although some of these gains were temporarily lost immediately after the war, they ultimately became the foundation of lasting opportunities for African Americans.

NOTES

1. Cheryl Lynn Greenberg, *Or Does it Explode: Black Harlem in the Great Depression* (New York: Oxford University Press, 1991), 114–39.
2. "WPA Defense Job Opportunities," *New York Amsterdam News*, November 30, 1940; "Seek Race Employment in Defense Industries," *New York Amsterdam News*, December 7, 1940; Editorial page, untitled, *New York Amsterdam News*, December 7, 1940; Editorial page, "Must Better Themselves," *New York Amsterdam News*, December 14, 1940; Editorial page, "Give Negroes Jobs," *New York Amsterdam News*, January 18, 1941; "Means by which Defense Commission can Eliminate Discrimination Suggested," *New York Amsterdam News*, February 15, 1941; Editorial page, "Millions of Negroes Idle," *New York Amsterdam News*, March 1, 1941; "Real Bottleneck of Defense Program," *New York Amsterdam News*, December 21, 1940.
3. "It Just Doesn't Make Sense," *New York Amsterdam News*, January 18, 1941; "Airplane Firm Said Bending to Pressure," *New York Amsterdam News*, August 23, 1941.
4. "NAACP Maps Huge Confab: Walter White to Give Main Talk at Boys' High Meeting," *New York Amsterdam News*, January 25, 1941; "Defense Bias Will Be Aired," *New York Amsterdam News*, January 25, 1941; "Drive Against Program Bias," *New York Amsterdam News*, January 18, 1941.
5. John Roman, "People's Court Plans Quiz on Harlem Conditions," *New York Amsterdam News*, February 1, 1941; Greenberg, *Or Does it Explode*, 133, 203; "Pressure Planned by Harlem Group," *New York Times*, November 13, 1941.

6. Washburn quoted in "Governor's Man Blasts Brooklyn," *Voice*, March 21, 1942; "Discrimination Against Races Prevails Here," *Brooklyn Citizen*, March 18, 1942, New York State Committee on Discrimination Archives, New York State Archives, Albany, NY (hereafter cited as "NYCOD Archives"), Box 4, Folder 209.
7. "Rally To Determine Negro's Part in Defense," *New York Amsterdam News*, January 25, 1941; "Boro NAACP Conference Assails Discrimination," *New York Amsterdam News*, February 1, 1941; R.E. Gillmor, "How Can the Negro Hold His Job? [1945]," Public Information and Advertising Department Records, Series II, Box 18, Folder 4, Sperry Gyroscope Company Records, Hagley Library, Wilmington, DE; "Letter from E. Frederic Morrow to Fred Turner," February 3, 1941, Legal Papers of the NAACP, Part 15, Series A, Legal Department Complaints and Responses, 1940–1955, Series A: Legal Department Files, Discrimination Sperry, 1941–1943 Folder, microfilm reel 7 (Bethesda: University Publications of America, 1991).
8. "Harlem Assemblymen Spur Movement to Air Racial Discrimination in State," *New York Amsterdam News*, March 1, 1941; Greenberg, *Or Does It Explode*, 203; "Cecilia Ager Meets The State Industrial Commissioner," *New York PM*, March 12, 1942, NYCOD Archives, Box 4, Folder 209.
9. "To Demand FDR Issue Exec Order Banning Bias," *New York Amsterdam News*, April 12, 1941.
10. "A. F. of L. Threatens to Drop Union Said to Bar Working with Negroes," *New York Times*, February 18, 1942.
11. New York Urban League 1985 commemorative pamphlet, *National Urban League, Inc. 75th Anniversary, 1910–1985*, 17; "Negro Associations Interested in Training and Placement," March 15, 1943, New York State War Council Committee on Discrimination Papers, New York State Archives, Albany, NY (hereafter cited as "War Council Papers"), Box 4, Folder 202; "Letter from Lorenzo Davis, Industrial Secretary of the Brooklyn Urban League, to Charles Berkley, Executive Director, of the Committee on Discrimination," August 6, 1943, NYCOD Archives, Box 7, Folder 340; "Letter from Lorenzo Davis to Charles Berkley, July 24, 1943," War Council Papers, Box 7, Folder 340.
12. "Labor Market and Development Reports," April 15–May 31, 1943, New York Metropolitan Region, United States Employment Service of the War Manpower Commission, June 1943, War Council Papers, Box 6, Folder 271; "Negro Worker Asset or Liability? America Must Decide," Semi-Annual Report of the Brooklyn Urban League Industrial Department, August 1943, NYCOD Archives, Box 7, Folder 340.
13. "Labor Market Development Report," New York Metropolitan Region, February-March 1945, 14, War Council Papers, Box 7, Folder 319.
14. Rear Admiral Kelly, "Scores Navy Yard Racial Bias," *New York Amsterdam News*, October 9, 1943; "Letter from Lorenzo Davis to the Commandant of the United States Navy Yard, January 5, 1943" and "Letter from Lorenzo Davis to members of the Citizen's Anti-Discrimination Committee on the Brooklyn Navy Yard, December 17, 1943," both in National Negro Congress Papers, Schomburg Research Library, New York Public Library, New York, NY (hereafter cited as "NNC Papers"), Part 4, Box 73, Folder 16; Untitled Entry 70, Box 562, Fair Employment Practices Commission Papers (Record Group 228), National Archives and Records Administration, Northeast Region, New York, NY.
15. Negro Labor Victory Committee, "Correspondence, Fact Sheet and List of Offices," NNC Papers, Part 4, Box 73, Folder 1; Alvin C. Hughes, "Let Us Do Our Part: The New York City Based Negro Labor Victory Committee,

1941–1945," *Afro-Americans in New York Life and History* 10:1 (January 1986): 19–29.

16. "Expansion in Industrial Relations," *Urban League of New York Reports to Its Friends*, 4–5 in Olivia Frost Papers, Box 2, Folder 11, New York Public Library, New York, NY.
17. "Statement by M. Moran Weston at National Urban League Conference," Fall 1944, NNC Papers, Part 4, Box 80, Folder 122a; "Press Release September 5, 1945," NNC Papers, Part 4, Box 79, Folder 99.

4 Early Economic Civil Rights in Washington, DC

The New Negro Alliance, Howard University, and the Interracial Workshop

Derek Charles Catsam

Alabama native John Lewis had never been to the nation's capital prior to his 1961 arrival for a pre-departure training session for the Freedom Rides. He was astonished by what he saw. From the Greyhound bus station that marked his introduction to the city, Lewis could see the tops of the Washington Monument and the U.S. Capitol. This was all new for him. "I had been in big cities before. But this was more than big," he wrote. "This was the seat of the nation's government, the place where laws were made, the center of all that the country stood for. That, combined with the purpose for which I had come, made the moment overwhelming, truly magical."[1]

Washington, DC may have symbolized to some citizens all the good things that America stood for, but many of the city's black denizens had a different perspective. In addition to its symbolic significance as the nation's capital, its role as the seat of the federal government, and its status as the site of some of our country's most important monuments, at certain times Washington had also become a strategic locus for the black freedom struggle. Although a series of municipal statutes in the late 1800s had actually eliminated *de jure* segregation, Washington was no doubt a Jim Crow city. The overwhelming majority of Washington's restaurants, bars, cafés, and lunch counters were segregated. With few exceptions—cafeterias in government buildings, the Young Women's Christian Association, and Union Station—downtown Washington's eating and restroom facilities were off-limits to African Americans. The journalist I.F. Stone wrote of his experience with the segregated nature of eateries in Washington when he tried to have lunch with Judge William Hastie at the National Press Club and they were refused service. In *The Nation*, Stone wrote that "it takes a little while to catch the extent to which Washington is a Jim Crow town," before quitting the National Press Club.[2]

As a segregated city and the nation's capital, Washington played an important, if largely overlooked, role in the black fight for equality, especially during the 1930s and 1940s. Furthermore, civil rights campaigns in Washington reveal the remarkable extent that economic opportunity played a role in the long civil rights movement. Commerce and employment were front and center; there was always an economic aspect to demands for racial justice. This chapter explores a series of movements that took place in Washington, DC during the World War II era. Although not directly connected, these actions built upon each other, becoming more complex over the years and presaging a number of campaigns that would not flourish until the 1960s. Although DC does not get much attention as a center of black resistance, the events of the 1930s and 1940s suggest otherwise. In particular, the civil rights activities of the New Negro Alliance, The March on Washington Campaign, Howard University student groups, and the Interracial Workshop deserve a place in the telling of civil rights history as important antecedents to the full-fledged movement for racial justice that would emerge nationwide over the next three decades.

THE NEW NEGRO ALLIANCE

African American organizations mobilized against segregation and economic inequalities long before the Montgomery Bus Boycott. The New Negro Alliance (NNA), for example, was a Washington-based organization founded in 1933 that used direct-action protests such as pickets to promote civil rights. In the decade or so prior to the onset of World War II, the NNA was probably the largest and most effective local organization to use economic boycotts to challenge Jim Crow. The NNA came into existence when the white-owned Hamburger Grill fired three black employees and replaced them with whites. A neighborhood group of black men led by twenty-one-year-old Williams College graduate John Aubry Davis decided to boycott the restaurant. Within two days the boycott proved effective, as the Hamburger Grill rehired the three black workers.[3]

Realizing that their tactic had long-range potential, Davis and the others formed the NNA to mobilize blacks and whites to challenge discriminatory hiring practices, demand promotion of African American workers, and fight discrimination. Building on its Hamburger Grill protests the Alliance engaged in "Don't Buy Where You Can't Work" and "Jobs for Negroes" campaigns throughout the city. They scored several victories between 1933–35 over white-owned businesses including the A&P grocery chain and the *Evening Star* newspaper, as well as a number of smaller businesses. By choosing its targets wisely, the NNA often achieved its goals through negotiation rather than by the use of pickets.[4]

The organization's biggest victory came when the Sanitary Grocery Company (which changed its name to Safeway in 1938) took the NNA to court for conducting illegal pickets. Congress had passed the 1932 Norris-LaGuardia Act in order to protect the rights of protesters, but some area businesses, including Kaufman's department store and High's ice cream parlor, had nonetheless used court injunctions to prevent NNA pickets. Lower courts had ruled that the NNA represented neither employees nor a competing business that could be harmed by the hiring practices of the picketed stores. The Supreme Court, however, in *New Negro Alliance v. Sanitary Grocery Company, Inc.*, saw differently. By a 6–3 majority, led by Justice Charles Evans Hughes, the court ruled that "those having a direct or indirect interest" in matters of employment "should be at liberty to" take action against discrimination and "peacefully persuade others to concur in their views respecting an employer's practices."[5]

Although the Supreme Court's decision led to the formation of "Don't Buy Where You Can't Work" campaigns across the country and the NNA's actions were an important precursor to the student movement of the 1960s, the organization did not ultimately prove successful. It lost a protracted standoff with the People's Drug Store chain. Although it defeated Sanitary Grocery Company in court for the right to picket, the company still refused to yield to NNA demands. The NNA's failure to achieve victories in its campaigns against Safeway and People's Drug Store led to its demise in 1941.[6]

The NNA's dismantling notwithstanding, Washington became an important backdrop for the national civil rights agenda when in 1941 A. Philip Randolph, head of the Brotherhood of Sleeping Car Porters and one of the most important African American leaders of the twentieth century, made his famous call for a "March on Washington" to protest segregation and discrimination. Following an unsatisfying meeting between President Franklin Roosevelt, Randolph, NAACP Secretary Walter White, and T. Arnold Hill of the National Urban League in September 1940 in which they asked Roosevelt to integrate the U.S. Armed Forces and open defense jobs to blacks, Randolph called for a July 1, 1941 March on Washington. Randolph would use his sway over the Brotherhood of Sleeping Car Porters, which numbered some 10,000 members, as well as his ties to other organizations to generate a massive demonstration.[7]

Roosevelt recognized what a potential embarrassment this might be for his administration and to the nation; to avert it he called a meeting with Randolph and White for June 18, 1941. By this time White and Randolph estimated that they would have 100,000 participants in the march. Roosevelt compromised. On June 25 he issued Executive Order 8802, which outlawed discrimination in federal employment. Roosevelt did not desegregate the military, but his executive order placated Randolph, White, and other civil rights activists temporarily and prevented a march that might have discredited Roosevelt at a time when the President hoped to mobilize support for U.S. involvement in the cauldron that had become world affairs. Roosevelt's actions also served to make groups such as the New Negro Alliance less necessary.

Randolph was not fully satisfied with the executive order, even if he decided not to go through with the March on Washington. During 1942 he organized the "March on Washington Movement," which did not march in DC but instead brought together African American groups in mass meetings to advocate an eight-point program of civil rights. These eight points included the full elimination of Jim Crow laws; enforcement of the Fifth and Fourteenth Amendments, particularly to eliminate lynching; protection of all voting rights, including the elimination of poll taxes; abolition of segregation in the armed services; an end to discrimination in jobs and job training and a granting of permanent status for the federal Fair Employment Practices Commission; the withholding of all federal funds from any agency that practiced discrimination; the establishment of African American representation in all government administrative agencies; and black representation on all missions related to the peace after the end of the war. Economic freedom, if not at the very core of all these points, is clearly connected to most of them.[8]

THE HOWARD UNIVERSITY STUDENT MOVEMENT

With the exception of those that developed out of Howard University's student body, Washington's civil rights organizations were largely quiescent during World War II. Howard was the nation's premiere black university, a distinction particularly noteworthy in an era when many schools and virtually all of those in the South were segregated either by law or by custom. Howard drew the cream of the crop of African American college and graduate students from across the country. Howard carried an elite status for blacks like Ivy League schools did among white Americans. World War II awakened many Howard students—some of whom had been as blissfully unaware of social and political realities as their white Ivy League counterparts—to the disconnect between America's stated ideals in fighting a war for freedom and democracy abroad (and using African American troops in segregated units to do so) and the realities blacks faced in the United States. Most Howard students were well aware of the racism endemic to American society but many believed, as their parents did, that the best way to overcome inequalities was through education. By the 1940s, however, a small cadre of students was no longer prepared to sit back and accept the indignities of daily life in the nation's capital.

Students began to use direct action to challenge segregation in restaurants and cafés near the Howard campus in 1943. Many had grown tired of the treatment they received at local establishments where they spent their money. Coupled with a general sense of discontent over the plight of the many Howard students called to serve in the segregated military, these protests fueled the early sit-in movement in Washington. The university's law school students were especially militant. William Hastie, who was on a leave of absence as dean of Howard Law School, resigned his post as civilian aide to Secretary of War Henry L. Stimson to protest segregation in the armed services. A number of law students followed Hastie's act of conscience by defying or circumventing their draft orders. Some Howard student leaders embraced Gandhian nonviolent protest and Randolph's March on Washington movement, both of which resonated among their peers. Several off-campus racial incidents exacerbated the sense of discontentment among the student body. One of these confrontations proved to be a catalyst for a little-known but remarkably resilient campaign among Howard students in their Washington neighborhood.[9]

Three sophomore women, Ruth Powell from Massachusetts and Ohioans Marianne Musgrave and Juanita Morrow, ordered hot chocolates in a United Cigar store on Pennsylvania Avenue. At first they were refused service and the manager summoned police. When the police came, however, it appeared as if the manager's plan had backfired. The police officer ordered the waitress to serve the women. When they received their bill, Powell, Musgrave, and Morrow realized that they had been charged twenty-five cents for each of their drinks. The normal cost was ten cents. When they placed a total of thirty-five cents on the counter and got up to leave they were arrested. In humiliating fashion the police dragged them away in paddy wagons, searched them, and threw them in jail. Ruth Powell later reported that the arresting officers told them that they were under investigation because there was no proof that they were not subversive agents. After a few hours in jail one of the college deans discovered the women's arrest and bailed them out. The police did not file charges, so clearly this was a case of harassment and intimidation of students who had broken no laws but rather had crossed the line of racial mores.[10]

When word of the arrests circulated around campus, the Howard community was outraged. University officials entreated students to work through their NAACP chapter rather than engage in independent protest actions, but a student named William C. Raines had a different idea. He argued for a tactic that he called "the stool-sitting technique." In a foreshadowing of what a future generation of students would do in an epochal moment in civil rights history, Raines argued: "Let's go downtown some lunch hour when they're crowded, and if they won't serve us, we'll just sit there and read our books. They'll lose trade while that seat is out of circulation. If enough people occupy seats, they'll lose so much trade they'll start thinking."[11]

Most students did not embrace Raines' idea right away, but there were some adherents like Ruth Powell, who engaged for some time in a one-woman protest along the lines of what Raines had concocted. Powell first encountered Jim Crow as a sophomore. Coming from the Boston suburbs, Powell went to college having experienced little of the discrimination that was commonplace for many of her classmates, but she felt that many of her peers had grown complacent about segregation. Rather than try to lead a direct-action campaign during the repressive early years of the war, she instead engaged in a one-woman sit-in movement. She would go to a restaurant, ask for service, and when denied would sit, often for hours at a time. She would focus on one member of the staff and stare at him or her, making them feel uncomfortable and oftentimes guilty. Her activities culminated in her arrest at United Cigar with her two friends. The event pushed members of the Howard community to follow Powell's example and take the sort of action that Raines had advocated before he left the university to enter Tuskegee's flight program. An organization called the Student Committee on Campus Opinion polled 292 students. Ninety-seven percent of them said that they did not believe that blacks should wait until the war was over to mobilize against Jim Crow and 96 percent believed that students should be at the forefront of such a movement. The Howard chapter of the NAACP facilitated the formation of a student-led civil rights committee. Students also formed a subcommittee on direct action, which Powell chaired.[12]

Drawing from some of the most talented students on campus, the direct-action subcommittee planned sit-ins at local restaurants. Its first targets were on the neighboring stretch of U Street that was a central location of Washington's black community but where the businesses mostly catered to whites only. The subcommittee targeted the Little Palace restaurant. The proprietor, Mr. W.S. Choconas, was committed to keeping his restaurant all-white. After several days of fundraising, conducting educational and strategic meetings, and planning the course of events, the first challenge at the Little Palace came on April 17, 1943. Students occupied the tables, armed with magazines, textbooks, and the accoutrements of student life. Outside, other students picketed, carrying signs reading "Our Boys, Our Bonds, Our Brothers are fighting for YOU! Why can't we eat together?" and "There's No Segregation Law in DC. What's Your Story Little Palace?" Choconas called the police, but as the students were violating no laws, the officers left without arresting anyone or breaking up the protest, and the students continued until Choconas closed early. This protest took place on a Saturday. The students resumed their action when the restaurant reopened on Monday and by Wednesday Choconas had capitulated. The students were able to desegregate one more restaurant that spring before exams and summer vacation.[13]

A year later Howard students engaged in another protest, this time at a restaurant that was part of a local chain called Thompson's. Fifty-six students gathered at the restaurant on April 22 under the auspices of the university's civil rights committee. All of the students had signed a pledge indicating that they opposed discrimination and believed that all Americans, especially those fighting overseas, deserved to share in the "Four Freedoms" that President Roosevelt had celebrated. The students also promised to conduct themselves respectably. They entered the restaurant in groups of two and three, requested service, and were denied. Then the students took seats. Leaders of the organization entered into negotiations with restaurant management, who after some time called local police as student picketers carrying signs with slogans such as "Are you for HITLER's Way (Race Supremacy) or the AMERICAN Way (Equality)? Make Up Your Mind!" gathered outside drawing crowds of onlookers, some of whom supported the cause whereas others voiced their disapproval. Eventually the management, apparently at the behest of the restaurant company's Chicago headquarters, agreed to serve the students in hopes of stanching an exodus of its paying customers. When waitresses refused, a manager and district supervisor took over their duties.[14]

The victory was meaningful but the movement soon met fatal resistance. When a small group of students returned to Thompson's a few days later they were refused service. Student protesters were preparing for negotiations and planning further action when they were stopped by an unexpected opponent, Howard University President Dr. Mordecai W. Johnson. Johnson determined that the students were in violation of university bylaws by virtue of there being no policy explicitly allowing student organizations "to engage in a program of direct action in the city of Washington for the purpose of accomplishing social reform affecting institutions other than Howard University itself." The university policy effectively appeared to be that student rights had to be explicitly enumerated in order to be valid. Students were at first reluctant to get behind this seemingly capricious ruling but relented after university officials explained to them Howard's precarious economic status. The administration discouraged student protest because the school was vulnerable to the whims of segregationist politicians. The chair of the Congressional committee that apportioned most of the university's funding was none other than Mississippi's staunch segregationist Senator Theodore G. Bilbo. Although Johnson was sometimes described as a militant defender of black rights, direct action was too much for him to allow during the politically fraught wartime era. But for many of the Howard students their struggle revealed the possibilities of direct action, possibilities that others would bring to full fruition less than two decades later.[15]

THE INTERRACIAL WORKSHOP

With the end of the war came a re-emergence of civil rights activities in Washington, DC. Perhaps the most active and effective effort came from the Interracial Workshop (IW), which first met in July 1947. Thirty-two congregants gathered from around the country to gain insight and experience at the hands of some of the movement's most experienced practitioners in working direct-action campaigns. The Congress of Racial Equality, a civil rights organization dedicated to gaining black rights through nonviolent protest, and the Fellowship of Reconciliation, a pacifist human rights organization, sponsored the IW. In April 1947, the two groups joined for a "Journey of Reconciliation" to test the application of the Supreme Court's 1946 decision in *Morgan v. Virginia* outlawing Jim Crow seating for interstate passengers. They brought this experience to their work with the IW.[16]

The IW had three aims: to demonstrate that persons of differing backgrounds could live together harmoniously, to study the race problem and nonviolent techniques for dealing with it, and perhaps most importantly to apply and dramatize effective nonviolent techniques for combating discrimination. In addition to direct-action campaigns, the group engaged in recreational activities such as parties and outings in the region. They heard several prominent speakers including Mary McLeod Bethune (who had the group to her home at the headquarters of the National Council of Negro Women), Howard University sociologist E. Franklin Frazier, and Washington NAACP counsel Leon Ransom.[17]

The Interracial Workshop was a comprehensive endeavor. Unlike the Howard students, members of the workshop did not focus solely on integrating restaurants. Unlike the New Negro Alliance, the IW did not emphasize employment possibilities over all others. Instead, the organization strove to improve the lives of Washington's blacks through various direct-action protests. Soon after its formation the group engaged in several efforts that drew attention from the African American press. The IW protested discrimination in city eateries, including one cafeteria at the Methodist Building next door to the Supreme Court, challenged Jim Crow at the Young Men's Christian Association (YMCA), and tested segregated seating and service policies at the National Zoo. Within a few weeks the YMCA agreed to end discriminatory policies after several protests. The National Zoo took a bit longer. An anonymous epistle that the Workshop received indicated one extreme of local attitudes about its endeavors, claiming that baboons "have more intelligence than the niggers who gape at us and most of us look more like humans that [sic] these gorillas." The IW received daily postcards and letters of support, shock, outrage, and hate. It pressed on until zoo officials agreed to follow a committee's recommendations for addressing discrimination.[18]

Most of the IW's protests concerned the participation of African Americans in the city's economic life. It distributed "Where Can I Eat?" lists that told black patrons which downtown restaurants accepted their trade. The group also handed out leaflets at bus stations informing passengers of the Supreme Court's *Morgan* decision that had ruled segregation on interstate conveyances to be unconstitutional and encouraging them to assert their rights under that ruling. The group handed out 5,000 copies of the leaflet over the course of a three-day campaign.[19]

The IW gained publicity through a number of measures, including the composition and production of songs. Bayard Rustin, whose musical talent was legendary within the movement, collaborated with several others to produce "You Don't Have to Ride Jim Crow." The song had seven stanzas and appropriated the melody of the familiar tune "There's No Hidin' Place Down Here." The first stanza went as follows:

> You Don't Have To Ride Jim Crow,
> You Don't Have to Ride Jim Crow,
> On June The Third
> The High Court Said
> If You Ride Interstate Jim Crow is Dead.
> You Don't Have to Ride Jim Crow.

The group distributed more than 30,000 leaflets on various other topics, such as its call for volunteers, "Non-Violent Direct Action"; "Let Us Break Bread Together," which they distributed at the YMCA; "Democracy in the Balance" which they prepared for the Methodist Building; and "What's The Interracial Workshop?" The leaflets also included announcements of mass meetings.[20]

The IW produced a comprehensive report that included broad observations about race relations and the state of black protest in Washington. It paid particular attention to the relationships between U.S. foreign policy and the African American freedom struggle at home. Workshop participants noted, for example, that the Cold War had become a consistent thorn in the sides of activists: "The 'RED SCARE' in the United States is having its effect upon all non-totalitarian groups attempting to bring about real social change." IW participants stated that anticommunism was primarily "aimed at undermining liberals by rendering their progressive programs ineffective" and feared that the Cold War would remain a problem for groups committed to nonviolent direct action.[21]

Workshop participants also believed that America's moral authority as a defender of democracy abroad was compromised by segregation and resistance to integration. In its efforts to desegregate the YMCA, for example, IW activists found that not only African Americans but also Indian nationals were targeted for discrimination. American racial mores could have international impact. After observing an Indian engineering student denied service at the YMCA, one of his countrymen wrote in a letter to New York's leftist *PM* newspaper about the hypocrisy of the situation: "India, which has had to take the nagging from the USA for our practice of the caste system" when American policies "have not proved to have done any good for your own people." Ultimately, as scholar Mary Dudziak has convincingly argued, this tension between Cold War ideals and segregationist practices would play a major role in government responses to civil rights efforts over the next fifteen years.[22]

The report firmly established the IW's dedication to direct action as the vanguard civil rights tactic. Continued pressure on the government would be the only way to assure the continued integration of Washington, DC. The report also stressed the importance of communicating and working with area police, cultivating ties with the media, and responding to the needs of community members. Workshop participants believed strongly that they had set something good in motion and that they had gained a lot from their experience. As one noted, "I have appreciated the opportunity of living for a couple of weeks with an interracial group. Now I *know* it can be done!" Another felt that she could take her experience and apply it in the South. "I think I now know what approaches may be possible in my new work in Kingsley House Settlement in New Orleans." The IW sputtered along for another two years, but with money tight and the environment not yet fully ready to support the sort of nonviolent direct-action campaigns that it advocated, the group's high water mark continued to be that stretch in July 1947 when it showed some of the potential for its approach to civil rights questions. Members hoped that others would follow through with what they had started.[23]

Several other organizations also sprang up to join the battle for racial equality in the nation's capital during the 1940s. Lawyer Leon Ransom founded the Committee for Racial Democracy in the Nation's Capital, which lasted from 1946–48. Its goal was to "encourage unity of action among the many civic, labor, religious, cooperative and women's organizations" in Washington and to pull together leaders to "achieve a combination of good neighbor relations and good legislation which will spell the end to segregation and discrimination." Although it rallied middle-class black Washingtonians to develop a commitment to equality, the organization's unwillingness to pick up the mantle of direct action rendered it largely ineffective. The New Negro Alliance tried to re-form in hopes of resuming where it had left off a decade earlier, but struggled to recapture its past glory as the Washington NAACP became the city's most prominent civil rights organization. The late 1940s were a good time for these nascent groups to try to fight Jim Crow, but after an initial modicum of success they were unable to gain the wholesale foothold for which they had hoped.[24]

The efforts of various organizations in the late 1940s may have contributed to the slow changes that began to take place in Washington during the 1950s. Many of these changes came in the form of coattails victories that came down in the wake of the series of Supreme Court cases like *Brown v. Board of Education* that helped blacks nationwide. The Washington-based 1954 case *Bolling v. Sharpe* buttressed *Brown* when the Supreme Court ruled that the federal government, and not just the states, could not maintain segregated schools. Some area businesses began to accept integration, although many more did not. The DC schools integrated, sometimes without a hitch and sometimes to the improvement of educational standards for blacks. During this time period Washington was on its way to becoming a predominantly African American city. Many segregationist organizations in the Deep South used this change to paint a bleak picture and to scare southerners into believing that the federal government wanted the rest of the South to be like the nation's capital. Had these rabble rousers only known how much Washington resembled the Jim Crow South, however, they may well have taken a more charitable view of the city.[25]

We should not overlook the civil rights contributions that came out of Washington, DC during the 1930s and 1940s. Many of these campaigns presaged what would occur during the civil rights and black power movements of the 1960s and 1970s. Boycotts and other economic direct-action tactics that would become commonplace in later decades were proven effective early on in Washington. The multi-front campaign by the Interracial Workshop anticipated the agendas of several 1960s-era civil rights groups. Sit-ins by Howard University students happened two decades before such protests became the direct-action tactic of choice for young African Americans. Although Washington remained segregated as the World War II era came to an end, the actions there by civil rights organizations proved to be important precursors to what would happen a generation later, including A. Philip Randolph's 1963 March on Washington for Jobs and Freedom, the largest civil rights protest in American history.

NOTES

1. John Lewis, *Walking With the Wind* (New York: Simon & Schuster, 1998), 136. For more on the Freedom Rides, see Derek Charles Catsam, *Freedom's Main Line: The Journey of Reconciliation and the Freedom Rides* (Lexington: University Press of Kentucky, 2009) and Raymond Arsenault, *Freedom Riders: 1961 and the Struggle for Racial Justice* (New York: Oxford University Press, 2006).
2. Kenesaw M. Landis, *Segregation in Washington: A Report of the National Committee on Segregation in the Nation's Capital, November 1948* excerpted in John H. Bracey, Jr., August Meier, and Elliott Rudwick, eds., *The Afro-Americans: Selected Documents* (Boston: Allyn and Bacon, 1972), 622–36. See also Haynes Johnson's nine-part series, "The Negro in Washington," which ran from May 21 to May 30, 1961 in the *Washington Star*; Flora Bryant Brown, "NAACP Sponsored Sit-ins by Howard University Students in Washington, D.C., 1943–1944," *Journal of Negro History* 85:4 (Autumn 2000): 275; *Fellowship*, September 1947 and "Interracial Workshop: Progress Report," both in Swarthmore Peace Collection, Swarthmore College (hereafter cited as "Swarthmore Peace Collection"), Document Group 13, Series E, Box 19; Pauli Murray, *Song In a Weary Throat: An American Pilgrimage* (New York: Harper & Row, 1987), 200; I.F. Stone, "Capitol Notes," *The Nation*, April 10, 1943, 512–13.
3. Bart Barnes, "John Aubrey Davis Sr.; Scholar, Rights Activist Who Led Boycotts," *Washington Post*, December 21, 2002; Derek Catsam, "New Negro Alliance," in Nina Mjagkij, ed. *Organizing Black America: An Encyclopedia of African American Organizations* (New York: Garland Publishing, 2001), 514–15.
4. Michele F. Pacifico, "'Don't Buy Where You Can't Work': The New Negro Alliance of Washington," *Washington History* 6:1 (Spring-Summer 1994): 66–88.
5. *New Negro Alliance v. Sanitary Grocery Company, Inc.* (303 U.S. 552): 562–63.
6. Catsam, "New Negro Alliance," 514–15; Pacifico, "'Don't Buy Where You Can't Work,'" 66–88.
7. A. Philip Randolph, "Why Should We March?," *Survey Graphic*, November 1942, 488–89; Harvey Wish, ed., *The Negro Since Emancipation* (Englewood Cliffs: Prentice-Hall, 1964), 158–62; "Excerpts from Keynote Address to the Policy Conference of the March on Washington Movement," in Joanne Grant, ed., *Black Protest: History, Document, and Analyses* (New York: Ballantine, 1986), 243–50; Lucy G. Barber, *Marching on Washington: The Forging of An American Political Tradition* (Berkeley: University of California Press, 2004), especially 108–40; March on Washington Committee, "Call to Negro America: To March on Washington for Jobs and Equal Participation in National Defense," *The Black Worker*, May 1941; Beth Tompkins Bates, *Pullman Porters and the Rise of Protest Politics in Black*

America, 1925–1945 (Chapel Hill: University of North Carolina Press, 2001), 148–74.

8. Randolph, "Why Should We March?," 489; Wish, *The Negro Since Emancipation*, 162.
9. Murray, *Song in a Weary Throat*, 198–209; Brown, "NAACP Sponsored Sit-ins," 202–203, 274–86.
10. Brown, "NAACP Sponsored Sit-ins," 202–203.
11. Raines quoted in Brown, "NAACP Sponsored Sit-ins," 203.
12. Brown, "NAACP Sponsored Sit-ins," 204–206, 277–78.
13. Murray, *Song in a Weary Throat*, 206–209. Murray spelled the proprietor's name "Chaconas." The April 23, 1943 *Baltimore Afro-American* spelled it "Choconas."
14. Brown, "NAACP Sponsored Sit-ins," 279–81; Murray, *Song in a Weary Throat*, 222–25; Steven F. Lawson, *Running For Freedom: Civil Rights and Black Politics in Americas Since 1941*, 3rd Edition (Malden: Wiley-Blackwell, [1990] 2009), 12–13.
15. Johnson quoted in Brown, "NAACP Sponsored Sit-ins," 280.
16. Catsam, *Freedom's Main Line*, 13–45 and 77–78.
17. Catsam, *Freedom's Main Line*, 13–45 and 77–78.
18. "Interracial Workshop: Progress Report".
19. *Fellowship*, September 1947; Catsam, *Freedom's Main Line*, 14–18; "Interracial Workshop: Progress Report"; "Interracial Workshop Puts Religious Groups 'On Spot,'" *Baltimore Afro-American*, July 15, 1947.
20. On the Journey of Reconciliation see Catsam, *Freedom's Main Line*, 13–46; "You Don't Have To Ride Jim Crow," Swarthmore Peace Collection, Document Group 13, Series E, Box 19; "Interracial Workshop: Progress Report"; "Interracial Workshop Puts".
21. "Interracial Workshop: Progress Report".
22. *PM* quoted in "Interracial Workshop: Progress Report"; Mary Dudziak, *Cold War Civil Rights: Race and the Image of American Democracy* (Princeton: Princeton University Press, 2000).
23. "Interracial Workshop: Progress Report". For more on the Interracial Workshop's later work see Washington Interracial Workshop Papers, Albert Mindlin Collection, State Historical Society of Wisconsin, Madison, WI, Box 1, Folders 3 and 4.
24. See "Personal and Family Papers: Committee for Racial Democracy in the Nation's Capital 1946–1948," Leon Ransom Papers, Howard University, Moorland-Spingarn Research Center, Box 1, Folder 84.
25. "The Truth About Desegregation in Washington's Schools," *Washington Post and Times Herald*, December 22 through December 28, 1958, reprinted by The Turnpike Press, Annandale, VA in Payne Papers, William Stanley Hoole Special Collections Library, University of Alabama, Box 3 (hereafter cited as "Payne Papers"). Also see Citizens Councils of Alabama, "What Integration Has Done to Your Nation's Capitol [sic]," Payne Papers, Box 3. On the *Bolling* decision see *Bolling v. Sharpe* (347 U.S. 497); Lisa A. Crooms, "Race, Education and the District of Columbia: The Meaning and Legacy of *Bolling v. Sharpe*," and Bell Clement, "Pushback: The White Community's Dissent from *Bolling*," both in *Washington History* 16:2 (Fall/Winter 2004–2005): 14–25, 86–109.

5 The Moral Economy of Postwar Radical Interracial Summer Camping

Orion A. Teal

In December 1945, a group of children gathered for a reunion of Camp Wo-Chi-Ca (Workers' Children's Camp), a New Jersey summer camp with ties to the Communist Party (CP). While renewing friendships forged during the previous summer, the youngsters explored the possibilities for the postwar United States by imagining their "World of Tomorrow." Their vision was a place filled with "houses straight and tall," where "Health is not bought with money," "Schools are free for all people," and "Brown and white people go hand in hand [s]haring the fruits of the people's struggles." This utopia was a distinctly urban vision, simultaneously titled the "City of Tomorrow." In their city, "the Ghettos and Chinatowns and Harlems" would disappear, to be replaced by equal housing regardless of class, race, or ethnicity. "In order to help carry out these beliefs," the youngsters declared, "we pledge ourselves to keep racial equality in our camp and to try to spread the idea of racial equality wherever we go." The ex-campers' idealism so moved Wo-Chi-Ca administrators that they made the World of Tomorrow part of the camp's official credo. The youngsters' critique of racial capitalism captured the spirit of a fleeting alliance between the labor movement, civil rights activists, and leftwing political organizations during and immediately after World War II.[1]

Few groups forwarded a more penetrating critique of race and class during this period than the Communist Party. Communists protested discrimination in public housing, schools, and workplaces; threw their support behind African Americans wrongly tried for crimes, including the Trenton Six, Rosa Lee Ingram, and Willie McGee; celebrated black history and culture; fought against "white chauvinism" within its own ranks; and practiced affirmative action. Although critics have questioned the motivation behind communists' civil rights activism, the fact remains that the Party was the only majority-white organization willing to take up black civil rights with such force and commitment. African Americans never joined the communist movement in large numbers, but many welcomed its vocal denunciations of racism and worked closely with Party members in local affairs. As historian Martha Biondi has shown, these connections were particularly strong in New York City, the headquarters of the American communist movement. There, Communist Party members, labor leaders, and civil rights activists forged a social democratic vision that united civil rights, labor rights, and civil liberties under the banner of human rights. Wo-Chi-Ca was a living extension of these connections.[2]

The 1940s black freedom struggle's social democratic impulse could not, however, escape its red taint. As Americans turned from the fight against fascism to the fight against international communism, many civil rights and labor activists distanced themselves from the Left. Recast as the enemies of democracy, communists found little room for their open participation in the mainstream civil rights movement. The National Association for the Advancement of Colored People (NAACP), in fact, undertook its own internal anticommunist campaign, purging thousands of communists and suspected communists from its ranks. By the mid-1950s, the Communist Party freely admitted its total isolation from black communities and the civil rights struggle.[3]

Historians disagree widely over how the postwar Red Scare shaped the movement. Many bemoan how anticommunism shifted civil rights discourse from economic concerns and a concept of civil rights as human rights toward narrower legal strategies centered on desegregation. Others have shown how civil rights leaders used the specter of international communism to forward civil rights demands such as school desegregation. The class-based critique of racism at the heart of the Wo-Chi-Cans' World of Tomorrow, a naively idealistic dream, would appear to be evidence of subversive indoctrination in the eyes of many Americans.[4]

Although effectively marginalized in the civil rights movement, radicals with roots in the communist milieu did not cease all activity. Many had been participating in "Mass Work" with groups like the NAACP, the Urban League, unions, local PTAs, and neighborhood organizations for years and continued this work with or without the Party's guidance. At its 1957 convention, the CP endorsed its members' work in the NAACP for the first time in nearly a decade. NAACP Executive Secretary Roy Wilkins quickly denounced this overture, although individuals with connections to the CP continued to play important roles in the NAACP well into the 1960s. Radical interracial summer camping was another way in which many in New York and the surrounding area remained engaged with the civil rights movement during the "doldrums" of the 1950s.[5]

This chapter demonstrates how radicals in the progressive milieu surrounding the Communist Party in New York created and maintained a number of interracial summer camps during the first few decades after World War II. In particular, it focuses on the "moral economy" of such ventures, that is, the tension and interaction between ideological and economic concerns. The summer camps examined here were all private, not-for-profit organizations that required a good deal of cooperative labor and a number of financial sacrifices to remain in operation. This piece looks at three summer camps serving New York City and its environs. The story of Camp Wo-Chi-Ca documents how staff and campers created a radical antiracist children's culture that drew on the Left's civil rights activity. Wo-Chi-Ca's demise in the early 1950s also provides a case study of the political pressures that threatened radical summer camps during the early Cold War. Camp Woodland, located in the heart of New York's Catskill Mountains, managed to be successful in the 1950s despite its political orientation. At Camp Midvale, near Ringwood, New Jersey, we see the problems that emerged within the camp community over interracialism and anticommunism. Collectively, these stories attest to the various economic and political difficulties that faced radical interracial summer camps during the period.

THE RED SCARE AND THE COMMITMENT TO INTERRACIALISM

In the 1920s, radicals with ties to the Communist Party founded a network of summer colonies within driving distance of New York City. These camps were constructed with funds and labor from the mostly working-class, largely immigrant population that comprised the contemporary CP. These vacation spots took many forms, from lodges and hotels serving adults to family-centered bungalow colonies and children's summer camps. Attendance at children's summer camps peaked during World War II, as the economic boom brought busy parents more work and more pay and more of a need to send their children somewhere during the summer months. Although the Red Scare in the war's aftermath put great pressure on these camps to fold, it was their commitment to interracialism that sustained them through these difficult times.[6]

As the Cold War escalated, radical summer camps came under the scrutiny of government officials and law enforcement. Federal Bureau of Investigation agents frequently visited the camps to observe activities and record visitors' license plate numbers. Camp administrators were called before the House Un-American Activities Committee. This unwanted attention made many progressives less eager to vacation at a radical resort or send their children to a camp deemed "subversive" by authorities. Nevertheless, by the mid-1950s, an investigation by the New York Legislature revealed at least twenty-seven leftwing summer camps operating in New York State alone.[7]

The Red Scare posed a number of financial problems for summer camps. Several unions stopped sending children on scholarships for fear of being associated with "reds" after Congress passed the anticommunist Taft-Hartley Bill requiring union leaders to sign loyalty oaths. In 1947, Attorney General Thomas Clark placed the International Workers Order (IWO), a large leftwing mutual aid organization and insurance provider, and the Nature Friends of America, an ecology and outdoors society, on the "List of Subversive Organizations." Placement on the Attorney General's list jeopardized camps run by these groups, including Wo-Chi-Ca, Kinderland, and Midvale because law disqualified "subversive" organizations from federal tax exemptions. Camp administrators also faced resistance from state and local authorities, such as when New Jersey's liquor board revoked Camp Midvale's license in 1949, cutting off an important source of revenue. The Communist *Daily Worker* assailed the move, calling it "an attempt to hound a progressive operation through petty 'pocketbook' recriminations."[8]

As the Cold War escalated it became harder for progressive summer camps to operate, but the fact that they weathered this adversity illustrated just how important these endeavors were to their constituents. During the early 1950s, the IWO became embroiled in a costly legal battle with the New York State Insurance Board after it ruled that the fraternal order's radical politics endangered its policyholders. The IWO's summer camps were caught in the middle. Wo-Chi-Ca managed to transfer its ownership and avoid closure. But Camp Kinderland, an avowedly interracial but predominantly Jewish camp in upstate New York, did not escape the IWO's legal troubles so easily. When the State Insurance Board liquidated the IWO in 1954, it assumed control of the camp's mortgage and tried to foreclose on the property. Miraculously, however, Kinderland's supporters managed to raise $100,000 in three days and kept the camp open. That the camp's supporters were willing and able to raise this kind of money at a time when many leftists' livelihoods were in peril and their pockets stretched thin by other fund-raising campaigns indicates that summer camps were essential to the survival of the New York Left's social world. As one latter-day visitor put it, "Kinderland has survived because it's not just a camp, but a cause."[9]

The Red Scare's greatest impact on summer camps came when the New York State Legislature's Committee on Philanthropic and Charitable Organizations, known as the Larkin Committee, launched a much-publicized investigation of "subversive" activities in New York-area camps. Due to the investigation, the New York State Commerce Department began requiring that camp directors and staff sign loyalty oaths before it would grant the approval required for operation. Patronage slackened at many camps as a result of the negative publicity whipped up by the Committee's hearings. At Kinderland, for example, the number of campers fell from 417 in 1955 to just below 200 in 1957. Although staff was cut and debt mounted, the camp managed to hang on and even began growing again by the end of the decade. Most radical summer camps remained in operation throughout the 1950s despite the many attempts to shut them down. Some, like Camp Woodland, even prospered despite close governmental scrutiny. Their endurance demonstrated that they were not simply business enterprises that provided summer recreation, but ideological causes to be defended and protected.[10]

A continuing commitment to interracialism helped sustain radical summer camps throughout the Red Scare. Summer camps with roots in the communist world always embraced the most utopian aspects of the Left's political ideology. They were moored to the CP through personal connections, but never fully wedded to its fortunes. After a string of CP leaders were jailed under the Smith Act in the early 1950s, several thousand American communists went "underground" to avoid arrest. Ironically, the Party was further weakened just as McCarthyism began to thaw in the mid-1950s, when "de-Stalinization" and the Soviet suppression of Hungarian rebels prompted all but the most loyal members to leave the CP. The skeleton of an organization that remained was said to contain more FBI agents than authentic members by the late 1950s. Summer camps were community-based institutions that required patronage beyond the dwindling ranks of the CP to survive. As the 1950s wore on, summer camps, like many individuals in progressive circles, tempered their radicalism. With a less dogmatic outlook, summer camp programs embraced the mainstream civil rights movement agendas of the Student Nonviolent Coordinating Committee, Congress of Racial Equality (CORE), and the NAACP. By focusing on the integrated social worlds created in leftwing summer camps during the period, we get insight into a forgotten story overshadowed by the demise of the American Communist Party that inspired the creation of these camps but never fully defined their direction and meaning.[11]

Radicals' efforts at creating integrated, egalitarian spaces within their movement contrasted sharply with New York City's racial geography. Although known as a progressive city at mid-century, minorities there nevertheless suffered widespread discrimination. Segregation in housing was enforced through formal and informal means by way of racial covenants in deeds and discrimination in home loans and rental applications. Businesses and industries, too, found ways to keep people of color in the dirtiest, most dangerous, and lowest- paying work. Radical summer camps addressed such inequalities in two ways: designing cultural programs focused on interracialism and African American history and the simple act of creating recreational opportunities for children, black and white, which helped break down the social, economic, and spatial barriers that perpetuated racism. Summer vacation spots were particularly affected by the color line. Widespread discrimination prevailed in vacation destinations under the code phrase "restricted clientele." Such discrimination led Jews and other European immigrant communities to establish their own vacationing sites. But African Americans established few summer camps and resorts. Whereas white and ethnic newspapers brimmed with advertisements for summer camps in the spring and early summer, black ones revealed relatively few opportunities for summer recreation.

Radical summer camps challenged these inequalities and filled a significant void for African American youth. Although day camps run by the Young Men's Christian Association (YMCA) began integrating in the 1940s and the National Council of Christians and Jews established a number of "Brotherhood Camps" around urban areas in the mid-1950s, most private camps would continue to draw a firm color line into the 1960s. When the more liberal private camps experimented with even token integration, white people often simply left. "Urban black families were enthusiastic about camps, but they generally had few camp options," writes historian Leslie Paris, "White families could vote with their feet." Radical camps were quite unique as private ventures that actively sold interracialism as a feature of the camp experience. The political orientation of some camps proved hazy enough to allow the American Camping Association (ACA), the largest private camping organization, to praise leftwing camps' commitment to interracial camping while embracing anticommunism. As one former Wo-Chi-Ca staff member wrote, "many thought of Wo-Chi-Ca as a socialist camp, but for the [ACA] and for those involved with it, it served as a model for harmonious integration." After all, although liberals argued for increased integration in mainstream summer camps, it was leftist ones that dominated the short list of those that actually had interracial rosters.[12]

TEACHING RACE AT CAMP WO-CHI-CA

Camp Wo-Chi-Ca embodied the radical antiracism of the postwar period more than any other children's camp in the communist milieu. In 1935, IWO members founded the camp on 130 acres outside Hackettstown, New Jersey as a healthful recreation site for working-class children suffering in the depths of the Great Depression. Although initially populated mostly by ethnic whites from New York City, the camp took up Popular Front civil rights causes like the Angelo Herndon and Scottsboro Boys cases. Wo-Chi-Ca grew quickly, especially during World War II, when parents busy with defense work and flush with cash from the wartime economic boom searched for places to send their children. In the 1940s, more than 600 children attended the camp each summer and nearly 1,000 more were on a waiting list. Wo-Chi-Ca was one of the only radical summer camps that did not advertise in the *Daily Worker*, *National Guardian*, or any other African American or leftwing periodicals during the period. Word-of-mouth seemed to suffice. Camp directors recruited heavily through progressive unions and the IWO, drawing on both groups' recent growth among African Americans and Puerto Ricans in New York. Because of these connections, Wo-Chi-Ca more successfully recruited minorities than other camps. Children of color made up 20 percent of the camp roster by 1947 and that year the staff was over 25 percent non-white.[13]

Antiracism suffused all activities at Wo-Chi-Ca, from athletics to music to the arts. A host of important African American painters and illustrators taught at the camp, including John Wilson, Jacob Lawrence, Elizabeth Catlett, Charles White, and Ernest Crichlow. African American modern dancer Pearl Primus taught the children routines with social-justice themes. Paul Robeson, the camp's most venerated patron, visited throughout the 1940s, prompting celebrations of interracial solidarity. The camp also hosted the children of Rosa Lee Ingram and possibly Willie McGee, two civil rights *cause célèbres*. Even recreation was a time for transmitting racial politics, such as softball games that provided opportunities to discuss Jackie Robinson and the color bar in Major League Baseball.[14]

The unique camp culture offered administrators many chances to teach children about racism. Older campers received the strongest lessons, attending lectures on African American history and the "Negro Question" by Doxey Wilkerson, a Communist Party official who served as the head of the Jefferson School of Social Science, a New York-based "school for Marxist studies." But even young campers took up explicitly antiracist activities at the camp. In 1949, for example, Wo-Chi-Cans campaigned against racist children's toys, taking aim at the All-Metal Products Company for producing a "Sambo Target" game that featured a racist caricature. For several weeks, the camp displayed the letters they received from the toymaker, under a banner reading "Children's games spread prejudice. . . . We're fighting it."[15]

Young people understood the larger implications of such campaigns. Camper Crystal Field noted in the 1948 yearbook that the discussion around the game "brought us a very important lesson in how to live together." She predicted, "I think when we get back to the city we'll be much more alert to attacks on people in any form because of [what] happened this summer." Camp administrators believed in children's innate antiracism and encouraged their every activist impulse. Few summer camps, if any, would make an economic boycott against racist toys part of its activities. Of course, Wo-Chi-Cans did their share of playing and laughing, too, but their time at camp always had a radical edge that cut sharpest in its critique of racism. Even the camp's physical space was imbued with racial meaning. During the summers of 1947–49, campers helped construct the foundation of the Paul Robeson Playhouse and Recreation Hall. Like a number of sites at Wo-Chi-Ca, campers imagined the playhouse structure to have symbolic importance far beyond the physical function it served. For Laurel Field, age twelve, the building represented not only Paul Robeson, but also African American aspirations for freedom. She wrote:

> It stands majestic, straight and tall.
> On firm foundations it is built,
> It symbolizes big hearted Paul
> Whose spirit will never wilt.
>
> Like the courage of the Negro people
> His great will shall never fall.
> His spirit has been captured by
> The Robeson Recreation Hall.[16]

Wo-Chi-Ca's unique programs made it vulnerable to physical attacks and accusations of political subversion. Halfway through the summer of 1950, tensions with the local community reached a breaking point when a group of men, allegedly American Legion and Ku Klux Klan members, threatened to destroy the camp if the administration did not remove the sign dedicating its playhouse to Robeson. The men were initially rebuffed, but returned with reinforcements the next day. Fearing that the confrontation could devolve into a melee not unlike the riot at Robeson's Peekskill, New York concert the previous summer, camp administrators removed the sign after a spirited debate. Removing the sign seemed to violate the interracial spirit of the camp, but it was deemed necessary to protect the children. Perhaps one of the reasons radicals invested such energy in the black freedom movement was the set of common enemies they shared.[17]

Although the summer drew to a close without further incident, it would prove to be Camp Wo-Chi-Ca's last season. The following year, a group of Wo-Chi-Ca administrators purchased the camp's mortgage from the IWO and changed its name to Wyandot in a naïve attempt to quell controversy, but frictions with locals persisted. The camp then moved to Mount Tremper, New York where it operated for several seasons until a polio epidemic in 1953 killed one camper and infected more than 100 others. Unable to recover, Wyandot closed after one more season. Wo-Chi-Ca's undoing was tragic for all involved because of the great investment so many staff, administrators, parents, and campers had made in the camp's physical space and moral economy during its sixteen years of operation.[18]

CAMP WOODLAND: A SUCCESS STORY

As Camp Wo-Chi-Ca's demise demonstrated, leftwing interracial summer camps operating in rural areas had to interact carefully with surrounding communities as anticommunism grew during the postwar period. Like all summer camps, they were dependent on local businesses for food, building supplies, and labor. The vitriolic politics of the early Cold War strained these relationships. Among the leftwing interracial summer camps, Camp Woodland fared best in its interactions with the local community even while pursuing a civil rights agenda. Under the direction of Norman Studer, who led the camp each year from its inception in 1940 to his 1961 resignation, Woodland's cooperation with residents helped it to not only resist the pressures of anticommunism, but even to change the culture of the area.

Woodland's focus on regional history and folklore helped it earn the respect of locals and avoid the sort of racial backlash that led to Wo-Chi-Ca's demise. Woodland brought city children to the Catskills for recreation and summer education. Studer created a curriculum around local history, music, and folkways. The camp held folk festivals each summer, established a museum of Catskills culture, and collected hours of oral histories and songs from local people. Studer drew heavily on his experiences as an educator in New York City, where he directed an interracial private school and worked with Kenneth and Mamie Clark, the noted African American psychologists who served as important witnesses in one of the cases leading directly to the *Brown v. Board* decision. Studer blended his interests in local history and integration at Woodland in ways that did not offend the sensibilities of area residents. The camp did much, for example, to renew local interest in African American activist Sojourner Truth, who spent much of her early life in the Catskills. Woodland even sponsored a Fourth of July celebration with the Phoenicia branch of the American Legion in 1952, just a few years after Legion members led the mob that attacked leftwing concertgoers at Paul Robeson's Peekskill performance.[19]

The impact that the camp had on the local culture was evidenced in 1949, when the Camp Woodland Parents' Association started an Intercultural Committee to monitor segregation at nearby resorts. It was formed after the nearby Pan-American Hotel housed a visiting African American parent in a separate and inadequate room. The hotel claimed the discriminatory practice to be the result of a misunderstanding and quickly corrected the mistake. Yet members of the Parents' Association felt the incident was indicative of a larger pattern of discrimination in Catskill area resorts. The Intercultural Committee encouraged parents to patronize only those proprietors that did not draw a color line. "As parents of children who enjoy the advantages of Camp Woodland, not the least of which is the absence of discrimination. . . . [W]e cannot accept or ignore discrimination against visiting parents at nearby resorts or hotels," wrote Chairman Miriam Grossman. The boycott was remarkable effective. In 1949, only two resorts in the area accepted African American lodgers; five years later Grossman could recommend twenty non-discriminatory resorts. The Parents' Association continued its efforts throughout the 1950s with great success. By 1960, thirty-seven area resorts offered equal lodging regardless of color. By making something as simple as lodging on parents' weekend a political act, the Parents' Association extended Camp Woodland's philosophy into the surrounding community and changed its customs and culture.[20]

Effectively balancing local needs with his political agenda, Studer used his position of respect to openly challenge anticommunism without exposing his camp to Red Scare paranoia. Shortly after the Larkin Committee began its investigation of subversive influences in summer camps, the New York State Commerce Department imposed mandatory loyalty oaths for summer camp directors and staff. The ACA considered similar rules for its influential list of approved summer camps. Studer resisted, calling such moves "a threat to all camps, as it opens the door to state control of this important field of child education and development." Studer urged the New York section of the ACA—which had contacted lawyers about the legality of the oaths—to go on the record against this anticommunist tactic. Drawing a connection between civil liberties and civil rights, Studer warned that "Interracial camping, always a suspect in conservative circles, is likely to be the next target of our lawmakers." The Camp Woodland Parents'

Association also opposed the investigation, which in 1954 it decried as a "threat to the American principle of free institutions and a usurpation of the parent's prerogative of selecting the educational program and philosophy to meet the needs and desires of their children." Using contemporary patriotic rhetoric, it called the investigation an "infringement of free enterprise in the development of programs endeavoring to educate our children to enable them to participate in the true American ideals of democratic living for all." Whereas many radical summer camps lost enrollment during this period, Woodland remained relatively unscathed. In fact, it even began turning a profit for the first time in five years in the 1955 season during the Larkin Committee's high-profile hearings. Profits continued during the remainder of the decade even as the camp expanded its scholarship program for low-income campers. Studer's thoughtful approach to Woodland's mission played a significant role in its survival.[21]

The camp's interracialism contributed to its success during these trying times by imbuing its members with the same sense of purpose that had strengthened contemporary labor unions. Unions such as Local 1199 Drug and Hospital Workers Union and Retail, Wholesale, and Department Store Union District 65 managed to keep the spirit of interracial unionism alive throughout the 1950s. Camp Woodland recruited heavily through Local 1199 during this period, resulting in significant numbers of African American and Puerto Rican children winning scholarships annually to attend the camp. Both Local 1199 and District 65 created internal cultures devoted to the civil rights movement and drew praise from the NAACP and Martin Luther King, Jr., who called them his "favorite unions." Like these unions, Woodland prospered through its focus on interracialism. By the end of the decade, Woodland counted as many children of color—roughly 20 percent of the total—as Camp Wo-Chi-Ca had in the late 1940s. Studer's last summer, 1961, witnessed the camp's highest African American enrollment, which Studer interpreted as "a continued vote of confidence on the part of the Negro people."[22]

The 1957 case of Katy Wechsler illustrates the moral economy that governed radical summer camps and empowered those involved. That year, Wechsler's parents helped an African American couple, Bill and Daisy Myers, move into the house next door to their home in Levittown, Pennsylvania, one of the nation's largest postwar suburban developments. The integration of this all-white neighborhood was met with violent resistance. The Weschlers were ostracized immediately. The Ku Klux Klan made threats against their lives and burned a cross on their lawn. Seeking an escape, Katy applied for admission to Camp Woodland, although her parents could not afford the tuition. She wrote an impassioned letter explaining her family's recent hardships and struggles. Moved by the story, Studer found money for a scholarship. Weschler attended Woodland for four years and encountered racial politics more in line with her parents' values than what had reared its racist head in Levittown. "At camp I learned from, and grew in an atmosphere of love and brotherhood. . . . [E]veryone lived as one family," Weschler wrote to Norman and Hannah Studer several years later. "The best part," she added, "was that the family continued after the summer; it was these friendships which made it possible for me to live in Levittown."[23]

The camp's moral economy was undone not by outsiders but rather internal greed. Woodland's success prompted a group of inactive but still legally vested board members to wrest control from Norman and Hannah Studer and turn the camp into a for-profit venture. Such a change would forever alter the moral economy of the camp. The Woodland Parents' Association wrote in a plea to patrons: "if their effort is successful it will mean an end to those special qualities of Camp Woodland which have made it so unique; its genuinely integrated and inter-racial character, its scholarship program which makes this possible, its dedication to democratic principles and its program of inter-cultural education."[24]

Although former campers like Katy Wechsler wrote testimonials after the summer of 1961 in hopes of saving Woodland, the legal battle left a bad taste in Norman Studer's mouth and led him to resign after twenty-three seasons as director. His replacements modernized the camp's facilities, but Studer proved irreplaceable. The community that sustained Woodland through such trying times cared deeply about the unique interracial environment created on its acres; they held less regard for new recreational facilities. In July 1963, after one less-than-successful season under new management, much of Camp Woodland burned in a mysterious fire. It was the deathblow to one of the Left's most successful interracial camps.[25]

STRUGGLES OVER INTERRACIAL SPACE AT CAMP MIDVALE

Like Camp Woodland, Camp Midvale (near Ringwood, New Jersey) relied upon its commitment to interracialism to remain in operation despite efforts to close it down. Midvale, however, witnessed far more internal conflict over the moral economy of interracialism than did Woodland. German and Austrian immigrants founded Camp Midvale in 1921 as the central meeting place for the American wing of *Die Naturfreunde* or "Nature Friends," a European working-class recreation and outdoor tourism movement. The property included a nature preserve, a bungalow colony, recreational facilities, and a summer camp serving roughly 100 children from nursery school through their teenage years. Nature Friends built trails and established camps in New York, New Jersey, Pennsylvania, Wisconsin, and California. The group promoted ecology when few other groups took up the call. They prided themselves as a rugged bunch. The Nature Friends had an almost evangelical regard for work. Residents and regular visitors to Camp Midvale contributed a great deal of communal labor including building and repairing trails, cleaning the dormitory, mucking leaves from the camp pool, or serving food. Everyone was expected to do his or her part. Most early members came out of the Social Democratic tradition in Europe and brought their leftwing political outlooks to the camp. In the early 1930s, Nature Friends marched in May Day parades with banners against fascism. Around the same time, the all-white day camp became active in civil rights issues through the Scottsboro case.[26]

Even as anticommunism imperiled its sense of collective identity in the postwar period, the camp touted interracialism and recruited African Americans from New York and Newark to attend. In 1947, the Nature Friends was named on Attorney General Clark's list of subversive organizations, causing an immediate rift between older German socialists who feared the camp would be destroyed and a younger, communist-influenced, heavily Jewish group that sought to challenge anticommunism. Following lawyers' advice, the Midvale Nature Friends branch reorganized as the Metropolitan Recreation Association. The new organization devoted itself to interracialism, but not without external resistance. Campers at Midvale awoke to a large wooden cross burning on their flagpole one morning in August 1948. An attached sign, presumably left by the Ku Klux Klan, provided the warning: "This is the U.S.A. not Russia. If there's any trouble, you communist bastards get it first."[27]

The camp's impressive freshwater pool, still in operation today, was a primary recruiting draw for inner-city youth and was symbolic of the camp's commitment to racial equality. Prior to its construction in the mid-1930s, Midvale campers swam in a pond on a nearby farm that locals also used. One morning when Midvale campers arrived at the watering hole along with a few African American visitors, they were turned away. The camp responded by constructing its own pool. Longtime camper Ethyl Kirschner remembered: "With our own pool, well, we could have [whomever] we want come and swim." The pool assumed central importance as a symbol of the camp's interracial spirit. Such efforts were not lost on African American campers like Al Hodges, who upon returning home to Newark wondered why "the city couldn't be like the camp, why couldn't there be a pool where everybody could go?"[28]

Midvale's commitment to serving the underprivileged complicated its precarious financial situation. Robert Erhlich, Midvale's manager from 1951–58, recalls the camp being full most weekends during the period, especially on hot Sundays when hundreds drove up from Newark and New York City to swim, hike, and picnic. Yet the camp never turned a profit. Erhlich notes that the camp wanted "[a]n integrated, cooperative atmosphere on a non-profit basis" but admits, "we probably overdid the non-profit part of it" by trying so hard to attract "people that couldn't afford anywhere else."[29]

Friction grew over finances and the commitment to interracialism. Under Erhlich's direction, the camp extended an open invitation to the "Jackson-Whites" or Ramapo Mountain Indians, a community outside Ringwood descended from runaway slaves and white settlers who mixed with Native

Americans. Believing they constituted the "closest thing to a black community in Northern Jersey," Erhlich and others invited the group to use Midvale's facilities at no charge. But many felt that they should pay, furthering longstanding tensions between the socialist German group and the younger, mostly Jewish and communist generation. As the camp's physical plant, facilities, and constituency aged, fewer and fewer paying campers attended. Facing mounting bills and lacking much of its former clientele, Midvale limped into the 1960s.[30]

On October 4, 1966, a blaze engulfed the social hall, burning records kept in an adjoining office. Although the local fire chief asserted that there was no reason to suspect arson, campers alleged that a rightwing militant organization called the Minutemen was behind it. Weeks later, in fact, several Minutemen in New York were arrested for plotting to firebomb a number of leftwing sites, including Midvale. Regardless of who was responsible, the loss of the social hall was devastating for the camp. Membership records were lost, making it nearly impossible to collect rebuilding money from former campers and their families. Facing growing tax debts, Midvale donated its land to the Ethical Culture Society in 1968, which eventually founded the Weiss Ecology Center that operates in the space today.[31]

Camp Midvale's influence as a site of radical interracialism is difficult to assess, in part for a lack of material. Without records or ephemera, we can only uncover how children made sense of its interracialism through personal reminiscence. Longtime camper Carl Kirschner "always viewed the camp as a place that was interracial first, and heavily political second, [although] being interracial was a political statement in and of itself . . . I was less aware of the politics, but aware that it was interracial because of the people." For Kirschner, the most influential member of the Midvale community was Ernest Raymond "Ray" Washington, the camp's African American lifeguard in the 1950s. Washington took a keen interest in Kirschner's development as a swimmer, coaching him at his neighborhood YMCA and at Camp Midvale, despite the fact that Kirschner, as he put it, "was not going to be an Olympic swimmer." Looking back on his time at Midvale, Kirschner credited Washington with inspiring him to join Brooklyn CORE and attend the 1963 March on Washington. Attending the historic event and supporting the civil rights movement was not just a personal choice; it was an important result of Midvale's communal identity and moral economy.[32]

The interracial spirit that helped radical summer camps endure despite the Red Scare would be carried through its members' participation in the civil rights movement. Many of the children that passed through these camps, like Carl Kirschner, took part in the civil rights movement of the 1960s. Although it is difficult to know precisely what they carried with them from their time at camp, these early interracial experiences undoubtedly had a lasting effect and provided another strand of continuity between the class-based, global understanding of race that emerged during World War II and the movement's later "heroic phase" during the late 1950s and early 1960s. Radicals viewed summer camping as an essential arena of activism for putting their social values into practice. That they undertook this enterprise at great cost, and with surprising success, during the American Left's nadir forces scholars of civil rights and radical political movements to rethink historical narratives of the postwar period. Anticommunism may have persisted in the civil rights movement, but so did the movement's radical allies.

One of the ways the Left managed to survive the 1950s was by preserving social spaces where it could pass on its values. To achieve this goal, summer camp staff tried to create interracial sites where children could, for only the summer perhaps, participate in a "living democracy." Campers and staff also wanted to have fun, let off a little steam, and escape the heat of the city. The two impulses are not mutually exclusive; by imbuing daily life with racial meaning, radicals assured that both would have social significance. As ephemeral and besieged these summer spaces were, it is remarkable how many survived the period. The camps endured the financial and political costs of the Red Scare because of the incalculable sacrifices required to preserve moral economies built around interracialism.

NOTES

1. Wo-Chi-Ca, "The Road to Tomorrow," 1945, 6–9 in Camp Wo-Chi-Ca Records, Tamiment Library, New York University, Box 1, Folder 1. Also quoted in Paul C. Mishler, *Raising Reds: The Young Pioneers, Radical Summer Camps, and Communist Political Culture in the United States* (New York: Columbia University Press, 1999), 99.
2. On the role of African Americans and civil rights in the Communist movement, see Mark Naison, *Communists in Harlem during the Depression* (Urbana: University of Illinois Press, 1983); Robin D.G. Kelley, *Hammer and Hoe: Alabama Communists During the Great Depression* (Chapel Hill: University of North Carolina Press, 1990); Mark Solomon, *The Cry Was Unity: Communists and African Americans, 1917–1936* (Jackson: University of Mississippi Press, 1998); Cedric J. Robinson, *Black Marxism: The Making of the Black Radical Tradition* (Chapel Hill: University of North Carolina Press, 2000); Robert Korstad, *Civil Rights Unionism: Tobacco Workers and the Struggle for Democracy in the Mid-Twentieth-Century South* (Chapel Hill: University of North Carolina Press, 2003); Gerald Horne, *Red Seas: Ferdinand Smith and Radical Black Sailors in the United States and Jamaica* (New York: NYU Press, 2005); Glenda Gilmore, *Defying Dixie: The Radical Roots of Civil Rights, 1919–1950* (New York: W.W. Norton & Co., 2008); Martha Biondi, *To Stand and Fight: The Struggle for Civil Rights in Postwar New York City* (Cambridge: Harvard University Press, 2003). Biondi terms the 1940s African American alliance with labor and the Left in New York as the "Black Popular Front."
3. On the NAACP's campaign against communists in its ranks, see "Introduction," Robbie Lieberman and Clarence Lang, eds., *Anticommunism and the African American Freedom Movement: "Another Side of the Story"* (New York: Palgrave Macmillan, 2009); Manfred Berg, "Black Civil Rights and Liberal Anticommunism: The NAACP in the Early Cold War," *Journal of*

American History 94:1 (June 2007): 75–96; Carol Anderson, "Bleached Souls and Red Negroes: The NAACP and Black Communists in the Early Cold War, 1948–1952," in Brenda Gayle Plummer, ed., *Window on Freedom: Race, Civil Rights, and Foreign Affairs, 1945–1988* (Chapel Hill: University of North Carolina Press, 2003), 93–114. Several months before the *Brown* decision, one African American Communist official criticized the "persistent sectarian isolation of the Left from the mainstream of Negro life." Doxey Wilkerson, "The Historic Fight to Abolish School Segregation in the United States," February 1954, 1, Jefferson School of Social Science Records, Tamiment Library, New York University, Box 3, Folder 10.

4. For a synthesis and critique of historians' views on the Cold War's impact on the civil rights movement, see Jacquelyn Dowd Hall, "The Long Civil Rights Movement and the Political Uses of the Past," *Journal of American History* 91:4 (March 2005): 1233–63. Some civil rights advances rested squarely on discrediting the Left, a move that historian Mary Dudziak feels "*simultaneously* harmed the movement and created an opportunity for limited reform." See Mary L. Dudziak, "*Brown* as a Cold War Case," *The Journal of American History* 91:1 (June 2004): 41. Carol Anderson and several other historians have argued that the narrowing of the NACCP's agenda tragically abandoned the United Nations' formulation of human rights, a demand around which both the Left and mainstream often coalesced. See Carol Anderson, *Eyes off the Prize: The United Nations and the African American Struggle for Human Rights, 1944–1955* (Cambridge: Cambridge University Press, 2003); Anderson, "Bleached Souls and Red Negroes," 93–114.
5. "Communists Seek Appeal to Negroes," *New York Amsterdam News*, February 23, 1957. The CP's "Mass Work" in the late 1950s and early 1960s is difficult to assess, because the work was clandestine and intentionally did not leave a paper trail. Stanley Aronowitz and Maurice Isserman interview, July 11, 1984, Maurice Isserman Oral Histories, Tamiment Library, New York University; Maurice Isserman, *If I Had a Hammer . . . : The Death of the Old Left and the Birth of the New Left* (New York: Basic Books, 1987).
6. David Leviatin, *Followers of the Trail: Jewish Working Class Radicals in America* (New Haven: Yale University Press, 1989); Mishler, *Raising Reds*; June Levine and Gene Gordon, *Tales of Wo-Chi-Ca: Blacks, Whites, and Reds at Camp* (San Rafael: Avon Springs Press, 2002); Leslie Paris, *Children's Nature: The Rise and Fall of the American Summer Camp* (New York: New York University Press, 2008). Memoirs recalling time spent at radical summer camps include: David Horowitz, *Radical Son: A Journey Through Our Times* (New York: Free Press, 1997); Frances Barrett White with Anne Scott, *Reaches of the Heart* (New York: Barricade Books, 1994); Ronald Radosh, *Commies: A Journey through the Old Left, the New Left, and the Leftover Left* (San Francisco: Encounter Books, 2001); Dexter Jefferies, *Triple Exposure: Black, Jewish, and Red in the 1950s* (New York: Kensington Publishing, 2003); Bettina Aptheker, *Intimate Politics: How I Grew up Red, Fought for Free Speech, and Became a Feminist Rebel* (Emeryville: Seal Press, 2006). See also Judy Kaplan and Linn Shapiro, *Red Diapers: Growing up in the Communist Left* (Urbana: University of Illinois Press, 1998).
7. State of New York, *Report of the Joint Legislative Committee on Charitable and Philanthropic Agencies and Organizations* (1956): 10, 13.
8. "Terming Camp Red, ABC Would Revoke Liquor License," *Jersey Journal*, January 26, 1949; "Nature Camp Snubs ABC Hearing," *Newark Star-Ledger*, March 16, 1949; "Hock Suspends License of Nature Friends Camp," *Passaic Herald-News*, April 30, 1949; "No 'Sabotage'—So Ledger Tries Liquor Ban for Size," *Daily Worker*, February 6, 1949.

9. "44th Anniversary Script for Musical Salute," 1967, 6, Camp Kinderland Records, Tamiment Library, New York University (hereafter cited as "Camp Kinderland Records"), Box 1, Folder 3; Suzanne Ruta, "Social Studies," *Wigwag*, August 1990, 14.
10. "Board of Directors Meeting Minutes," October 18, 1956 and May 21, 1957, Camp Kinderland Records, Box 2, Folder 1.
11. See Joseph Starobin, *American Communism in Crisis, 1943–1957* (Cambridge: Harvard University Press, 1972); Maurice Isserman, "The 1956 Generation: An Alternative Approach to the History of American Communism," *Radical America* 14:2 (March–April 1980): 43–51; Maurice Isserman, *If I Had a Hammer.*
12. See David E. Bergh, *Your Child and the Summer Camp* (New York: Odyssey Press, 1946); Marguerite Tuttle, *A Guide to Summer Camps and Summer Schools and Summer Travel* (New York: American Camping Association, 1946); Marie Lafferty Cortell, *Camping With Purpose* (New York: Woman's Press [Young Women's Christian Association], 1950); Frank L. Irwin, *The Theory of Camping: An Introduction to Camping in Education* (New York: A.S. Barnes and Co., 1950). In these remarkably integrated summer camps, young people absorbed an antiracist identity quite similar to that of leftwing camps like Wo-Chi-Ca, although far less of an emphasis was placed on the structural and economic underpinnings of racism. See, for examples, Phyllis Palmer, *Living as Equals: How Three White Communities Struggled to Make Interracial Connections during the Civil Rights Era* (Nashville: Vanderbilt University Press, 2008), 25–92; Paris, *Children's Nature*, 269; White, *Reaches of the Heart*, 44; Mishler, *Raising Reds*, 95.
13. Although camp staff used the term "Negro," it would be inappropriate to substitute the term "African American," because a number of the campers counted as "Negro" or "black" were undoubtedly West Indian or Puerto Rican. The proportion of minority campers grew during the 1940s, reaching over 20 percent by the close of the decade. Paris, *Children's Nature*, 219. See foreword to "Program for Second Annual Concert (Benefit Camp Wo-Chi-Ca), January 14, 1947, Hunter College Auditorium, New York City," 13. Document provided from private collection of June Levine and Gene Gordon.
14. For a sampling of antiracist activities and black personalities at Wo-Chi-Ca, see Levine and Gordon, *Tales of Wo-Chi-Ca*, 17–28, 55–71. Although Levine and Gordon and others claim that Willie McGee's children attended the camp, biographer Alex Heard could only find evidence of preparations to send the McGee children to Camp Kinderland in the summer of 1950. Alex Heard, *The Eyes of Willie McGee: A Tragedy of Race, Class, and Secrets in the Jim Crow South* (New York: HarperCollins, 2010), 227, 368n12. James and Charles Ingram's visit to Wo-Chi-Ca under the auspices of the IWO in 1948 was well-documented in the fraternal order's journal. Beryle Banfield, "Just Like Brothers: a Day with the Ingram Boys at Camp Wo-Chi-Ca," *Fraternal Outlook*, August–September 1948, 15.
15. *Wo-Chi-Ca 1949 Yearbook*, 24–25.
16. *Wo-Chi-Ca 1949 Yearbook*, 24–25; Laurel Field, "Dedication," *Wo-Chi-Ca 1948 Yearbook*, 8.
17. Levine and Gordon, *Tales of Wo-Chi-Ca*, 174–75.
18. Telephone interview with John Vago, October, 4, 2007; "141 Here From Camp Hit by Polio," *New York Times*, August 15, 1953; Farnsworth Fowle, "Parents' Siege Wins Anti-Polio Injections," *New York Times*, August 22, 1953; "94 Pints of Blood 'Pay' for Globulin," *New York Times*, September 27, 1953.

19. Studer, in fact, had been a founding member of the American Legion post in his Ohio hometown shortly after World War I. Ronald Radosh, "Celebrating the Fourth at Home," *Neighbors*, 1952, in Norman Studer Papers, M.E. Grenander Department of Special Collections & Archives, State University of New York at Albany (hereafter cited as "Studer Papers"), Box 14, Folder 4; Interview with Joan Studer Levine, New York, NY, November 16, 2009.
20. "Staff Meeting Notes," August 9, 1949, Studer Papers, Box 37, Folder 14; Intercultural Committee Memo, July 1, 1954 and July 4, 1960, Studer Papers, Box 37, Folder 13.
21. "Norman Studer to Betty Huff," July 23, 1954, Studer Papers, Box 37, Folder 7; "Camp Woodland Parents Association," July 25, 1954, Studer Papers, Box 37, Folder 7; "Annual Financial Records for 1944–1959," Studer Papers, Box 11, Folders 1–16.
22. Maurice Isserman interview with Ronald Radosh, July 10, 1984, Maurice Isserman Papers, Tamiment Library, New York University; "Summer of 1961," Studer Papers, Box 37, Folder 14.
23. See David Kushner, *Levittown: Two Families, One Tycoon, and the Fight for Civil Rights in America's Legendary Suburb* (New York: Walker and Company, 2009); "Katy Wechsler to Norman and Hannah Studer," September 12, 1961, Studer Papers, Box 11, Folder 26.
24. Camp Woodland Parents' Association, "Dear Camp Parent," August 21, 1961, Studer Papers, Box 37, Folder 11.
25. Joan Studer Levine interview; "Memo," July 8, 1963, Studer Papers, Box 37, Folder 11.
26. Leon Kuhle interview, August 29, 1987, Camp Midvale Oral History Collection, Tamiment Library, New York University (hereafter cited as "Midvale Collection").
27. "Red Sabotage Camp at Wanaque Bared," *Newark Star-Ledger*, January 30, 1949; Bertha Blocksberg interview, August 4, 1987, Midvale Collection.
28. Ethyl Kirschner interview, December 19, 1987 and Al and Judy Hodges interview, August 7, 1987, both in Midvale Collection. Hodges was so impressed with the camp's interracialism that he returned again and again. He met his wife Judy and raised his children at the camp.
29. Robert and Kornelia Erhlich interview, June 6, 1987, Midvale Collection.
30. Saul Erhlich interview, November 8, 1987, Midvale Collection.
31. Camp Midvale Federal Bureau of Investigation Records, Newark 65–859, Sec. 1, Camp Midvale/Nature Friends of America FOIA Files, Tamiment Library, New York University.
32. Carl Kirschner interview, January 22, 1988, Midvale Collection.

6 The NAACP Boycott of the *Amos 'n' Andy Show*

Justin T. Lorts

The long-running radio show *Amos 'n' Andy* made its first television appearance in 1951 after the Columbia Broadcasting Service (CBS) paid a record $2.5 million for its rights and Blatz Beer agreed to sponsor the program. The show tracked the wacky adventures of African American southern migrants Amos Jones and Andrew Brown as they struggled to make their way in Harlem as proprietors of the Fresh Air Taxi Company. Amos and Andy experienced a variety of ups-and-downs, marriage, parenthood, as well as a laundry list of failed business ventures and get-rich-quick schemes. Since its debut in 1929 through its phenomenal success during the Great Depression and decline thereafter, *Amos 'n' Andy* and most of its characters had been voiced by the show's creators Freeman Gosden and Charles Correll, both of whom were white. Throughout this time, although the program had been periodically condemned for its portrayals of African Americans, the characters in *Amos 'n' Andy* remained among the most popular and recognized ones in show business. CBS recognized that casting for the television version would be important and it held a talent search for black actors to fill the lead roles. Amid a flurry of press coverage, millions of Americans awaited the reintroduction of the show.[1]

It did not take long for the television version of *Amos 'n' Andy* to spark a backlash among African Americans. Advance reviews by the black press had already put people on edge, and at the national convention of the National Association for the Advancement of Colored People (NAACP), which happened to take place the week of the show's debut, delegates were outraged by what they saw. The program confirmed their worst fears. The convention passed a resolution decreeing that by portraying blacks in "a stereotyped and derogatory manner," *Amos 'n' Andy* strengthened "the conclusion among un-informed or prejudiced people that Negroes . . . are inferior, lazy, dumb and dishonest." The organization also argued that the show would "seriously hamper and retard the development of the work of [the NAACP] and other interested groups and associations to promote intelligent appraisal of all human beings as individuals." The NAACP vowed to use "every means at their disposal" to remove the show from television, including "resorting to the boycott of the goods, products or services of the sponsors and promoters." Joined by a broad coalition of labor, liberal, and civil rights organizations, the NAACP pressured Blatz to end its sponsorship and CBS to take the show off the air.[2]

NAACP leaders viewed the representation of blacks on television as critical to the success of the civil rights struggle. The resistance to *Amos 'n' Andy* was part of a larger campaign against racial stereotypes in entertainment. The organization had previously passed resolutions denouncing such portrayals. Its biggest point of contention was the "misrepresentation of the black middle class . . . that demeaned aspiration, burlesqued the complex distinctions that marked social classes, and presented to a national white audience an image of maddening oversimplicity." NAACP leaders believed that if *Amos 'n' Andy* was allowed to appear on the air unchecked, a new generation of Americans would come to view blacks as unworthy of social equality. By challenging *Amos 'n' Andy* while it was also pursuing school desegregation cases, the NAACP illuminated linkages between the two struggles.[3]

The NAACP's decision to incite through its local branches a nationwide boycott of the show illustrated both the organization's acknowledgment of the significant role that African American consumer power could have on the black freedom struggle and its limitations in effectively mobilizing such strategies. In its press organ *Crisis*, the NAACP had for several decades used the threat of the boycott in an attempt to temper "rabid anti-Negro propaganda" in the form of mass-media stereotypes, urging blacks to leverage their considerable buying might to force changes in the entertainment industry. But the *Amos 'n' Andy* protest marked the NAACP's first attempt to follow through on this threat. Press releases, opinion pieces, and personal correspondence from the period all indicate that NAACP leaders were confident that black consumers were strong enough to force changes in the depictions of the race in the mass media. At the same time, however, the attempted boycott of *Amos 'n' Andy* revealed the shortcomings of using economic power to force cultural change. Unlike for more traditional concerns like the desegregation of public facilities, voting rights, and fair employment, the civil rights community did not unite against *The Amos 'n' Andy Show*. Black entertainers voiced their own economic interests that the protest deprived them of their livelihood. Liberal allies resisted what they viewed as the NAACP's attempt at censorship. And most black viewers simply did not see the harm in *Amos 'n' Andy*. These challenges would limit the effectiveness of the boycott and prevent it from developing into a national civil rights protest.[4]

MEDIA STEREOTYPES AND THE EXPANSION OF TELEVISION

The NAACP campaign against *Amos 'n' Andy* came during a watershed moment in civil rights history marked by the federal government's increased engagement in the struggle and corresponding successes of black organizations. Through an executive order, President Harry Truman established the multiracial Civil Rights Committee whose report *To Secure These Rights* recommended a broad expansion of federal civil rights reform. Historian Steven F. Lawson writes, "*To Secure These Rights* loudly proclaimed the opening salvo of the federal government's campaign for civil rights." Truman became the first president to address the NAACP and his re-election in 1948 was partly attributable to his strong civil rights stand, which he often framed within the rhetoric of Cold War patriotism. Emboldened by this federal support, the NAACP had scored a series of landmark judicial victories during this postwar period, including *Sweatt v. Painter* and *McLaurin v. Oklahoma*. The cases that would comprise the historic *Brown v. Board of Education* were also winding their way through the courts. Buoyed by these wins, the 1951 NAACP annual convention launched an aggressive assault on segregation that would "wipe out jim crow [sic] on Dixie street cars, buses, theaters, restaurants, public parks and even separate drinking fountains." In the keynote address, Assistant Secretary Roy Wilkins announced the goal of "full and complete equality, without any shocking and humiliating discrimination and segregation. We don't want equality next year, or in the next generation, we want it now."[5]

Television's rapid expansion during the postwar years made it a potent potential force for achieving the NAACP's goal of integration. Although it had been in the works since the late 1920s, the medium's implementation had been delayed by the Great Depression and World War II. Production of network television began in earnest after the war when the Federal Communications Commission adopted universal standards and began allocating frequencies and issuing broadcast licenses. Fueled by a dramatic increase in the disposable income of American workers, television caught on quickly. The number of sets sold jumped from six million in 1950 to sixteen million the next year, encompassing about a quarter of all American households. This rapid expansion of the television market undercut the popularity of movies, radio, live sporting events, restaurants, nightclubs, jukeboxes, and libraries.[6]

Early programming suggested that the new medium might positively impact race relations. The proliferation of television sets and stations created demand for shows of all kinds that opened doors for black performers. *Variety* opined that black actors were looking to take advantage of television's "insatiable demand for talent" because "by being accepted as artists in their own rights during these early days of video, the colored entertainers can escape the stereotyping which they feel handicapped them" on radio and in movies. By 1950, there were as many as ten all-black shows on television, including one in the South. Black celebrities made frequent appearances on the three major variety shows hosted by white celebrities Milton Berle, Arthur Godfrey, and Ed Sullivan while black entertainers Bob Howard, Willie Bryant, Hadda Brooks, and Amanda Randolph hosted or starred in their own shows without having to "stoop to the Uncle Tom pattern which is usually the Negro thespian's lot on radio shows and in

Hollywood movies." Both at the time and decades later, observers concluded that the early days were promising. *Ebony* claimed that the sheer number of blacks on TV was a "sure sign that television is free of racial barriers." Media historian J. Fred McDonald writes that "on the surface, early television seemed to be almost colorblind."[7]

Ed Sullivan, who was one of the most powerful figures in the industry, believed that the fledging medium would propel the black freedom struggle and help crack America's color line. "Television is not only just what the doctor ordered for Negro performers," he wrote, "television subtly has supplied ten league boots to the Negro in his fight to win what the Constitution of this country guarantees as his birthright." Sullivan believed that whites needed to get to know blacks better if they were to unburden themselves of racism. Television would provide them that opportunity. He argued, "It has taken his long crusade to the living rooms of American homes where public opinion is formed and the Negro is winning." Television allowed a black person to "become a welcome visitor, not only for the white adult, but to the white children, who finally will put Jim Crow to rest." This oversimplification notwithstanding, Sullivan's vision presaged what would happen a decade later, when broadcast images of Southern violence and oppression generated invaluable sympathy and support for the civil rights cause.[8]

The NAACP understood the importance of television but was wary of it, which explains its vigilant response to *Amos 'n' Andy*. Many of its board members believed that TV was ripe for the same stereotypes that had plagued radio and film. "Such misrepresentations on television may be even more damaging than similar distortions in radio, film and stage," read a 1951 resolution. "Accordingly, it is necessary to act before this pattern has been completely set in this new medium." In the weeks before and after the show's premiere, NAACP Secretary Walter White urged executives at CBS and Schenley Industries, the parent company of Blatz Beer, to reconsider their commitments. White also met with CBS Vice President Sig Mickelson, who agreed to screen future episodes of the show privately for a group of prominent progressives and NAACP members. White praised Mickelson for his cooperation and CBS as being "the most liberal of the radio and television networks in treatment of the Negro." He also noted that given the vast sums of money CBS had already invested in *Amos 'n' Andy*, the meeting would focus on recommendations for the show's improvement rather than its outright cancellation. But not all elements of the organization were as compromising. As its national leaders worked behind the scenes, local leaders lobbied for a national boycott of the show and its sponsor Blatz Beer. C.L. Dellums, president of the Alameda County NAACP branch and vice president of the Brotherhood of Sleeping Car Porters, insisted that "no stone should be left unturned to keep black-faced comedians, minstrels, bad english [sic], and dialect off" television. He urged Walter White to initiate a "national fight" to sack *Amos 'n' Andy*. The New York NAACP sent correspondence threatening to take action against Schenley Industries.[9]

White-owned companies had to temper their desire to tap into rapidly expanding postwar black buying power with careful marketing campaigns that would not backfire and hurt sales. African American consumers, numbering fifteen million with annual expenditures estimated at $15 billion, represented a potential gold mine that exceeded the value of all U.S. exports combined. Advertising trade magazine *Tide* devoted its July 1951 cover story to surveying the powers, promises, and pitfalls of the black consumer market. Other publications were also filled with articles proclaiming the untapped potential of black consumers (for example "The Forgotten 15,000,000" and "The Negro Market: $15,000,000,000 to Spend") and suggesting specific ways to target that market. The editor of *Variety* grandly declared that blacks were "the most important, financially potent, and sales-and-advertising serenaded 'minority' in the land." African Americans were a large, urban-centered, and brand-conscious population that was experiencing a dramatic rise in education, household wealth, and consumer purchasing power, described by *Tide* as "rich, ripe and ready" for those companies willing to "get with the program" by advertising in black periodicals, on black-owned radio stations, and on television stations in urban areas. But *Tide* also warned that the same old ads wouldn't work for this new generation of African Americans and that even the use of seemingly benign copy could cause unintended consequences. White-owned companies would have to "maintain careful diplomatic relations" and treat blacks as "proud and sensitive American citizen[s]," if they were to court them successfully.[10]

THE FAILED NAACP BOYCOTT

NAACP leaders understood the significance of black consumerism and calculated it into the decision to take the boycott of Blatz Beer nationwide. Blatz had always focused a good deal of its marketing efforts on the black community via print media advertisements, promotions with local retailers, and in neighborhood bars. The *Amos 'n' Andy* campaign took things to a higher level. It was among the largest such drives ever undertaken in the beer industry, reportedly costing several million dollars annually. In a memo to Walter White, Roy Wilkins wrote that "they [Schenley] are vulnerable on a boycott on Blatz because of the very tight fight among a dozen beers for the national leadership . . . even a fair effort on the part of the colored people could drop them down in the sales picture." White used his syndicated newspaper column to chide Blatz and Schenley for sponsoring a product that alienated the consumer audience it was trying to reach and for its belief that the employment gained by the *Amos 'n' Andy* actors and Schenley salesmen was "considered adequate compensation for perpetuation of harmful stereotypes." To sponsors like Blatz, whose unenlightened approach perpetuated the "inaccurate and resented traditions stemming from the minstrel shows of a century ago," rather than "pioneering in creation of such new concepts," White warned that "an incalculable amount of good will and patronage seems certain to be the price which the sponsors may be forced to pay for their lack of intelligence." NAACP Director of Branches Gloster Current charged local chapters with organizing protests and urging churches, labor unions, and civic organizations to adopt their own resolutions and forward them to CBS, its affiliates, Blatz Brewing Company, Schenley Industries, and the national NAACP. NAACP locals were also given the green light to boycott Blatz and Schenley products and to persuade tavern and store owners to do likewise. The national NAACP had a history of keeping its distance from boycott efforts, such as the "Don't Buy Where You Can't Work" campaigns of the 1930s. That it finally stimulated such action signaled the significance it attached to television images as well as its awareness of the powerful potential relationship between civil rights and the black consumer market.[11]

Strong feelings about the connections between societal treatment of African Americans and their representation in the media fueled opposition to *Amos 'n' Andy* from the black press and public in addition to the NAACP. "How in the world are we going to win civil rights or equality as long as we are portrayed to those who must grant them to us as clowns or fools?" asked the *New York Amsterdam News*. A petition authored by black Chicagoans read: "So long as we tolerate such shows as Amos 'n' Andy . . . will we be faced with segregation, discrimination and race prejudice." Cleveland NAACP President L. Pearl Mitchell noted that "there has . . . been an awakening in the North and even more in the courageous South" that "calls for *freedom now*, for acceptance in every field, for no patronizing or special consideration, but acceptance because of merit." Mitchell argued that, "To attain this goal the people feel it is most important to have a true picture of the colored people." Past gains made by blacks would be "thrown for a loss" if the "vicious propaganda" of *Amos 'n' Andy* continued "to flood the homes of the nation," argued a local NAACP member. The ultimate future promise of racial equality that the legal challenge to *Plessy* embodied would be unattainable if blacks continued to be portrayed as inferior on television and in American culture.[12]

NAACP action inspired encouragement from other organizations, particularly labor. Over 100 civil rights, cultural, professional, and religious groups expressed support for the campaign. They passed resolutions condemning *Amos 'n' Andy*, initiated letter-writing drives, and led direct-action protests. The Congress of Racial Equality picketed stores and stations when it joined the boycott in early 1952. The United Auto Workers–Congress of Industrial Organizations was also a staunch ally. William Oliver, one of its officers, urged union locals to support the boycott. He also wrote the NAACP suggesting a national conference on *Amos 'n' Andy* in either Chicago or Milwaukee (home to Blatz Brewing Company). "I feel that unless we institute some action in this direction, we face the possibility of being defeated on the important issue of Negroes in the new field of television," Oliver asserted. "We should revitalize this campaign and attempt to interpret more forcibly the basic reasons for our objections to the AMOS 'N' ANDY TV show."[13]

One of the most important aspects of the *Amos 'n' Andy* boycott is that it bridged earlier forms of activism with the emerging national civil rights movement. Longstanding NAACP concerns over the influence that the entertainment media had on the quality of African American life took on even greater importance in the face of television's emergence. The tactics used by the NAACP-led coalition further indicated that the black freedom struggle was moving in a new direction. The *Amos 'n' Andy* campaign was more militant, localized, and based on direct action than previous protest efforts. In Milwaukee, with help from local business groups, political organizations, and media, the coalition forced the program's temporary removal from the air. This victory justified the NAACP's use of the boycott and fueled hope that other localities would soon follow. "The feeling was expressed that if we could get Blatz' home city station to discontinue the show, it would help branches throughout the country as well as individuals and other organizations," Milwaukee NAACP President Ardie Halyard stated in a letter to the NAACP's national leaders.[14]

The Milwaukee campaign, however, failed to coalesce into a national movement. The most significant barrier was the stark disagreement within the ranks of those who constituted the contemporary civil rights coalition. Unlike the unified front it had on issues like access to quality education, voting rights, equal justice, and fair labor practices, there lacked a consensus on how to deal with *Amos 'n' Andy*. Blacks and white liberals challenged NAACP tactics, rhetoric, and goals. Some questioned the prudence of a boycott and chafed at the idea of censoring the show regardless of its content. African Americans in the entertainment industry resented the NAACP's jeopardizing their livelihood. Most significantly, audiences disagreed with the Association's reading of the show and did not think it merited boycotting. There was not enough popular support to sustain the campaign. When combined with the difficulty of overcoming the powerful financial resources of the television and advertising industries, these obstacles short-circuited efforts to take the protest national.

The fierce support of *Amos 'n' Andy* by entertainment industry blacks provided a powerful counterpoint to the NAACP campaign. To find an all-black cast for the television version of the show CBS conducted a nationwide search. Its employees traveled 25,000 miles, interviewed 800 actors, and conducted fifty screen tests. A virtual who's who of the African American theatrical world auditioned, including Cab Calloway, Pigmeat Markham, Sidney Poitier, and Ossie Davis. The public took particular interest in the casting of "Kingfish," who was one of the most popular characters in radio history. Even President Harry Truman and General Dwight Eisenhower offered suggestions. Some members of the black press were delighted with the results. *Pittsburgh Courier* entertainment columnist Billy Rowe called the ensemble "one of the most brilliant casts in the history of show business. . . . Not only is this a cast of Negro actors and actresses—it is a cast of top notch performers who can hold their own anywhere."[15]

Blacks in the entertainment industry, including actors, writers, and backstage workers made up a significant portion of the growing black middle class and for them *Amos 'n' Andy* represented upward mobility, the reinforcement of their class status, and an excellent professional opportunity. Without a concrete plan to replace *Amos 'n' Andy* with an equally lucrative show, the NAACP crusade threatened to put a lot of actors out of work. Actress Ruby Dandridge urged the NAACP to not "take money from anyone's pocket unless you can put more in." Actress Eva Taylor warned that "the movement such as the NAACP advocates would close the door to the Negro in the theater, and, in addition, bring back the blackface comedian." She also questioned whether the NAACP understood the problems that black actors faced and worried that "the resolution of the NAACP can only do us more harm than good." Author Jessie Fauset defended *Amos 'n' Andy* as farce, writing, "We cannot afford to listen to the short-sighted advice of those urging us to pass by the avenues where our precious natural talents can be displayed and utilized, and, instead, bury those talents to the detriment of our welfare." Arna Bontemps, whose own musical *St. Louis Woman* was a target of NAACP protests five years earlier, agreed, "This new departure by the NAACP is a step toward the kind of controls usually attempted by censors."[16]

White liberal allies like the American Jewish Committee (AJC) hesitated to join the boycott due to the campaign's strategy and tactics and because of their own financial concerns. AJC had always maintained a relatively conservative approach to civil rights, preferring lobbying and legislation to direct confrontation. In a meeting with Walter White, AJC Executive Director Edwin Lukas pointed out that Jews were disturbed by the television program *The Goldbergs*, which they felt presented an outdated image of Jewish life. "[We] have been plagued with problems not unlike the one that faces you now," wrote Lukas in a follow-up correspondence, but the way to force change was through "Pressures, consultations and negotiations by influential [people]." Lukas recommended the enlistment of social scientists to suggest possible changes to the script. Lukas also offered his own suggestions to Sig Mickelson at CBS, including minimizing the role of the Kingfish character, having the actors appear briefly at the end of each episode out of character (to underscore that the show was a deliberate caricature), and having the show air "clever, one-minute jingles" to promote good intergroup relations. The AJC's willingness to support the boycott also may have been compromised by its relationship with Lewis Rosenstiel, head of Schenley Industries, who was a generous patron of the AJC and other civil rights causes and organizations, including the National Urban League.[17]

Hesitancy toward the boycott by white liberal groups like the AJC and the American Civil Liberties Union (ACLU) reflected fissures on the left over the issue of censorship. The era's hysterical anticommunist witch hunts and the cultural politics of the Cold War exposed Hollywood's vulnerability on this issue. Artists who were even suspected of harboring communist sympathies could be blacklisted for life or called before the House Un-American Activities Committee. Although the NAACP denied that the *Amos 'n' Andy* campaign constituted censorship, its white liberal allies were inclined to disagree. Both the AJC and ACLU had actively defended members of the entertainment community accused of being communists and had drafted official policies condemning pressure group censorship. For them, the NAACP campaign stepped dangerously close to the tactics of the anticommunists. ACLU Executive Director Patrick Malin wrote Walter White to tell him that although his organization shared the NAACP's goals of "equality and non-discrimination," the ACLU urged the NAACP not to resort to a boycott of Blatz Beer and would "actively oppose" a national boycott of Schenley Industries. Malin felt compelled to remind White harshly to "remember how much Negroes have suffered from the lack of free expression, and how much they and members of other minority groups . . . will suffer if opponents of civil liberties are given the opportunity to say that the Negroes are not interested in <u>all</u> civil liberties for <u>everybody</u>, as the fundamental necessity of democracy, but are interested only in <u>some</u> civil liberties for <u>themselves</u>." The NAACP struggled to muster the support of white liberal allies that had been sensitized by contemporary attacks on free speech.[18]

Ultimately, however, it was not white liberal resistance to the boycott that caused its doom but rather the inability of the NAACP to convince its members and African Americans at large that the show perpetuated negative stereotypes and represented a real threat to civil rights gains. Many blacks saw the humor and characters so feared by the NAACP as mere entertainment, farce, satire, parody, or comedy. "Far from picturing the Negro race as degraded and lazy, it shows them to be very human and charming," wrote one NAACP member. "If they are shown in situations where they are always trying to get 'something for nothing,' or to avoid hard work, is that not a common weakness of us all?" One public opinion poll showed that New York and New Jersey blacks overwhelmingly approved of the show and considered it a good thing to see. Only 8.6 percent of respondents thought the show degraded and made fun of African Americans whereas a whopping 86.5 percent wanted to keep it on the air. Black support for the show would continue throughout *Amos 'n' Andy*'s primetime run, as suggested by a *Pittsburgh Courier* poll that ranked it the fourth most popular television show among its readers in 1952–53. The show remained on primetime television until 1953, when declining ratings and Blatz Beer's decision to end its sponsorship led CBS to film thirteen more episodes and then place the show into syndication, where it would be aired by the network's 100 local affiliates. *Amos 'n' Andy* remained on the air until 1966, when the victories of the civil rights movement rendered the show unacceptable even in reruns.[19]

Although the *Amos 'n' Andy* boycott failed to generate much enthusiasm outside of a core group of NAACP and civil rights leaders, its strategy of using militant, localized, boycott-based protests to achieve national civil rights gains would become fundamental to the classical 1960s phase of the civil rights movement. In the years immediately following the *Amos 'n' Andy* campaign, bus boycotts in Baton Rouge in 1953 and Montgomery in 1955–56 forced white city officials to compromise with civil rights groups and led to important gains for African Americans. These boycotts illustrated the economic power of the black community and ushered in "the direct action phase of the modern civil rights movement," in the words of scholar Aldon Morris. Although overlooked by most civil rights historians, the *Amos 'n' Andy* boycott was the NAACP's attempt to do the same thing two years earlier.[20]

NOTES

1. For the most thorough history of *The Amos 'n' Andy Show* and its impact on American culture see Melvin Patrick Ely, *The Adventures of Amos 'n' Andy: A Social History of an American Phenomenon* (New York: Free Press, 1991). See also Thomas Cripps, "*Amos 'n' Andy* and the Debate over American Racial Integration," in Joanne Morreale, ed., *Critiquing the Sitcom: A Reader* (Syracuse: Syracuse University Press, 2003).
2. "Resolution passed at the 42nd Annual Convention, Atlanta, GA," June 1951, Papers of the National Association for the Advancement of Colored People, Microfilm Collection, Elmer Holmes Bobst Library, New York University (hereafter cited as "NAACP Papers"), Part 15, Series B, Reel 9.
3. For a history of NAACP protests against stereotyped images of blacks in popular culture see Leonard C. Archer, *Black Images in the American Theater: NAACP Protest Campaigns—Stage, Screen, Radio and Television* (Brooklyn: Pageant-Poseidon, 1973); Cripps, "*Amos 'n' Andy*," 26. For more on the class dimensions of *TheAmos 'n' Andy Show* see George Lipsitz, *Time Passages: Collective Memory and American Culture* (Minneapolis: University of Minnesota Press, 1990), 39–96.
4. Loren Miller, "Uncle Tom in Hollywood," *Crisis*, November 1934, 329.
5. John LeFlore, "NAACP Launches War on Jim Crow," *Chicago Defender*, July 7, 1951; Wilkins quoted in "NAACP Plans All Out Battle," *New York Amsterdam News*, June 30, 1951; Steven F. Lawson, "Introduction: Setting the Agenda for the Civil Rights Movement," in Steven F. Lawson, ed., *To Secure These Rights: The Report of President Harry S. Truman's Committee on Civil Rights* (New York: Bedford/St. Martin's, 2004), 1. For more on these cases, see Richard Kluger, *Simple Justice: The History of Brown v. Board of Education and Black America's Struggle for Equality* (New York: Knopf, 1976); Mark V. Tushnet, *The NAACP's Legal Strategy Against Segregated Education, 1925–1950* (Chapel Hill: University of North Carolina Press, 2004).
6. See Erik Barnouw, *Tube of Plenty: The Evolution of American Television* (New York: Oxford University Press, [1975] 1990, 2nd Rev. Ed.), 99–116; J.

Fred MacDonald, *One Nation Under Television: The Rise and Decline of Network TV* (New York: Pantheon Books, 1990), 43; Gerald Jones, *Honey, I'm Home! Sitcoms: Selling the American Dream* (New York: Grove Weidenfeld, 1992), 29–37, 62–75; James Von Schilling, *The Magic Window, American Television, 1939–1953* (New York: Hawthorne Press, 2003), 125.

7. "Hadda Brooks," *Ebony*, April 1951, 101–104; "Negro Talent Coming Into Own on TV . . . Without Use of Stereotypes," *Variety*, May 3, 1950; "Television," *Ebony*, June 1950, 22–23; J. Fred MacDonald, *Blacks and White TV: Afro-Americans in Television since 1948* (Chicago: Nelson Hall Publishers, 1983), 3–4.
8. Ed Sullivan, "Can TV Crack America's Color Line?," *Ebony*, June 1951, 58–65. For the important role that television played in the civil rights movement see Julian Bond, "The Media and the Movement: Looking Back from the Southern Front," in Brian Ward, ed., *Media, Culture, and the Modern African American Freedom Struggle* (Gainesville: University of Florida Press, 2001), 16–40; Allison Graham, *Framing the South: Hollywood, Television, and Race During the Civil Rights Struggle* (Baltimore: Johns Hopkins University Press, 2001); Sasha Torres, *Black, White, and In Color: Television and Black Civil Rights* (Princeton: Princeton University Press, 2003).
9. "Resolution adopted by the NAACP Board of Directors," May 14, 1951 quoted in "Letter to Jean Bach from Edna Freeman," December 4, 1952, NAACP Papers, Part 15, Series B, Reel 14; "Memorandum to the Files: From the Secretary," July 11, 1951, NAACP Papers, Part 15, Series B, Reel 10; Walter White, memorandum, July 11, 1951, NAACP Papers, Part 15, Series B, Reel 10; "Conference with Sig Mickelson," NAACP Papers, Part 15, Series B, Reel 14; "Letter to NAACP from Nathan Klein," March 1, 1949, NAACP Papers, Part 15, Series B, Reel 14; "Letter to Walter White from C.L. Dellums," December 6, 1950, NAACP Papers, Part 15, Series B, Reel 9; "Letter to Lewis Rosensthiel from Lindsay White and James Allen," June 27, 1951, NAACP Papers, Part 15, Series B, Reel 9.
10. "Selling The Negro Market," *Tide*, July 20, 1951, 37–44 in NAACP Papers, Part 15, Series B, Reel 10; Robert E. Weems, Jr., *Desegregating the Dollar: African American Consumerism in the Twentieth Century* (New York: New York University Press, 1998), 31–55; Kathy M. Newman, "The Forgotten Fifteen Million: Black Radio, Radicalism, and the Construction of the 'Negro Market,'" in Susan Merrill Squire, ed., *Communities of the Air: Radio Century, Radio Culture* (Durham: Duke University Press, 2003), 109–33; MacDonald, *Blacks and White TV*, 3, 7; Lizabeth Cohen, *A Consumer's Republic: The Politics of Mass Consumption in Postwar America* (New York: Knopf, 2003), 7.
11. Walter White, syndicated column, July 12 and August 2, 1951 in Roy Wilkins Papers, Manuscript Division, Library of Congress, Washington, DC, Box 34; W. Richard Bruner, "Amos 'n' Andy Hassle Won't Stop TV Show," *Printer's Ink*, August 24, 1951, 30; "Memo to W. White from R. Wilkins," July 19, 1951, NAACP Papers, Part 15, Series B, Reel 9; "Letter to Branch Leaders from Gloster Current," July 16, 1951, NAACP Papers, Part 15, Series B, Reel 9. For information on the "Don't Buy Where You Can't Work" campaigns see Beth Tompkins Bates, "A New Crowd Challenges the Agenda of the Old Guard in the NAACP, 1933–41," *American Historical Review* 102:2 (April 1997): 347–50; August Meier and Elliot Rudwick, *Along the Color Line: Explorations in the Black Experience* (Urbana and Chicago: University of Illinois Press, 1976), esp. 315–53.
12. Earl Brown, "Truth Vs. Entertainment," *New York Amsterdam News*, August 4, 1951; L.F. Palmer, Jr., "Amos 'n' Andy Bow (Even Lower) on

Video So Your Scribe Spends a Dull Half Hour," *Chicago Defender,* July 7, 1951; "Why Take Amos 'n' Andy Show Off Television," NAACP Papers, Part 15, Series B, Reel 10; "Launch Drive to Ban 'Amos 'n' Andy' Television Show," *Chicago Defender,* August 25, 1951; "L. Pearl Mitchell to Editors of Cleveland Plain Dealer," July 12, 1951, NAACP Papers, Part 15, Series B, Reel 9; "Errold Collymore to Edward Lashin," January 14, 1950, NAACP Papers, Part 15, Series B, Reel 13.

13. Supporting organizations included: Students for Democratic Action, New York Council of the Arts, Sciences and Professions, American Federation of Labor, Communist Party USA, Transportation Workers Union of America, American Civil Liberties Union, American Jewish Committee, Michigan Federation of Teachers, Chicago Urban League, Phi Beta Sigma Fraternity, National Beauty Culturist League, Hotel & Restaurant Employees and Bartenders International Union, United Church Women, and Mount Olivet Baptist Church. "Launch Drive to Ban," *Chicago Defender,* August 25, 1951. Also see generally NAACP Papers, Part 15, Series B, Reel 10; "Labor, Liberals Join NAACP Protest Against Amos 'n' Andy," *The Auto Worker,* August 1951 in NAACP Papers, Part 15, Series B, Reel 10; Robert Korstad and Nelson Lichtenstein, "Opportunities Found and Lost: Labor, Radicals, and the Early Civil Rights Movement," *Journal of American History* 75:3 (December 1998): 794.
14. "Letter to Gloster Current from Ardie Halyard," July 27, 1951, NAACP Papers, Part 15, Series B, Reel 9.
15. "An Inside Story: It Took 4 Years to Find Actors to Play Amos, Andy, Kingfish," *New York Amsterdam News,* June 23, 1951; Ely, *The Adventures of Amos 'n' Andy,* 203–204; "People Interviewed—Audition for Amos + Andy," Flournoy E. Miller Papers, Box 2, Folder 1 in the Helen Armstead-Johnson Theater Collection, Schomburg Center for Research in Black Culture, New York Public Library, New York, NY; "It' Out Now! 'Shuffle Along' Miller Dug Up Video's 'Andy,'" *Chicago Defender* August 11, 1951; "TV's Kingfish, Tim Moore, Started in Show Biz at 12," *Los Angeles Sentinel,* June 14, 1951; Chester L. Washington, "Amos 'n' Andy on TV: Loaded with Race Talent," *Pittsburgh Courier,* June 23, 1951; "Billy Rowe's Notebook," *Pittsburgh Courier,* April 22, 1950 and July 7, 1951.
16. All quotes from "Many Say NAACP Stand Endangers Artists' Future," *Pittsburgh Courier,* November 10, 1951.
17. For the AJC's approach to civil rights and its relationship with the NAACP see Naomi W. Cohen, *Not Free to Desist: The American Jewish Committee, 1906–1966* (Philadelphia: The Jewish Publication Society of America, 1972), 383–89. "Letter to Walter White from Edwin Lukas," July 19, 1951, NAACP Papers, Part 15, Series B, Reel 10; "Memorandum re: Conference with Mr. Edwin Lukas of the American Jewish Committee," July 10, 1951, NAACP Papers, Part 15, Series B, Reel 10; "Letter to Walter White from Edwin Lukas," August 7, 1951, NAACP Papers, Part 15, Series B, Reel 10; "Memorandum RE: Conference with Lukas," July 10, 1951, NAACP Papers, Part 15, Series B, Reel 10; "Letter to L. Rosenstiel from L. Granger," May 24, 1951 in Papers of the National Urban League, Manuscripts Division, Library of Congress, Washington, DC, Series VII, Box 1.
18. "Letter to Hobart Lagrone from Roy Wilkins," July 25, 1951, NAACP Papers, Part 15, Series B, Reel 9; Barnouw, *Tube of Plenty,* 109–10, 123–25; "Letter to Walter White from Patrick Malin," July 27, 1951, NAACP Papers, Part 15, Series B, Reel 9; "Pressure Group Censorship: The Policy of the American Civil Liberties Union," April 16, 1951 in Papers of the American Civil Liberties Union, Department of Rare Books and Special Collections,

Mudd Library, Princeton University, Box 764, Folder 6. Copies of Malin's letter were distributed to media outlets, sponsors, and in an ACLU press release as the organization's official position on the matter. For the relationship between the NAACP and the ACLU see Samuel Walker, *In Defense of American Liberties: A History of the ACLU* (New York: Oxford University Press, 1990), 162–66 and 237–39.

19. "Letter to Walter White from Bessie Donchian," July 23, 1951, NAACP Papers, Part 15, Series B, Reel 9; "Advertest Shows Most Negroes OK Blatz 'Amos' Show," *Advertising Age,* August 13, 1951, 1, 36; "Best Television Show," *Pittsburgh Courier,* April 25, 1953.
20. Aldon D. Morris, *The Origins of the Civil Rights Movement: Black Communities Organizing for Change* (New York: Free Press, 1984), 17–25.

Part II

African American Campaigns for Economic Power During the Civil Rights Era and Beyond

7 Economic Civil Rights Activism in Pensacola, Florida

J. Michael Butler

The impact that economic interests had on different aspects of America's civil rights struggle is undeniable. Protests in Montgomery, Tallahassee, Nashville, Albany, Birmingham, and Atlanta, just to name a few significant locales, lend credence to the contention that the civil rights movement had clear economic goals and consequences. Economic considerations inspired the opinions, actions, and decisions of many different groups involved in civil rights activities. National organizations, student protestors, indigenous groups, white businessmen, black churches, and various other factions had to acknowledge and address economic issues at some point during their conflicts concerning segregated public accommodations in the Jim Crow South. One such conflict was the 1961 campaign for integrated facilities in downtown Pensacola, Florida, which involved all of the groups mentioned and proved exceptional for many reasons. The Pensacola movement utilized local elements in both unique and familiar ways to achieve all of its primary goals after weeks of meticulously organized nonviolent demonstrations.[1]

Pensacola has a long history as a site for multicultural economic opportunity. The Florida Panhandle's colonial legacy and physical location gave it a degree of religious diversity, economic prosperity, and ethnic variation absent in much of the South. The seat of Escambia County, the westernmost county in Florida, Pensacola has served as a key port on the Gulf of Mexico since its initial settlement and had a tremendous impact on the development of race relations in the area. Its bountiful employment opportunities and relative multiculturalism attracted large numbers of freedmen to Escambia County and contributed to the rise of a confident, assertive black middle class in Pensacola during the post-Civil War era. African Americans joined interracial labor unions, established thriving businesses, and successfully challenged a law that segregated city streetcars. One of the keys to increased economic opportunity and political representation for the area's black community was the 1919 establishment of a National Association for the Advancement of Colored People (NAACP) branch, one of only two chapters in the Sunshine State. In 1928, the Pensacola NAACP filed a lawsuit to end the white primary in Florida. Residents also started the

Escambia County Voter's League, an indigenous voting rights organization that operated independently from the NAACP.[2]

Black activism and white resistance increased following World War II. Whites from throughout the rural South came to port cities like Pensacola to fill wartime jobs and brought with them cultural mores, including a fervent commitment to the principle of white supremacy. Thousands remained in the city after the war ended, but their employment opportunities deteriorated as production levels dropped. Consequently, a storm of racial angst built among disillusioned whites. Their frustration only grew with the monumental *Brown v. Board of Education* ruling and the bus boycotts that occurred in Montgomery and Tallahassee. Anti-black organizations such as the White Citizen's Council and the Federation for Constitutional Government of Escambia County drew from this population.[3]

The first of a wave of local challenges to Jim Crow began on February 1, 1960, when five NAACP-backed African American plaintiffs filed a class-action lawsuit against the Escambia County School Board and superintendent to desegregate the district's public schools in what became known as *Augustus v. Escambia County School Board*. The case attracted nationwide media attention and intense local scrutiny. *Southern School News* called it "Florida's most sweeping court challenge" to segregated schools, noting, "it was filed in Pensacola, at the tip of the state's northwest panhandle, where segregation sentiment is strongest." The *Pensacola News* hoped the suit "may take months, perhaps years, to settle" and urged the board to "spend several thousand dollars" to combat integration. Ten days after the suit was filed the county school board took action. It unanimously declared "an all-out defense" against the case and with county funds hired two Pensacola law firms for representation. The defense team sent copies of the suit to Florida's attorney general, school superintendent, and every county school board to inform them of the pending legal showdown that had potential ramifications for schools throughout the state. The long struggle to integrate schools in Escambia County had begun, but it had relatively little immediate effect upon the community because the national NAACP wanted to keep movement activities in the courtroom and off the street. Local African Americans needed to focus their efforts upon another form of racial injustice in order to bring substantive changes to the racial status quo in Pensacola.[4]

While *Augustus* slowly progressed through the courts, a separate black protest movement developed and transformed Northwest Florida in unprecedented fashion. The social, economic, and political conditions that existed in the area during the late 1950s proved conducive to a momentous local movement. This series of challenges to Jim Crow differed substantially from the effort to integrate schools. Protesters targeted stores in downtown Pensacola that depended upon black patronage, yet segregated their dining facilities and refused to hire blacks in positions of meaningful employment. The downtown campaign utilized direct action and depended upon mass participation to achieve its goals, tactics that the national NAACP discouraged and often refused to endorse. Activities in the business district also drew the attention of black students, who provided the numbers and enthusiasm that court cases could not muster. African American churches in Pensacola served as both logistical and emotional centers of the public demonstrations; they emerged as the most significant threat to Jim Crow in the Florida Panhandle.

THE PENSACOLA MOVEMENT LED BY W.C. DOBBINS

The movement found a charismatic leader to galvanize it in Reverend William Curtis Dobbins, who left a church in Montgomery, Alabama to become the minister of Pensacola's St. Paul United Methodist Church in 1959. W.C. Dobbins was born in Athens, Alabama in 1934. He entered the ministry as a teenager and received degrees from Alabama A&M, Scarritt College, and Gammon Theological Seminary. Soon after his arrival in Pensacola, Dobbins became a member of the local NAACP. He first captured attention when he tried to attend a service at Pensacola's all-white First Baptist Church. Although deacons stationed in front of the chapel doors refused to let him in, Dobbins gained entrance to the church weeks later. His insistence upon equality during the worship hour did not surprise those who knew the preacher. Like Reverend Martin Luther King, Jr., Dobbins made social justice the focus of his ministry and used Biblical teachings to justify civil rights activism. As Christians, he argued, southern blacks had an obligation to work for social change. Dobbins drummed up support not only from his congregation but also from fellow ministers, which led to the formation of the significant Pensacola Council of Ministers (PCM) in 1960. The group consisted of nearly every local black clergy from various denominations and dedicated itself to achieving racial equality in the county. The involvement of area ministers and their congregations in the Pensacola black freedom struggle marked a turning point in the local movement. From then on, the church played a central role in leading and organizing the African American community's fight for justice in Escambia County.[5]

Dobbins believed that young people had to become active components of the movement if it was to succeed. Before his arrival, the local NAACP Youth Council existed in name alone; its advisor Raymon Harvey referred to it as "dormant." It had at most five teenaged members and never applied for formal recognition from the national office. Dobbins wanted to wake up the moribund organization. Sensing the opportunity, Harvey voluntarily relinquished his leadership role to Dobbins, primarily because Dobbins possessed more status in the black community due to his occupation as a minister. Harvey also recognized that Dobbins had demonstrated the leadership abilities that African Americans in Pensacola needed. Dobbins named Harvey the group's co-advisor and relied heavily upon the Pensacola native during his work with the Youth Council. Harvey, in turn, considered Dobbins his mentor and the primary reason he became actively involved in the area freedom struggle. In 1959, Dobbins sent the Pensacola NAACP Youth Council's application to the national headquarters, where it was almost immediately accepted. At its initial meeting, twenty-one people ranging from twelve to twenty-five-years-old joined the Youth Council.[6]

Dobbins had a dramatic impact upon those who belonged to the group. Youth Council member Mary Harrison Washington remembered the minister as "a young, enthusiastic person who was very articulate and had a brilliant mind." Her peers, Washington recalled, likewise viewed Dobbins as "very impressive" and "very smart." Her younger brother Horace Harrison became a member of the Youth Council because of the "charisma" and "leadership qualities" that Dobbins possessed. According to Washington, "When Rev. Dobbins would speak, everyone would listen because he always had something important to say. He did not waste words." The Youth Council met with Dobbins and Harvey every Saturday afternoon at Central Life Insurance Company, a black-owned business, where they discussed local and national issues that pertained to African Americans. The education, confidence, and bravery Dobbins possessed inspired people of all ages, earning almost instantaneous community respect.[7]

By the beginning of 1960, the pieces were in place—a charismatic leader, an organized ministry, energized youth, and the right socioeconomic conditions—to wage a successful campaign against Jim Crow in the Florida Panhandle. The Pensacola Movement was triggered by the Greensboro sit-ins on February 1 when four North Carolina A&T students occupied a segregated Woolworth's lunch counter. Sit-ins quickly spread throughout the South, including Pensacola, and they became the city's first indigenous black direct-action campaign of the postwar era. The student sit-in campaigns proved particularly important to the development of America's civil rights movement, infusing the struggle with vigor and enthusiasm. The technique provided demonstrators with a strategy that proved both simple to implement and effective in its use of nonviolent resistance to protest segregated public facilities.

Pensacola residents could relate with what happened in Greensboro. Pensacola possessed a thriving downtown area with stores that black customers frequented. Only whites, however, could eat at their lunch counters. In addition, all downtown water fountains and restrooms were reserved for white use only. Only the Greyhound bus station provided a restroom for African American customers in the vicinity, and that was only because a white Tallahassee resident named Jefferson Poland had earlier informed federal authorities that the terminal maintained segregated waiting rooms and eating areas for interstate travelers. Poland, a member of the Congress of Racial Equality and the American Civil Liberties Union, traveled from Tallahassee to San Jose on a bus that stopped at the Pensacola station. He sat in the "colored section" of the restaurant and asked for service, but the station manager instead called police to remove Poland. He left before officers arrived but later wrote a letter about the encounter to Interstate Commerce Commission Chairman Everett Hutchinson. Poland accused terminal management of violating the Interstate Commerce Act and requested "that appropriate punitive measures be taken against Greyhound." After a federal inquiry into the situation, the Pensacola terminal integrated all of its facilities. Situations like this represented the most blatant reminder of white supremacy in Escambia County as throughout the South. With his attention fixed on Greensboro and the subsequent sit-ins that had spread across the region, Dobbins asked Youth Council members repeatedly, "What is Pensacola doing to end segregation?"[8]

The first step the students and their advisors took was to ask local merchants to desegregate their public dining facilities voluntarily. Dobbins and his Youth Council leaders wrote letters dated March 30 to the managers of S.H. Kress, Woolworth, and W.T. Grant stores in downtown Pensacola asking for cooperation. The letters cited "the courageous efforts of American youth to end the humiliation of segregation and discrimination in southern cities" as the Youth Council's motivation. The students wished to avoid "the necessity of such 'sit-down' or picketing demonstrations" to "correct any discriminatory practices" that business owners exercised. The notes concluded with an appeal and implicit threat to the economic interests of the owner. "We feel that you will be very happy to do whatever you can to retain the tremendous amount of business that comes to your store from many citizens who are denied certain privileges in your Pensacola" establishment. After all, African Americans represented over half of the clientele at businesses the council targeted. Dobbins also issued a press release explaining the Youth Council's actions. Although none of the letters threatened direct action if proprietors ignored their requests, each expressed hope that stores "will seek to end all discriminatory practices without the loss of any Negro business." Despite the appeal to their financial sensibilities, however, white businessmen ignored the demand.[9]

Dobbins and nine others entered the white-only dining area at the Pensacola Woolworth's on April 5. The group stood quietly and left approximately five minutes after their entrance. As they departed the store, group spokesman Raymon Harvey left a note that stated, "This is a phase of our protest demonstration against unfair, unethical, and unchristian practices of many nationwide variety stores." The letter promised future demonstrations and announced a black selective-buying boycott of downtown merchants during the upcoming Easter season. The *Pensacola Journal* called the action "a brief, almost unnoticed demonstration" while an Alabama reporter claimed the event "went almost unnoticed during the noon rush hour." Despite media efforts to downplay the episode, five robed Klansmen marched into the store the next day and offered their services to the manager in the case of any future demonstrations.[10]

For the rest of the year, Dobbins crusaded for the integration of Pensacola's downtown lunch counters, basing his plan on the Greensboro model. The Pensacola direct-action protests reflected a great deal of planning and required strong local support to succeed. Dobbins coordinated the operations under the auspices of the PCM, the NAACP Youth Council, and the Pensacola NAACP branch. Dobbins believed that the PCM would provide leadership by spreading news of the protests. Because they possessed both economic autonomy and a highly regarded position, ministers played a crucial role in the success of this indigenous civil rights campaign. PCM members prepared their congregations for direct action by preaching on a regular basis against racial inequalities. The NAACP Youth Council met weekly and was enthusiastic about demonstrating. Dobbins planned to use these students in lunch counter sit-ins, believing that whites would be less likely to attack young people. Dobbins also utilized the Pensacola NAACP to recruit volunteers and engineered an NAACP membership drive in October 1960. Dobbins' St. Paul United Methodist base was also vital to the protest's success. Many NAACP members and local civic leaders attended the church, including physicians, dentists, teachers, and attorneys. Their advocacy of the demonstrations carried weight both in the African American community and among white merchants who would lose their substantial business.[11]

DIRECT-ACTION PROTESTS DESEGREGATE DOWNTOWN PENSACOLA

The campaign began in January 1961 when Dobbins and others from the PCM and Pensacola NAACP approached downtown business managers individually and asked them to both integrate their lunch counters and hire at least one black employee. The PCM simultaneously placed a full-page advertisement in the *Pensacola News Journal* that listed its demands. It named the downtown businesses that possessed segregated lunch counters and refused to hire black employees, asking that they implement PCM objectives voluntarily as a sign of good faith to their black customers. The appeal urged the black community not to patronize those stores until their owners complied. When none of them did, PCM representatives followed up a month later and met with a coalition of local white businessmen called the Pensacola Retail Merchants' Association. The group further resisted African American demands. One of the businessmen declared, "You cannot force us to hire anybody that we don't want to hire," while another promised, "We won't serve any nigger at our [dining] counters." PCM representative H.K. Matthews told the owners, "If you want to keep your business all-white, then we will help you keep it all-white." Shortly after these tense and unsuccessful meetings the PCM decided unanimously to initiate the sit-ins and support a selective-buying campaign in downtown Pensacola.[12]

While negotiations with white merchants continued, Dobbins and Harvey chose five teens to participate in the first downtown sit-in. They met privately in the office of local civil rights attorney Charles Wilson with those who were selected. The students did not know the purpose of the meeting until the minister spoke. Dobbins explained why he picked them; he wanted the protesters to be at least fifteen years old, active NAACP Youth Council members, and good students. Whites would no doubt accuse them of being troublemakers, so an emphasis was placed on character. Each student had a good reputation with no past disciplinary problems. They had to be brave enough to face hostility but disciplined enough not to respond to it. Dobbins also chose them based on their parents' employment situations. He did not want any people to lose their jobs because of their children's activities, so parents had to own their own businesses or work for a black employer. Each parent also had to grant their children permission to participate in the demonstrations. Most importantly, Dobbins and Harvey had to trust each student completely. They wanted the sit-ins to come as a surprise to local whites. Dobbins told the assembled youth that any leaked information would give downtown merchants the upper hand. They could lock out all blacks, call the police, or assemble a mob of hostile onlookers. If the white community found out, violence could transpire. All five of the students decided to take part in the protest.[13]

To these students and their advisors, the sit-ins represented more than a plea for integrated lunch counters; they were signs that the area's young African Americans would no longer tolerate segregation. Mary Harrison Washington participated because "somebody had to stand up and say that blacks were not going to accept inferior treatment." Her objective "was to show the white people in Pensacola that we did not want to be treated as second-class citizens any longer. White folks thought that black people were happy, that everything was just fine in Pensacola. We had to show them that everything wasn't fine." Raymon Harvey felt that the sit-ins "weren't about eating, they were about our dignity." Whereas the meticulous selection of the protesters and the secretive nature of the protests demonstrated that the Pensacola sit-ins were a highly organized endeavor that adult leaders carefully constructed, the energy, passion, and enthusiasm of the students also proved to be invaluable.[14]

The first Pensacola sit-in took place in June 1961. On the morning of the first demonstration, the five young activists met with Dobbins and Harvey for final instructions. The students had to have a book or magazine to read while sitting. They could not under any circumstances respond to the taunts and jeers of onlookers. They had to surrender nail files, penknives, or anything else that whites could label a weapon. They could not touch any merchandise in the store for fear of shoplifting accusations, and they had to possess a small amount of cash in the unlikely case that the restaurant served them. Dobbins gave each individual a dime in case they needed to use a pay phone. The two adults then drove the young volunteers to Woolworth's in separate vehicles at approximately 11:30 AM. Dobbins chose the protest time purposefully; he wanted the youth to make their statement during the café's lunchtime rush. To avoid arousing suspicion, each student entered separately and pretended to shop in the department store. Once all five arrived they walked together into the dining area and took seats at different tables in the café. According to Washington the employees "were in total shock" and "did not know what to do." The manager told them to leave but the students refused to acknowledge him. The few whites that were dining in the area left almost immediately. No other patrons entered. While the students quietly occupied their counters, Harvey and Dobbins watched their activities through the front window outside the store. After approximately two hours the students left Woolworth's to review the day's protest and coordinate activities for the following day. Within days of the initial demonstration other young people began to volunteer to participate in the sit-ins. Dobbins and the PCM carefully screened their backgrounds and motives before authorizing their participation.[15]

Approximately fifty African American youth would volunteer for the continued demonstrations. Their activities spread to include lunch counters at department stores like Kress, J.J. Newberry's, and Walgreen's. The protests all followed a similar pattern: students entered the stores simultaneously, individually sat at the counters, and asked to place an order. When café workers refused to serve them they remained in their seats and read in silence. Dobbins and Harvey always monitored from a distance and allowed no adults to join the demonstrations. The sit-ins occurred on different days of the week (except Sundays) and at various places and times so that whites could not predict their occurrence. The sit-ins were coordinated to maximize their economic impact. As they progressed, the number of whites who shopped at the targeted stores declined. Those who continued to patronize them would not enter the dining area if African Americans were there already. Furthermore, merchants unwittingly encouraged protesters when they closed their counters or locked their doors to prevent a demonstration because such actions accomplished the economic objectives of a boycott.[16]

Intense white resistance accompanied the sit-ins as crowds of curious and furious spectators gathered around affected lunch counters. These counter-demonstrators were emboldened by police that had no intention of providing meaningful protection to black youths engaged in civil disobedience. Verbal harangues escalated into violence as officers refused to protect African American demonstrators from physical assaults. Assailants burned one protestor with a cigarette and sprayed insecticide in the eyes of another during the June 15 sit-ins. The next day a white teenager stabbed a black teenager. The day after, a white onlooker threw battery acid in the face of a demonstrator. One African American witness saw a cook sprinkle crushed glass over food before he served it to a Youth Council member. Police made no arrests of whites and even encouraged additional assaults by laughing at or ignoring the actions. On the other hand, officers arrested blacks for a wide range of offenses including trespassing, illegal boycott, public cursing, loitering, vagrancy, jaywalking, unlawful assembly, resisting arrest, loitering, malicious destruction of private property, refusing to comply with a lawful order, "feeding a parking meter," and disorderly conduct. Policemen retrieved items from the store, placed them in demonstrators' pockets, and then arrested them for shoplifting. These experiences deepened the mistrust of law enforcement that later characterized the Pensacola movement. Authorities also incarcerated Dobbins for contributing to the delinquency of a minor and interfering with an officer in the discharge of his duties. Passersby fired shotgun blasts into his house and the Dobbins family slept in the homes of his congregation members during the first weeks of the sit-ins. Other adult NAACP members found signs posted on their property that read, "Don't let the sun set on your head in this town" and "Stay away from lunch counters, Niggers." The "KKK" signed each warning. *Pensacola News Journal* scarcely mentioned the sit-ins but it reported all of the arrests.[17]

Both the PCM and Pensacola NAACP played indispensable roles throughout the campaign. The PCM organized weekly mass meetings, many of which produced overflow crowds, at churches throughout the city to inform the community of protest activities. The PCM invited Dr. Martin Luther King, Jr. to speak. He did not come, but his confidant Ralph Abernathy did. PCM and Pensacola NAACP members took shifts at the city jail to ensure that police did not abuse the teens arrested in the sit-ins. They also packed the county courthouse, usually sitting in the section reserved for whites, when student activists had to face a judge. Both organizations collected money for bail, court fees, and fines. Each was also wise enough to allow NAACP Youth Council members, the protesters themselves, to participate by distributing a newsletter "to truthfully inform the community of the activity of the Youth Council, relative to sit-in demonstrations," in hopes that adults "will conscientiously support our efforts to achieve a just goal." These one-sheet documents summarized each day's activities and listed all arrests. The first such report noted that police incarcerated fourteen youth, all black, during six days of protests.[18]

The communication and cooperation between these three organizations led to the first of a resounding series of victories when the economic impact of the sit-ins became too much for local businesses to contend with and all of the targeted stores agreed to integrate their lunch counters, water fountains, and restrooms by the fall of 1961. Inspired by the NAACP Youth Council, who wanted to channel their energies into a new project almost immediately, Pensacola's activist community turned its attention back toward downtown businesses, this time for their refusal to hire African Americans. Dobbins suggested that the PCM and Pensacola NAACP establish picket lines in front of downtown establishments that refused to employ blacks. Adults would participate in this direct-action campaign because with school back in session, the NAACP Youth Council members would be occupied during business hours. Selective buying had always accompanied the sit-in campaign but now the boycott would take center stage.

Once again, the campaign was resoundingly effective; the boycott had a tremendous impact on area establishments and some Pensacola businessmen agreed to address the grievances only days after the demonstrations began. Nolan's, a downtown grocery store that refused to hire black cashiers, lost $10,000 and 90 percent of its business during the first month of protests. Only after Nolan's hired several African Americans did the boycott there cease. The campaigns followed a consistent pattern; protestors would march in shifts throughout the day. Youth Council members made placards and walked in the lines when they were not in class. The signs had a variety of slogans on them: "Justice Is Not Served," "Don't Shop Here," and "Your Dollar Is As Good As The Next," among others. When students participated, their numbers swelled picket lines down both sides of downtown Pensacola's main thoroughfare. Adults and youth alike passed out fliers that discouraged shoppers from entering stores that refused to hire African Americans. Youth Council member and sit-in participant Horace Harrison recalled that demonstrators particularly discouraged black consumers from crossing the picket lines and "would try to talk them out" of entering the businesses by explaining the purpose of the protests. Harrison estimates that 90 percent of the local black community stayed away from the downtown area during the campaign and shopped in other places, such as the suburban Town and Country Plaza.[19]

When Dobbins and other PCM members met again with the Pensacola Retail Merchants' Association, the white businessmen struck a different tone than they had at the beginning of the year. This time they admitted that they could not survive financially without black patronage but expressed concern that whites would abandon their stores if they hired black workers. The PCM understood that the hiring process had to progress at a reasonable pace so that the businesses would not lose all of their white customers to those that continued to segregate, but also insisted that downtown shops hire blacks "in meaningful positions of employment" and not just as menial laborers. PCM member H.K. Matthews reports, "We did not want them to lose their white customers by [our] being dogmatic, but we promised to resume the campaigns against them if the integration process was too slow."[20]

On March 6, 1962 all of Pensacola's department, variety, and drug stores desegregated their lunch counters officially. Elebash's Jewelry, owned by Pensacola Mayor Eugene Elebash, became the first downtown store to hire a black employee. By the end of 1961 over thirty such establishments had either hired black employees, integrated their dining facilities, or both. The *Montgomery Advertiser* called the Pensacola movement "extremely successful" and Dobbins estimated that the campaigns satisfied 80 percent of NAACP and PCM goals. Florida NAACP Field Secretary Robert W. Saunders noted in his 1962 "Annual Report" of state activities that the Pensacola Youth Council "in cooperation with local ministers . . . successfully desegregated all lunch counter facilities in downtown stores." Saunders declared the operation one of the most "outstanding activities" a Florida NAACP branch sponsored during the year even though neither the state office nor the national office offered any assistance to its panhandle locals. That the NAACP bureaucracy—which usually shunned direct action and instead preferred to work through the courts—recognized and praised a local campaign that utilized nonviolent resistance, student protestors, and its own adult branch members, indicated the campaign's undeniable effectiveness.[21]

The success of the Pensacola movement established the black church as the center of civil rights activity in the area while also conferring the importance of secular forces like the NAACP's local adult branch and youth council. City churches provided African Americans with the dynamic group of indigenous leaders that the Pensacola movement needed. The downtown campaign proved a watershed moment for race relations in Northwest Florida and required calculation, communication, and cooperation. The PCM, Pensacola NAACP, and NAACP Youth Council each played specific roles during the demonstrations and accomplished together what would have proved much more arduous for any one of them to obtain. The campaign illustrated that black economic power was a collective force that could be exercised by the engagement of a diverse range of community members—youth and adults, sacred and secular, men and women, rank-and-file and elite. The campaign provided people with a common experience in community mobilization and their success bred confidence in the rightness of their cause and effectiveness of their method. It was the first successful protest against Jim Crow in Escambia County with no help from outside organizations and thus a significant piece of local history.

NOTES

1. Gavin Wright, "The Civil Rights Revolution as Economic History," The Journal of Economic History 59:2 (June 1999): 267–89; Elizabeth Jacoway and David Colburn, eds., *Southern Businessmen and Desegregation* (Baton Rouge: LSU Press, 1982).
2. For more on the political activism of black Pensacola between Reconstruction and World War II see August Meier and Elliott Rudwick, "Negro Boycotts of Segregated Streetcars in Florida, 1901–1905," *South Atlantic Quarterly* 69:4 (Autumn 1970): 525–33; Jerrell H. Shofner, "The Pensacola Workingman's Association: A Militant Negro Labor Union During Reconstruction," *Labor History* 13:4 (Fall 1972): 556; Wayne Flynt, "Pensacola Labor Problems and Political Radicalism," *Florida Historical Quarterly* 43:4 (April 1965): 321; Eric Arnesen, "What's on the Black Worker's Mind?: African-American Labor and the Union Tradition on the Gulf Coast," *Gulf Coast Historical Review* 10:1 (Fall 1994): 7–30. The initial charter of the Pensacola NAACP can be found in "NAACP Branch files, Pensacola, Florida, 1919, 1921–28," in the National Association for the Advancement of Colored People Papers,

Library of Congress, Washington, DC (hereafter cited as "NAACP Papers"), Volume I, Box G42; Cindy West, "Civil Rights Tide Swept Bitter Water Into Pensacola," *Pensacola News Journal*, February 27, 1986. For more on the Pensacola NAACP's successful challenge to the state white primary, see NAACP Papers, "NAACP Legal File, Cases Supported, H. D. Goode, Mar–June 1928," Box D58.

3. Information concerning the foundation of the Escambia County White Citizen's Council and the Federation for Constitutional Government of Escambia County can be found in the "LeBaron family papers, 1907–72," University of West Florida Special Collections, Accession No. 1972–12, Files 38 and 39; "Some Would Make City Another Brooklyn—Harris," *Pensacola Journal*, February 22, 1958. For more on the impact that World War II had on port cities in the South, see Charles D. Chamberlain, *Victory at Home: Manpower and Race in the American South During World War II* (Athens: University of Georgia Press, 2003).
4. For more on the suit that integrated public schools in Escambia County, see *Augustus v. Escambia County School Board*, PCA 1064, Case File, Escambia County Clerk of Courts, Archives and Records Department, Pensacola, FL; Associated Press, "NAACP Begins a Suit in Florida," *New York Times*, February 2, 1960; Escambia County School Board Meeting Minutes Book, October 1958–August 1960, 351–52, Escambia County Public School Board, Pensacola, FL; Paul Jasper, "Hopeful Board Will Spend Thousands Over Mix Fight," *Pensacola News*, February 26, 1960; "School Desegregation Suit Filed in Escambia County," *Southern School News*, March 1960; "Florida—Bryant Defeats Candidate Backed by Collins," *Southern School News*, June 1960; *Karen Renee Augustus, a minor, etc., v. The Board of Public Instruction of Escambia County, etc.*, United States District Court, Northern District, Florida, Pensacola Division, June 23, 1960, September 7, 1960, 185 F. Supp. 450. The full opinion was published in *Race Relations Law Reporter* 5:4 (Fall 1960): 645–49.
5. "Journal of the Tennessee Annual Conference of the United Methodist Church," Sixteenth Session of the 170th Annual Conference, West End United Methodist Church, Nashville, TN, June 13–16, 1983, 256, The Methodist Archive Center, United Methodist Church Alabama–West Florida Conference records, Huntingdon College Library; "Ministers of Saint Paul Church, Pensacola, Escambia County, Florida," *Central Alabama Conference* Journal of the United Methodist Church, no date, Methodist Archive Center, UMC Alabama–West Florida Conference records, Huntingdon College; Telephone interview with Charles Carter Sr., July 10, 2002; In-person interviews with H.K. Matthews, Brewton, AL, October 27, 2000, September 16, 2001, and November 23, 2001.
6. "NAACP Youth File, Charter Applications, Florida, 1957–1965," NAACP Papers, Pensacola file, Group III, Box E17; In-person interview with Raymon Harvey, Pensacola, FL, May 15, 2010.
7. Telephone interview with Mary Harrison Washington, March 16, 2006.
8. "Report to Interstate Commerce Commission" and "Jefferson Poland to Interstate Commerce Commission Chairman Everett Hutchinson, February 7, 1961," Docket No. MC-C-3358, 1961, Box 214, National Archives II, College Park, MD.
9. Neither the *Pensacola Journal* nor the *Pensacola News* mentioned the NAACP's written demand. "NAACP Youth File, Florida, Pensacola-West Palm Beach, 1956–65," NAACP Papers, Pensacola file, Group III, Box E3; Harrison interview; Harvey interview; Washington interview.

10. "NAACP Youth File, Florida, Pensacola-West Palm Beach, 1956–65," NAACP Papers, Pensacola file, Group III, Box E; "Negroes Agitate in Variety Store," *Pensacola Journal*, April 6, 1960; Associated Press, "Negroes Demonstrate Briefly at Pensacola Variety Store," *Montgomery Advertiser*, April 6, 1960; Associated Press, "KKK Appearance," *St. Petersburg Times*, April 7, 1960.
11. Harrison interview; Harvey interview.
12. "NAACP Branch Department Files, Florida, Pensacola Branch, 1945–1970," NAACP Papers, Part 6, Box C83; Matthews interviews. For more on the Pensacola Merchants' Association and the meetings it had with the PCM, see "Escambia County Community Council, Special Committee Report," March 6, 1962, Howard King Papers, Pensacola Historical Society, Pensacola, FL.
13. Matthews interviews; Harvey interview; Washington interview.
14. Matthews interviews.
15. Harrison interview; Harvey interview; Washington interview.
16. Matthews interviews; Harrison interview; Harvey interview.
17. Associated Press, "Two Sit-Ins in Pensacola," *St. Petersburg Times*, June 14, 1961; "23 Negroes Sit at Counters; No Food Served," *Pensacola News*, June 16, 1961; Associated Press, "3 More Sit-Ins Held at Pensacola," *St. Petersburg Times*, June 16, 1961; United Press International, "Violence Charged," *St. Petersburg Times*, June 17, 1961; Matthews interviews; Carter interview; Harrison interview; Harvey interview; "Negro's Trial is Continued," *Pensacola News*, July 2, 1961; "Arrests Made for Boycott," *Pensacola News*, July 3, 1961; "Councilmen Fear 'Sit-in' Violence," *Pensacola Journal*, July 7, 1961; Pensacola NAACP Youth Council, "Newsletter," July 8, 1961, from private collection of Mary Harrison Washington; "Seven Found Guilty," *Pensacola News*, July 10, 1961; "Warning Sign Posted on Tree At Negro Home," *Pensacola News*, July 10, 1961; "Another KKK Sign Appears," *Pensacola News*, July 11, 1961; "Two 'Sit-ins' are Fined $100," *Pensacola Journal*, July 14, 1961. A city court judge found Dobbins guilty of both charges and fined him $300. See "Dobbins Fined $300 in Court," *Pensacola Journal*, July 13, 1961.
18. Harrison interview; Harvey interview; Pensacola NAACP Youth Council, "Newsletter".
19. Harrison interview; Matthews interviews.
20. Matthews interviews.
21. "Fla. Hospital Café Lowers Color Bar," *Baltimore Afro-American*, December 30, 1961; "Judge Halts Selective Buying Drive Against Fla. Grocery," *Baltimore Afro-American*, October 13, 1962; Associated Press, "Pensacola Desegregates Stores' Lunch Counters," *Montgomery Advertiser*, February 23, 1962; Matthews interviews; "Pensacola Stores Desegregate," *Philadelphia Tribune*, March 6, 1962; NAACP Field Secretary Robert W. Saunders, "Annual Report: Florida Assignment, 1962," NAACP Papers, Part 6, Box C29.

8 Muhammad Ali's Main Bout

African American Economic Power and the World Heavyweight Title

Michael Ezra

Muhammad Ali announced at a press conference in January 1966 that he had formed a new corporation called Main Bout, Inc. to manage the multimillion-dollar promotional rights to his fights. "I am vitally interested in the company," he said, "and in seeing that it will be one in which Negroes are not used as fronts, but as stockholders, officers, and production and promotion agents." Although racially integrated, Main Bout was led by the all-black Nation of Islam. Its rise to this position gave African Americans control of boxing's most valuable prize, the world heavyweight championship. Ali envisioned Main Bout as an economic network, a structure that would generate autonomy for African Americans.[1]

Main Bout encountered resistance from the beginning. It came initially from white sportswriters. But about a month after Main Bout's formation Ali's draft status changed to 1-A, which meant that he had become eligible for military service in the Vietnam War. When Ali then opposed the war publicly, politicians nationwide joined the press in attacking Main Bout. The political controversy surrounding Ali made it easier for Main Bout's economic competitors—rival promoters, closed-circuit television theater chains, and organized crime—to run the organization out of business. Money and politics were important elements of white resistance to Main Bout as was the organization's potential as a black power symbol.

Like his civil rights contemporaries, Muhammad Ali understood the importance of economic power. Main Bout had the potential to share with black communities the heavyweight title's enormous earning power. Ali told reporters at the press conference introducing Main Bout that the company would handle the ancillary rights to his fights, starting with a multimillion-dollar March 29 match in Chicago against Ernie Terrell. Prior to 1966, Ali was managed by an all-white group of millionaires from his hometown called the Louisville Sponsoring Group. Most accounts indicate an amicable and profitable relationship between Ali and these backers. But Ali's installation of Main Bout as his promotional team gave African Americans an unprecedented share of perhaps the most lucrative prize in sport, the ancillary rights to the heavyweight championship of the world. Main Bout's ownership of these ancillary rights gave them access to the vast majority of revenues from Ali's bouts. The ancillary promoter controlled the rights to live and delayed telecasts, radio broadcasts, fight films, and any further transmission or distribution of a bout, as opposed to the local promoter, who produced the live event and controlled its on-site ticket sales. The major monies from big-time boxing matches during this period came from closed-circuit television. Because seating and revenue from the hundreds of closed-circuit theaters nationwide greatly outnumbered what would be generated at the arena where a given fight took place, such fights usually had closed-circuit television takes much larger than from other sources such as radio broadcasts or live gates.[2]

Ali's three previous bouts, which were the first of his championship career, had proven no exception. His last match before forming Main Bout, a November 1965 contest with former champion Floyd Patterson, grossed approximately $4 million. At least 210 closed-circuit television venues showed the match. Nearly 260 locations with a seating capacity of 1.1 million telecast Ali's May 1965 rematch with Sonny Liston and gross receipts for the fight approached $4.3 million. Ali's first title fight against Liston in February 1964 was shown in about 250 theaters to nearly 550,000 spectators and the bout's gross receipts were about $4 million. For all three of these fights, well over half of the total revenues came from closed-circuit television. By comparison, on-site ticket sales were only $300,000 for Ali's fight with Patterson, $200,000 for the Liston rematch, and $400,000 for the first Liston bout. Ali's purses also reflected the riches associated with this broadcast medium. He earned approximately $750,000 for the Patterson bout and $600,000 for each of the two Liston matches.[3]

Main Bout had five stockholders. Herbert Muhammad, son of Nation of Islam leader Elijah Muhammad, was its president. John Ali, the Nation of Islam's national secretary, was Main Bout's treasurer. Together they controlled 50 percent of its stock and half of its board's six votes. The closed-circuit television operator Mike Malitz and his attorney Bob Arum were Main Bout's vice-president and secretary; each held 20 percent of Main Bout's stock and one vote. Jim Brown, the professional football player and Main Bout's vice-president in charge of publicity, controlled one vote and 10 percent of the company. Malitz and Arum were Main Bout's sole white members. They came up with the idea for the enterprise while promoting a 1965 fight for which they hired Brown to do closed-circuit television commentary. Malitz and Arum asked Brown to carry to the champion a proposal for a company that would allow Ali to control the finances of his fights and increase African American participation in their production. Brown passed the idea to Ali. Ali and the Nation of Islam approved the measure and Main Bout was the result.[4]

Jim Brown emphasized Main Bout's potential for increasing black economic power and control. He told a reporter, "Our goal is to use the money that we make—and hope to make in future ventures—to support the founding of business by Negroes. At first, we'll have to count basically on small businesses." Several months after Main Bout's formation, Brown retired from professional football and founded the National Negro Industrial and Economic Union. Although Main Bout was not formally connected to the National Negro Industrial and Economic Union, their goals were similar. Both wanted to increase African American economic power. Muhammad Ali recognized this and donated $10,000 to Brown's group.[5]

WHITE OPPOSITION TO MAIN BOUT

White sportswriters, including many of the day's top syndicated columnists, constituted the first wave of opposition to Main Bout. These reporters expressed fear over the Nation of Islam's ascent to power within professional boxing. Most were concerned with a black takeover of the sport. Gene Ward claimed, "Any way one sizes up this take-over of the heavyweight title by the Black Muslims, the fight game is going to be the worse for it. This could be the death blow." Jimmy Cannon wrote, "The fight racket has been turned into a crusade by the Muslims. . . . Herbert Muhammad, who is Elijah's kid, is the president of the firm that controls the Clay-Ernie Terrell promotion in Chicago. It is more than a fight. This is a fete to celebrate a religion that throws hate at people." Red Smith opined, "Except insofar as the Black Muslim leadership has a stake in the promotion, there is no good reason at present why the match should not be accepted." Doug Gilbert believed "that if the Muslims own Clay, and also own the television rights to all of his fights, they have what amounts to a hammerlock on all that's lucrative in boxing." The editorial boards of two Chicago newspapers, the *Daily News* and the *Tribune*, urged Illinois Governor Otto Kerner to ban the upcoming bout.[6]

In February 1966, less than a month after Main Bout's formation, the U.S. Selective Service reclassified Muhammad Ali as draft-eligible for the Vietnam War. In 1960, at age eighteen, Ali had registered with Selective Service Local Board 47 in Louisville and in 1962 was classified as draft-eligible (1-A). In 1964, however, Ali failed the mental aptitude section of the induction exam. Ali again flunked when asked to retest in front of Army psychologists and as a result he was reclassified as unqualified to serve (1-Y). In need of more soldiers for the Vietnam War, however, the Army lowered its mental aptitude requirement in early 1966 and Ali's score became a passing one. With members of Congress calling for his reclassification, Ali's local draft board reviewed his case in February. After the fighter's request for an appeal hearing was denied, he was again declared draft-eligible.[7]

When reporters called Ali for comment, he signified his political and religious opposition to the Vietnam War. He claimed that he had seen "lots of whites burning their draft cards on television. If they are against the war, and even some congressmen are against the war," Ali asked, "why should we Muslims be for it?" Ali also asserted that he had been singled out for unfair treatment: "I can't understand why, out of all the baseball players, all of the football players, all of the basketball players—they seek out me, who's the world's only heavyweight champion?" Quotes like these produced a backlash in the press and professional boxing.[8]

Ali's draft resistance and an escalating distrust of Main Bout unleashed furious attacks by Chicago newspapers and politicians who called for a ban of the upcoming match with Ernie Terrell. Editorials in two local dailies lobbied for cancellation of the fight, citing Ali's anti-Vietnam stance and his new promotional scheme. *Chicago's American* analyzed Ali's reasons for disputing the draft and concluded that "none of them [are] particularly convincing." The *Chicago Tribune* found it "deplorable that so many Chicagoans are unwittingly encouraging [Ali] by their interest in a fight whose profits will go largely to the Black Muslims." Twenty state newspaper executives released a joint announcement criticizing Governor Otto Kerner and the Illinois State Athletic Commission for allowing the bout to be sanctioned. For several days, the *Chicago Tribune* devoted its front page to opponents of the fight. It interviewed disgusted American GI's in Vietnam and highlighted their anti-Ali opinions. An area Veterans of Foreign Wars district representing 14,500 former soldiers passed a resolution urging Mayor Richard Daley and Governor Kerner to "intercede" and cancel the fight. Politicians and government appointees also registered their displeasure. State Representatives Clyde Choate and Arthur Gottschalk threatened to investigate the Illinois State Athletic Commission for approving the contest. State Senator Arthur Swanson called for Kerner to remove the match from Chicago. Charles Siragusa, the Illinois Crime Investigating Commission's executive director, felt that "it is an insult to the people of this state to permit a man like Clay who swears allegiance to an admitted cult of violence to reap a harvest of cash from the very citizens he has insulted with his whining attempts to avoid the draft." Police Superintendent Orlando Wilson offered critical opposition, telling reporters, "My main concern is with the possibility of disorder arising from the bout, but I am also disturbed by the unpatriotic statements attributed to Clay." This intersection of professional duties and personal beliefs characterized official resistance to Ali. Daley leaned on the Illinois State Athletic Commission to "reconsider" the bout, claiming that Chicago "could well do without this fight." Kerner called Ali's comments "disgusting and unpatriotic." Aided by the local press, white city and state politicians formed a nearly united front against the match within a matter of days.[9]

The Illinois State Athletic Commission held a hearing in which Ali was expected to apologize for his comments, but he refused. The hearing was a national event; fifty reporters, twenty-five lawyers, six state troopers, and several government officials packed the Illinois State Athletic Commission's Chicago office to see Ali testify. The commission asked him if he was sorry for his antiwar comments. Ali expressed regret, but not for his beliefs. He instead apologized "to the people who may be hurt financially. I am sorry I put the commission and Governor Kerner on the spot with my remarks. I did not mean to hurt the children and the sons of persons who are dying in Vietnam." Triner then asked Ali, "I want to know if you are apologizing to the people of the state of Illinois for the unpatriotic remarks you made." Ali insisted, "I'm not apologizing for anything like that because I don't have to." To make himself clear, he added, "I'm not here to make a showdown plea. I'm not here to apologize in any way that the press has predicted I would apologize." Flabbergasted by Ali's defiance, the Illinois State Athletic Commission adjourned the meeting and contemplated its next move.[10]

About a half-hour after the hearing, Illinois Attorney General William Clark declared the match illegal. Citing possible inconsistencies in the licensing procedures for Ali and Terrell and a widely ignored rule that any corporation promoting a boxing or wrestling event had to have at least fifty people in it, Clark advised the Illinois State Athletic Commission to "adjourn their meeting and to so advise the participants" that their promotion was finished in Chicago. Although Clark's legal claims were legitimate, such rules had always been loosely enforced, if not ignored. Ali's draft resistance almost certainly brought increased scrutiny over the licensing and promotion of his fight with Terrell. Mayor Daley backed the decision: "The attorney general has issued an opinion holding the fight illegal. All state officials are bound by the opinion of the attorney general. It seems to me the commission has no other choice but to follow the opinion." The Illinois State Athletic Commission acquiesced and canceled the match. The *Chicago Tribune* praised Daley, Kerner, and Clark for intervening.[11]

Refusing to apologize reinforced Ali's defiance and engendered nationwide opposition to his upcoming title fight with Terrell. Unwelcome in Chicago, Main Bout shopped the contest around the United States with little success. Area promoters in each locale greeted Main Bout with interest but state and local government officials rejected them. Main Bout's Bob Arum explained, "I got calls from promoters all over the country wanting to hold the fight, even from Huron, S.D.," but "the day after a promoter would call me, the governor of his state or the mayor would announce there'd be no Clay fight in his town or state." Promoters in Louisville completed negotiations with Main Bout and the Kentucky State Athletic Commission agreed to sanction the bout. Influenced by local veterans groups, however, members of the Kentucky State Senate announced the next day that they would block it. The Kentucky State Senate passed a resolution urging Ali to join the Army. State Senator William L. Sullivan called upon Ali to "abandon his reprehensible efforts to avoid duty in the country which afforded him the opportunity to achieve eminence." When promoters in Pittsburgh inquired about hosting the match, state legislators moved to bar it the following day. After local promoters and the Maine State Athletic Commission announced their interest in sponsoring the contest, Governor John Reed rebuffed them. Promoters in South Dakota, Rhode Island, Oklahoma, and Missouri also asked about holding the bout in their states but were blocked. The pattern was clear: as soon as the news broke somewhere that promoters were interested in the fight, government officials would oppose them. With the contest less than a month away, Main Bout had yet to secure a site.[12]

MAIN BOUT RESPONDS TO OPPOSITION

Main Bout shopped the match around Canada when the Louisville Draft Board granted Ali permission to perform there but the same pattern developed. Promoters in Montreal, Sorrels, Edmonton, and Verdun talked with Main Bout but their city governments blocked the fight in opposition to Ali's antiwar stance. The Ontario Minister of Labor finally agreed to host the contest in Toronto but even there the fight stirred controversy. The management of Maple Leaf Gardens, where the bout would be held, became embroiled in a bitter struggle. Hockey legend Conn Smythe, the founder of the Toronto Maple Leafs franchise, resigned in protest his position as the arena's director.[13]

Almost immediately after Toronto approved the contest, Ernie Terrell withdrew citing financial considerations, forcing Main Bout to find a substitute opponent in Canadian heavyweight George Chuvalo. Sportswriters then hurt Main Bout's cause further by labeling the fight a mismatch. Chuvalo was not as attractive an opponent as Terrell from a boxing standpoint. He had lost his previous bout to an unranked fighter and it was unsurprising that sportswriters believed he had little chance to win. Nevertheless, it is unlikely that the substitution of Chuvalo, *per se*, would make the promotion unprofitable. First, the popular Chuvalo's fighting in his hometown for the championship would probably increase the live gate and Canadian closed-circuit television sales. Second, Chuvalo's whiteness made the fight attractive to customers who invested boxing with racial significance. Third, Chuvalo had previously fought in matches that had done well financially. His February 1965 bout with Floyd Patterson at Madison Square Garden drew 19,000 fans paying $165,000. Sixty-four closed-circuit television venues with a seating capacity of 300,000 screened the bout.[14]

Nevertheless, the promotion had gone bust. A month earlier, the Associated Press had predicted gross receipts of over $4,000,000 and a minimum purse of $450,000 for Ali. This was an excellent guarantee for a fight against Terrell, who was not as well-known as Floyd Patterson or Sonny Liston. Ali's share would have been even larger if the fight did better than expected. The day after Main Bout announced that it had signed Chuvalo, however, the Associated Press reported that the fight's gross would be approximately $500,000. Although there had been radio broadcasts of all of Ali's previous title matches, only a handful of the fight's forty-two sponsors agreed to support the bout. The radio broadcast had to be canceled.[15]

Critics of Main Bout, Ali, and the Nation of Islam proposed a boycott of the closed-circuit broadcast. In Miami, where Ali had been based for years, a 2,700-member American Legion post said that it would picket any theater that showed the fight. No sites in Miami broadcast Ali versus Chuvalo. Other than a pair of demonstrators in Fort Worth and an unfounded bomb scare in Cleveland, however, the oft-threatened protests against operators showing the match did not materialize. Some sportswriters asked readers to stay away from the bout. Eddie Muller chastised any theater operators who "might take it upon themselves to accept the TV firm's promotion and make a quick dollar." Referring to a proposed local boycott of the fight, Muller commented, "If every state follows California's action perhaps it'll be a complete nationwide blackout, which is as it should be."[16]

The most crippling blow to the promotion, by far, was its abandonment by closed-circuit television theater chains. Main Bout had contracted 280 North American closed-circuit television venues to show the Terrell fight, but only thirty-two sites ended up showing the match against Chuvalo. Several cities that normally hosted Ali title fights in at least one area venue, including Cincinnati, Milwaukee, Kansas City, and Minneapolis-St. Paul, did not screen the bout. California's two biggest boxing promoters, Don Chargin and Aileen Eaton, met on March 6 and agreed to block the broadcast in their state. They announced that they would meet with theater owners in an effort to make sure that no venues in California showed the March 29 contest, "in deference to the many families that have loved ones fighting and dying in Vietnam." When Main Bout approached Ray Syufy, owner of twenty-one drive-in theaters in Northern California, to televise the match, it was turned down, although Syufy admitted that the company made him a "lucrative offer." In total, the fight was shown in only two California venues, both of them independent theaters. By contrast, Ali's previous bout against Floyd Patterson was shown in thirteen Los Angeles-area theaters alone. In New York, seven Loews' theaters withdrew 13,000 seats from the closed-circuit pool. Ernie Emerling, the firm's public relations vice-president claimed, "Too much silly-shallying over the site didn't leave us enough time to print tickets and advertise; we should have had six-to-eight weeks." New York's RKO theater chain canceled their offer to show the fight in ten area venues. Whereas twenty-five New York City venues with a seating capacity of 80,000 had shown Ali versus Patterson, only five New York City theaters with a seating capacity of 11,000 hosted Ali versus Chuvalo. In Chicago, Ed Seguin, representing the Balaban and Katz (B&K) chain of theaters, reported that his firm would not show the fight "because of all the uncertainty over where, and whether, it was coming off." Both the B&K and Warner theater chains canceled their arrangements with Main Bout nationwide. Main Bout needed cooperation from these chains because most of the theaters equipped to show fights belonged to motion picture concerns like Loews' and RKO. There were few independent operators capable of profiting from closed-circuit telecasts due to logistic and technical limitations, although Main Bout would help independent, black-owned theaters get involved in Ali's fights by lowering its percentage of the take.[17]

The Ali–Chuvalo fight was financially disastrous, although fans saw a good boxing match that Ali won by fifteen-round unanimous decision. The closed-circuit telecast sold about 46,000 tickets for $110,000. This gross take was twenty to forty times less than closed-circuit revenues from each of Ali's three previous championship fights. The $150,000 on-site, live gate was also lower than for each of Ali's previous title bouts. Furthermore, Ali's $60,000 purse was approximately a tenth of those for each of his three previous bouts and at least three times less than for any fight of his championship career. The Associated Press summarized, "Theater-television of last night's Cassius Clay-George Chuvalo heavyweight title fight proved a resounding dud, as expected." Eddie Muller crowed, "Forming the Main Bout, Inc. organization was a costly mistake. Whoever put money into the firm must wind up broke. There's no way, as far as we can see, of the organization recouping." Mike Malitz of Main Bout disputed this claim, telling reporters that Main Bout "made enough to pay the bills" and break even. Even Malitz had to admit, however, that the company was "grossly underpaid for the time and effort." The fiasco illustrated Main Bout's lack of control over the terms of Ali's fights. The organization would have to weigh its next move carefully if it, and Ali's career, were to survive.[18]

Several white sportswriters and at least one black reporter blamed Main Bout's incompetence for the promotion's collapse. Bob Stewart teased, "It all seemed so simple. You just formed a quickie corporation and put on a title fight." Eddie Muller called Main Bout a "fly-by-night enterprise which now louse[s] up the horizon." Jim Murray claimed, "Clay's corporation, which ironically, calls itself 'Main Bout, Inc.' and is run by a football player and a couple of guys whose sole qualification is they once subscribed to the Police Gazette." One of Ali's few consistent critics within the black press, A.S. "Doc" Young, insisted, "It was the stupidest sort of publicity for the Black Muslims to publicize their association with Main Bout, Inc." Sportswriters also compared Main Bout unfavorably to the Louisville Sponsoring Group.[19]

A number of African American observers disagreed and instead identified racism and a possible criminal conspiracy as reasons for the financial failure of the Ali–Chuvalo fight. "There are some reports of possible court action or civil rights agencies may be looking into the cancellations of the closed circuit television showings to ascertain if there was any overt racial discrimination involved," according to Clarence Matthews. "What columnists have tried to do is thwart the Black Muslims through castigation of Clay," wrote Marion Jackson, "It seems as though the Black Muslims for the first time ha[ve] projected a Negro group—Main Bout, Inc., in control of a nationwide closed circuit telecast." *Muhammad Speaks* accused white reporters of hiding their racism through so-called patriotic attacks on Ali.

"Outbursts over [Ali's] military draft status were [a] means of killing two birds with one red, white, and blue stone" and an "attempt to smear" Main Bout, according to the newspaper. The most strident response came from Moses Newson, who praised Main Bout for surviving "in face of the most vicious and concentrated 'kill them off' campaign ever joined in by the press, the Mafia, and politicians." Newson asserted that white "reporters, broadcasters, and others who tried to kill the fight scribbled and spouted bitter reams to a degree that they actually need to offer something more lest they themselves might be thought part of an unholy alliance that includes racists, hypocrites, and mobsters." At a press conference on Capitol Hill with Harlem Congressman Adam Clayton Powell, Main Bout's Jim Brown contended, "The ostensible reason" for the boycott "is because of Clay's so-called unpatriotic remarks about the draft, but that's just an excuse [to destroy Main Bout]." Powell vowed to have the U.S. Department of Justice and the Equal Employment Opportunity Commission investigate the situation, although it is unclear whether or not he did so.[20]

Although Main Bout had known as early as January that the mob was sabotaging their promotion, white sportswriters denied such a conspiracy. Even Robert Lipsyte, one of Ali's strongest supporters in the white press, called such a possibility "imaginative" because it suggested "an improbable plot of enormous complexity." Jack Berry asserted that such a scenario was "not evident here. There's only one difficulty in this whole affair and the name is Cassius Clay. He brought it all on himself." Jimmy Cannon denied that racism fueled anti-Main Bout sentiment but admitted that organized crime resented Main Bout's entry into boxing. "The fight mob detests Clay. Their revulsion isn't instigated by race," wrote Cannon in his syndicated column. "They want Chuvalo to beat him because Clay has made the greatest prize in sports worthless. This isn't temporary. He is in trouble for a long while."[21]

The Federal Bureau of Investigation (FBI) looked into the boycott. It suspected that Terrell withdrew not only because of financial concerns but also death threats to him and his manager Bernard Glickman by Chicago underworld figures that would no longer profit if the bout were moved to Canada. The FBI inquiry, however, proved inconclusive and no further federal investigation of the fight took place. The black *Pittsburgh Courier* sighed, "as usual, the casting of light on supported underworld control of boxing still remains unfulfilled." In response to the FBI investigation, some white sportswriters finally acknowledged the possibility of collusion to eliminate Main Bout and Ali from boxing. The difficulties surrounding Main Bout's initial closed-circuit venture were "apparently an outgrowth of boxing's current scramble for position in a future made uncertain by the troubles of Cassius Clay," wrote Robert Lipsyte. "To the underworld, the new organization meant only that 'a rival gang' had moved in and was in a position to 'ace them out' by not dealing with 'trusted' closed circuit television operators or exhibitors as well as the other businessmen who normally get pay days from a title fight." United Press International reported similarly, "New York Mafia interests were enraged at the attempt of the Muslims to take over closed circuit television rights and other revenues from professional boxing through Main Bout, Inc."[22]

Realizing that he might not be able to fight under Main Bout at home, Ali considered matches outside the United States. He was nervous about this possibility at first. "They want to stop me from fighting. They done run me out of the country. . . . This [the Chuvalo match] could be my last fight," the champion told Phil Pepe. He revealed to Milton Gross, "I don't want to go [abroad]. I want to defend my title here somewhere or even in a phone booth or on a barge at sea." By the end of March, however, Ali had reconciled his doubts. "I'm not fighting for money," he said, "but for the freedom of American black people to speak their minds." He admitted to a Louisville reporter that he would like to fight in the United States, "But they can put it in England, Nigeria, France, or Rome if they want to. I don't care about the money. It's a world title I got, not a U.S.A. title, and it can be defended anywhere in the world." During an interview with Larry Merchant, Ali fanned himself with a replica passport and insisted that he would fight wherever he would be allowed. Ali's most eloquent expression of this outlook was recorded by Robert Lipsyte: "Boxing is nothing, just satisfying some bloodthirsty people. I'm no longer Cassius Clay, a Negro from Kentucky. I belong to the world, the black world. I'll always have a home in Pakistan, in Algeria, in Ethiopia. This is more than money," he said. "I'm not disturbed and nervous. Why should I be? In a few hours I could fly to another country, in the East, in Africa, where people love me. Millions, all over the world want to see me. Why should I worry about losing a few dollars?" The champion concluded, "I'm not going to sell my manhood for a few dollars, or a smile. I'd rather be poor and free than rich and a slave." Such comments foreshadowed Main Bout's decision to take the champion's next three matches to Europe, where there had not been a world heavyweight title contest in more than thirty years. The three European fights earned Ali purses far more lucrative than he had received for the match in Canada with Chuvalo and re-established him as the top drawing power in boxing.[23]

Ali fought in May against Britain's Henry Cooper for a $350,000 purse, the first world heavyweight title fight in England since 1908. For the live U.S. television rights to the bout with Cooper, the American Broadcasting Company (ABC) paid Main Bout $75,000. Mexican and Canadian stations that picked up the signal also had to pay Main Bout a fee. Although smaller than successful U.S. closed-circuit telecasts, this sum was comparable to the $110,000 grossed by the broadcast of Ali versus Chuvalo. Equally important, the deal gave Main Bout and Ali increased independence from oppositional forces in the United States. Primarily through a huge on-site crowd and a successful British closed-circuit telecast, the Cooper fight raked in money. About 46,000 fans packed Arsenal Stadium. The $560,000 live gate was almost four times greater than that of the Chuvalo fight and set a British boxing record. Sixteen English closed-circuit theaters generated approximately 40,000 ticket sales and $280,000 in revenues. The fight grossed nearly $1.5 million.[24]

Ali fought again in England in August, garnering a $300,000 purse for his match against Brian London. Main Bout received fees in exchange for the European and international rights to the contest while Ali received a $270,000 minimum guarantee plus a share of the ancillary receipts. For the live North American television rights, ABC paid Main Bout $200,000. Ten thousand people paid to see the London fight, which took in $150,000 on-site. Closed-circuit returns neared $165,000. Even Ali critic Gene Ward had to admit, "In both of these European ventures, Clay will earn more than he ever could have in the United States, where his opposition to the draft has left him an unpopular figure."[25]

Ali defended his title in September for a $300,000 purse against Karl Mildenberger in Germany, where there had never been a world heavyweight championship fight. ABC paid Main Bout $200,000 for the live television rights. Forty thousand fans paid $500,000 on-site to see it in person. Although there was no closed-circuit television broadcast, other ancillary revenues (not including Main Bout's $200,000 deal with ABC) brought in another $250,000.[26]

In these three cases, rather than trying to work with a corrupt and hostile closed-circuit television industry at home, Main Bout instead negotiated to show the bouts live on free television in the United States (made possible by the Early Bird Satellite's successful launch a year earlier), on closed-circuit television in Europe, and on the radio in Africa, the Middle East, and Asia. Main Bout and Ali's independence from the established network of promoters in the United States allowed their return to North America for three fights in late 1966 and early 1967 under favorable terms. They earned millions of dollars without relinquishing any control of their prized championship commodity and Ali became the most active heavyweight champion since Joe Louis. Even against overmatched and relatively unknown opposition, Ali was making good money. The resistance Main Bout faced, however, greatly limited its effectiveness as a black economic power vehicle that could spread profits to large numbers of African Americans.

Ali's bout with Cleveland Williams in November 1966 did very well thanks to a successful closed-circuit broadcast that was stoked by Ali's popularity among African Americans. Thirty-five thousand fans watched the contest at the Houston Astrodome, paying $460,000 and breaking the American indoor attendance record for boxing. One hundred twenty-five U.S. closed-circuit television venues with a total seating capacity of 500,000 showed the match. Main Bout worked with previously uncooperative theater chains in a number of cities. Twenty-four New York closed-circuit locations with a seating capacity of 68,000 hosted the match, with tickets priced between $5 and $10 each. Loews' and RKO, theater chains that had refused to show Ali–Chuvalo, screened the fight. Three previously uncooperative Warner's theaters in New Jersey also telecast the match. Six Northern California venues showed the fight and at least one did superb business. The Warfield Theater in San Francisco sold 2,000 of 2,600 available seats for the match. Jack Fiske observed, "The theater audience was at least one-fourth Negro, perhaps the largest turnout for any Clay fight I recall." At least fourteen Los Angeles-area venues screened Ali–Williams; only two venues in California had shown Ali–Chuvalo. Chicago's B&K movie theater chain, which had declined to telecast Ali–Chuvalo, showed a feature movie before the Ali–Williams fight. Seven Chicago-area venues hosted the match. Leo Brown, the manager of the State-Lake movie theater, told the *Chicago Tribune*, "It wasn't a full house, but a good house." The *Tribune* reporter noted, "an unusually large number of Negro fans paid $7.50 for reserved seats." Total closed-circuit receipts probably topped $1,000,000. Main Bout also arranged for telecasts and films in forty-two countries. It sold live television rights to Mexican and Canadian stations and delayed telecast privileges to ABC. There was also a live U.S. radio broadcast of the match, which brought in an additional $100,000. Main Bout pocketed 32.5 percent of the ancillary gross. Ali's purse probably exceeded $750,000.[27]

Ali's long-awaited match with Ernie Terrell in February 1967 also proved lucrative. Thirty-seven thousand fans at the Astrodome paid $400,000 on-site. One hundred seventy-eight North American closed-circuit venues took in approximately $1,000,000. Main Bout pocketed 30 percent of the ancillaries. Ali's purse approached $1,000,000. At Madison Square Garden, one of eleven New York City venues to show the bout, 5,500 (of a possible 10,000) fans braved inclement weather and paid between $7.50 and $10 each. Main Bout again agreed to terms with previously uncooperative closed-circuit chains. In total, there were twenty-five New York Tri-State area venues with a seating capacity of 95,000, not including a pay-per-view home-TV arrangement in Hartford. Newark's Branford Theater, one of eight New Jersey venues, sold out. At least twelve Los Angeles-area venues broadcast the bout. There was also a live U.S. radio broadcast.[28]

Ali's March 1967 contest with Zora Folley was not as big as the other two matches but it yielded a solid $265,000 purse for Ali. The match was Madison Square Garden's first world heavyweight title bout in over fifteen years but terrible weather in New York limited the crowd to 14,000. They paid $244,000, an arena record, to see it in person. RKO Pictures purchased the worldwide rights to the match from Main Bout for $175,000 and made Ali versus Folley the first-ever heavyweight championship fight shown live on U.S. home television during primetime. Main Bout made no profit from the fight and did not promote it. The organization acted merely to broker the worldwide rights to RKO. Main Bout paid Ali $150,000 and Folley $25,000 of the fee it received. Ali also earned about 50 percent of the live gate.[29]

Following these successes, Main Bout arranged for a rematch between Ali and Floyd Patterson to take place prior to the champion's May induction date. The Nevada State Athletic Commission agreed to sanction the April 25 bout in Las Vegas. Main Bout announced that it would be broadcast on closed-circuit television in the United States and beamed via satellite to Japan and Europe. Contracts called for Ali to receive $225,000. By April 11, according to Mike Malitz, Main Bout had contracted eighty-five venues in the United States and a "large number of foreign outlets" to show the bout. He estimated that Main Bout had already received $150,000 in fees.[30]

As in Chicago a year earlier, however, an anti-Ali backlash ensued and the fight never took place. The press and government officials called for the cancellation of the match. Jimmy Cannon labeled the bout a "sanctioned atrocity." Las Vegas Sheriff Ralph Lamb warned local promoters that "they will not receive police protection from my department this time. Why should I risk some fine men getting hurt when the only ones who will profit from this fiasco will be the private promoters of the fight?" On April 11, Nevada Governor Paul Laxalt requested that the Nevada State Athletic Commission cancel the fight, which it did. "It would give Nevada a black eye," claimed Laxalt. Main Bout then shifted its attention to Pittsburgh. The Pennsylvania State Athletic Commission agreed to sanction the match. Laxalt called Pennsylvania Governor Raymond Shafer and asked him to block it, which Shafer did. New York was mentioned as a possible site. When asked about the fight, New York State Athletic Commissioner Edwin Dooley ended such speculation: "We have a reciprocity agreement with both the Nevada and Pennsylvania Commissions. They abide by our rulings and we abide by theirs." Although New Mexico Governor David Cargo offered Albuquerque as a last-minute site, Main Bout had run out of time. They risked another Toronto-type flop with just two weeks remaining before Ali's induction ceremony. The organization threw in the towel. Malitz told a reporter, "Once Pittsburgh was a dead issue, I felt it was all over." With his career stalled, Ali turned his attention to his trial.[31]

Muhammad Ali's conviction on draft evasion charges in June 1967 ended Main Bout's run after only seventeen months and seven fights, so it is difficult to assess the company's impact. Main Bout's economic goals seem to have been threefold: 1) negotiate good purses for Ali; 2) make money for its shareholders; 3) create wealth and employment for blacks. It would appear they accomplished the first two goals but not the third. Main Bout's early demise, however, makes it impossible to know if it could have become capable of making money and creating jobs for substantial numbers of African Americans.

Main Bout's collapse ultimately stemmed from its lack of political power rather than from economic pressure. State athletic commissions nationwide colluded to unanimously refuse Ali a boxing license after his indictment in May 1967. If any state athletic commission had sanctioned an Ali fight, he would have fought in that state. Following his conviction, Ali stayed out of prison on appeal, but his passport was invalidated, eliminating his chances of fighting abroad. Realizing Ali was finished, Arum, Malitz, and Brown left Main Bout to form their own company, Sports Action, Inc., which would promote the tournament designed to replace Ali as heavyweight champion. The Nation of Islam and Ali were frozen out of professional boxing and Ali did not fight professionally for the next three-and-a-half years.[32]

NOTES

1. Ali quoted in H.J. McFall, "Cassius Clay Tells Plans to Form a Negro Company," *Louisville Defender*, January 13, 1966.
2. Thomas Hauser, *Muhammad Ali: His Life and Times* (New York: Touchstone, 1991), 30; Claude Lewis, *Cassius Clay* (New York: MacFadden-Bartell Books, 1965), 39; Michael Ezra, *Muhammad Ali: The Making of an Icon* (Philadelphia: Temple University Press, 2009), 67–89.
3. Eddie Muller, "Fight Talk Today is $," *San Francisco Examiner*, November 19, 1965; Al Buck, "Cassius Clay: The 'Champion,'" *New York Post*, November 24, 1966; "The Fight of TV," *Chicago Sun-Times*, November 24, 1965; AP report, "Fight Facts and Figures," *Louisville Courier-Journal*, November 22, 1965; Paul Zimmerman, "Clay, Patterson to Offer Defense," *Los Angeles Times*, November 22, 1965; AP report, "Facts on Title Fight," *New York Times*, May 26, 1965; AP report, "Fight Facts, Figures," *San Francisco Examiner*, February 25, 1964; Robert Lipsyte, "Each Slice of Fight Pie is Rich, But Promoter's Going Hungry," *New York Times*, February 24, 1964; Leonard Koppett, "All the World's a Stage, via TV, for Title Fight," *New York Times*, February 23, 1964.
4. Although Main Bout had only five members the organization was split into six voting shares in order to give the Nation of Islam 50 percent control. Jimmy Cannon, "Theater TV, the Muslims . . . and Jim Brown," *Los Angeles Herald-Examiner*, January 10, 1966; Hauser, *Muhammad Ali*, 151–52; Robert Lipsyte, "Clay's Main Bout, Inc., Seen Final Step in a Project to Bolster Negro Business," *New York Times*, January 9, 1966; George Vass, "TV Firm Dictated Date of Title Bout," *Chicago Daily News*, January 28, 1966.
5. Brown quoted in Vass, "TV Firm Dictated Date"; Lipsyte, "Clay's Main Bout"; UPI report, "Cleveland Grid Star Brown Retires," *Montreal Star*, July 14, 1966; AP report, "Brown to Help Negro Economy," *Baltimore Sun*, July 15, 1966; Earl Ruby, "Has Brown Left Door Ajar? No ex-athletes in his Plan," *Louisville Courier-Journal*, July 22, 1966; Milton Gross, "Curiouser and Curiouser," *New York Post*, February 3, 1967.
6. Gene Ward, "Heavy Title, TV and All, Taken Over By Muslims," *Chicago's American*, February 13, 1966; Jimmy Cannon, "Malice Disguised as Banter in Clay's Evil Strain of Wit," *Miami Herald*, February 19, 1966; Cannon, "Theater-TV, the Muslims"; Doug Gilbert, "Clay-Terrell Package Wrapped in Muslims?," *Chicago's American*, February 5, 1966; Red Smith, "N.Y. Merits Clay-Terrell, It's Claimed," *Chicago Sun-Times*, February 7, 1966; Editorial page, "Throw the Bums Out," *Chicago Daily News*, February 5, 1966; Editorial page, "Sucker Bait," *Chicago Tribune*, February 14, 1966. For black press coverage of Main Bout, which was mixed but significantly more supportive than white press coverage, see "Clay Opens New 'Kettle of Fish,'" *New York Amsterdam News*, January 25, 1966; Cal Jacox, "From the Sidelines," *Cleveland Call and Post*, January 22, 1966; Ric Roberts,

"Change of Pace," *Pittsburgh Courier*, February 19, 1966; "'Mob' Ruled Boxers Retire Flat Broke," *Pittsburgh Courier*, February 12, 1966.

7. Hauser, *Muhammad Ali*, 142; UPI report, "Clay, Namath Targets in Draft Legislation," *Louisville Courier-Journal*, February 10, 1966; Chip Magnus, "Congressmen Seek Khaki for Clay, Namath," *Chicago Sun-Times*, February 10, 1966; UPI report, "Draft Heat On, but Lip Still Zipped," *Los Angeles Times*, February 12, 1966.
8. Ali quoted in Tom Fitzpatrick, "Cassius Appeals; 'Muslims Not at War,'" *Chicago Daily News*, February 18, 1966; Ali quoted in "Clay Sees Self as Boon to U.S. in Civilian Dress," *Chicago Tribune*, February 21, 1966.
9. Editorial page, "Cassius vs. the Draft," *Chicago's American*, February 19, 1966; Editorial page, "The Reluctant Hero," *Chicago Tribune*, February 19, 1966; "News Chiefs Rap Kerner, Boxing Board," *Chicago Tribune*, February 21, 1966; "VFW Urges Kerner to Block Clay Fight," *Chicago Tribune*, February 21, 1966; "2 Legislators Rip Clay Bout License," *Chicago Tribune*, February 21, 1966; "Senator Asks Kerner to Cancel Clay Bout," *Chicago Tribune*, February 22, 1966; Siragusa quoted in "Siragusa Raps Clay on Draft," *Chicago Tribune*, February 23, 1966; Wilson quoted in "Wilson Fears Disorders at Clay Fight: Joins Opposition With Howlett," *Chicago Tribune*, February 24, 1966; Daley quoted in Editorial page, "Mayor Daley's Good Advice," *Chicago Tribune*, February 23, 1966; Kerner quoted in "Clay Due Tomorrow as Fight Furor Grows," *Chicago's American*, February 23, 1966.
10. Ali quoted in Ed Sainsbury, "Illinois: Fight is Illegal . . . Clay No Apology," *New York World-Telegram and Sun*, February 25, 1966; Ed Stone, "Suspicion Clouds Clay-Terrell Sanction Here," *Chicago's American*, February 25, 1966; "Champ Refuses to Apologize to Commission," *Chicago Daily News*, February 25, 1966; Ali and Triner quoted in "Clay Fight Ruled Illegal," *Chicago's American*, February 26, 1966; Ali quoted in David Condon, "In the Wake of the News," *Chicago Tribune*, February 26, 1966.
11. Clark quoted in "Attorney General Clark's Statement," *Chicago's American*, February 25, 1966. Also see Jesse Abramson, "The Championship Fight Almost Nobody Wants," *New York Herald-Tribune*, March 2, 1966. Bentley and Schoenwald were the only members of the National Sports Promotion Corporation that promoted the live, on-site event. According to Clark, the licensing problems were: Ali didn't file a certificate of a resident physician with his license reapplication; Ali answered a 'moral character' question insufficiently; Ali failed to include his proper ring record in the license reapplication; and that he signed the application 'Muhammad Ali' instead of 'Cassius Clay.' Clark also cited Terrell for failing to file a physician's certificate. Daley quoted in Doug Gilbert, "Clay Title Fight on Ropes Here, Pittsburgh Next?," *Chicago's American*, February 26, 1966; Editorial page, "A Wise Decision at Last," *Chicago Tribune*, March 3, 1966.
12. Arum quoted in Jack Berry, "Clay: He Wouldn't Crawl," *Detroit Free Press*, March 10, 1966; Robert Lipsyte, "Clay-Terrell Fight for Title is Shifted to Louisville for March 29," *New York Times*, March 1, 1966; Robert Lipsyte, "Louisville Rejects Plans for a Clay-Terrell Go," *New York Times*, March 2, 1966; Sullivan quoted in UPI report, "Kentucky Senate Urges Clay to Enlist," *Philadelphia Daily News*, February 24, 1966; Gilbert, "Clay Title Fight"; UPI report, "Clay-Terrell Bout Gets No Pennsylvania Welcome," *New York Times*, February 27, 1966; AP report, "Boxing's Big Bout Bangor Bound?," *Los Angeles Herald-Examiner*, February 28, 1966; AP report, "No Decision on Clay Bout," *Baltimore Sun*, March 1, 1966; AP report, "Heavy Fight Bounces Back," *Baltimore Sun*, March 2, 1966.

13. UPI report, "Clay is Granted Permission to Leave Country For Bout," *New York Times*, March 18, 1966; Milton Gross, "Cassius Clay at the Brink," *Chicago Daily News*, March 28, 1966; Jesse Abramson, "The License Hasn't Been Granted Yet," *New York Herald-Tribune*, March 3, 1966; Combined Wire Services, "Funny Thing Happened To Clay Title Bout on Its Way to the Forum," *New York Herald-Tribune*, March 4, 1966; Jesse Abramson, "Clay Fails to Pass at Verdun, Tries New Front," *New York Herald-Tribune*, March 5, 1966; AP report, "5 Sites Considered for Clay Title Bout," *New York Herald-Tribune*, March 6, 1966; UPI report, "Montreal May Take Clay Bout," *Los Angeles Herald-Examiner*, March 3, 1966; Norm Miller, "Ill. Wind Blows Clay-Terrell Go to Montreal," *New York Daily News*, March 3, 1966; AP report, "Sorrels, Edmonton Display Interest," *New York Times*, March 5, 1966; Berry, "Clay: He Wouldn't Crawl"; Lester Bromberg, "Toronto: We'll Accept Clay-Terrell Fight," *New York World-Telegram and Sun*, March 8, 1966.
14. Lester Bromberg, "Clay-Terrell Fight for Title Appears Dead," *New York World-Telegram and Sun*, March 10, 1966; Jesse Abramson, "Clay Fights Chuvalo For Peanuts in Toronto," *New York Herald-Tribune*, March 29, 1966; Arthur Daley, "Is This Trip Necessary?," *New York Times*, March 29, 1966; Eddie Muller, "Clay-Chuvalo Talk Negative," *San Francisco Examiner*, March 25, 1966; Lester Bromberg, "Price is 6–5 Chuvalo Will Go 15 Rounds," *New York World-Telegram and Sun*, March 28, 1966; Prescott Sullivan, "Who'd Want to Miss It?," *San Francisco Examiner*, March 23, 1966; Robert Lipsyte, "Bettor's Eye View of Chuvalo: A Big Bum With a Lot of Heart," *New York Times*, March 26, 1966; Bob Stewart, "Just Maybe," *New York World-Telegram and Sun*, March 25, 1966; John P. Carmichael, "The Barber Shop," *Chicago Daily News*, March 26, 1966; Red Smith, "The Action," *New York Herald-Tribune*, March 29, 1966; Robert Lipsyte, "Patterson Gains Unanimous Decision Over Chuvalo in 12 Rounder," *New York Times*, February 2, 1965; "64 Theater Sites to Show Patterson-Chuvalo Bout," *New York Times*, January 27, 1965.
15. AP report, "Fight Facts and Figures," *Chicago Daily News*, February 9, 1966; AP report, "Fight Theater TV a Resounding Dud," *San Francisco Examiner*, March 30, 1966; *N.Y. Times-Chicago Tribune* Dispatch, "Advertisers Boycotting Clay Fight," *Chicago Tribune*, March 15, 1966; AP report, "Ad Sponsors Cool to Bout," *Baltimore Sun*, March 16, 1966.
16. AP report, "Miami Legion Post to Picket Theaters," *New York Herald-Tribune*, March 6, 1966; Berry, "Clay: He Wouldn't Crawl"; Eddie Muller, "Chargin, Ms. Eaton Swing Clay TV Ban," *San Francisco Examiner*, March 10, 1966; Norman Ross, "How to Vote Against Boxing: Don't Spend Money on It," *Chicago Daily News*, February 25, 1966; Robert Lipsyte, "Coast Backs Boycott," *New York Times*, March 10, 1966.
17. AP report, "Clay Beats Chuvalo in 15 Rounds," *Baltimore Sun*, March 30, 1966; Abramson, "Clay Fights Chuvalo"; AP report, "Theater-TV Lays an Egg at the Box Office," *New York World-Telegram and Sun*, March 30, 1966; AP report, "Clucking Sound at Clay Box Office," *San Francisco Examiner*, March 12, 1966; Eaton and Chargin quoted in John Washington, "Olympic Bans Clay TV," *Los Angeles Herald-Examiner*, March 8, 1966; Eddie Muller, "Clay Fight Blackout," *San Francisco Examiner*, March 8, 1966; Muller, "Chargin, Ms. Eaton"; Syufy quoted in Eddie Muller, "Syufy Spurns Clay Tee-Vee," *San Francisco Examiner*, March 19, 1966; Sullivan, "Who'd Want to Miss It?"; AP report, "Experts Flock to Chuvalo Camp," *San Francisco Examiner*, March 22, 1966; "Fight Tickets on Sale," *Los Angeles Herald-Examiner*, November 21, 1965; Emerling and Seguin quoted

in Lester Bromberg, "Only 1 Local Theater Chain Has Clay TV," *New York World-Telegram and Sun*, March 9, 1966; Paul Weisman, "Fight Facts . . . or Just Fiction?," *New York Herald-Tribune*, March 17, 1966; Dick Young, "Young Ideas," *New York Daily News*, November 17, 1965; Paul Weisman, " . . . Bout also Flops on the Popcorn Circuit," *New York Herald-Tribune*, March 29, 1966.

18. Muhammad Ali's birth name was Cassius Clay. Some reporters refused to acknowledge his 1964 renaming to Muhammad Ali by Nation of Islam leader Elijah Muhammad. AP report, "Clay Beats Chuvalo"; Melvin Durslag, "A Good Lively Match," *San Francisco Examiner*, March 30, 1966; Robert Lipsyte, "Clay Outpoints Chuvalo in Bruising, No-Knockdown 15-Rounder at Toronto," *New York Times*, March 30, 1966; "Clay Quiet, Chuvalo Proud," *New York World-Telegram and Sun*, March 30, 1966; AP report, "Fight Theater TV"; AP report, "Theater-TV Lays an Egg"; AP report, "Clucking Sound"; Muller, "Clay-Chuvalo Talk"; Malitz quoted in Dave Brady, "Home TV Carries Clay-Cooper Fight," *Washington Post*, April 27, 1966. If Malitz' claim was accurate, the profit margin for closed-circuit television was substantial.
19. Bob Stewart, "Flop in the Making," *New York World-Telegram and Sun*, March 9, 1966; Eddie Muller, "Fight Empire Not that Bad," *San Francisco Examiner*, March 6, 1966; Jim Murray, "'Enery Might Shut Him Up," *Des Moines Register*, April 26, 1966; A.S. Young, "Aw F'Heavens Sake," *New York Amsterdam News*, April 2, 1966; Larry Boeck, "Association With Muslims Has Cost Clay $2 Million Over Last Two Years, Backer Says," *Louisville Courier-Journal*, November 20, 1965; "Clay, Muslim Pals Figure to Strike It Rich Here," *Chicago Tribune*, February 21, 1966; "Clay Group to Stay With Him for Now; Reveal Appeal Plan," *Chicago Tribune*, February 22, 1966; Gene Ward, "Ward to the Wise," *New York Daily News*, March 1, 1966; Dick Young, "Young Ideas," *New York Daily News*, June 4, 1966.
20. Clarence Matthews, "Muhammad Ali Wins," *Louisville Defender*, April 7, 1966; Marion Jackson, "Views Sports of the World," *Atlanta Daily World*, March 13, 1966; "Champ Ali on Threshold of New Achievements," *Muhammad Speaks*, April 5, 1966; Moses J. Newson, "Cassius Clay, Main Bout, Inc. And a Boxing World Miracle," *Baltimore Afro-American*, April 9, 1966; Brown quoted in "Jim Brown Charges Fight Foes Oppose Negro TV Promoters," *Chicago Daily News*, March 10, 1966; "Jimmy Brown Defends Clay on Capitol Hill," *New York Herald-Tribune*, March 11, 1966.
21. Robert Lipsyte, "Boxing's Bogeyman's Back," *New York Times*, January 30, 1966; Berry, "Clay: He Wouldn't Crawl"; Jimmy Cannon, "This Mismatch is For Title, Despite Toronto's Billing," *Chicago Daily News*, March 29, 1966.
22. In a July 2002 interview with the author, Terrell denied being threatened by gangsters and claimed that Glickman had no mob ties. Terrell also denied talking to the FBI about his withdrawal from the Ali fight. The FBI, with help from the U.S. Department of Justice (it is unclear if they were responding to Powell's request) investigated the promotion and announced that it would hold grand jury hearings into death threats against Terrell. It also probed allegations that mobsters had threatened to kill Glickman for compromising the chances of a match between Ali and Terrell in New York, where the fight was originally scheduled to take place before being bumped to Chicago. The FBI also claimed that Chicago gangsters had threatened to murder Terrell if he faced Ali in Toronto. In all, eleven witnesses from the often-interrelated worlds of organized crime and professional boxing were on the docket. They were: Glickman; Irving Schoenwald; Bob Arum; Teddy Brenner and

Harry Markson, who together ran Madison Square Garden's boxing division; Joseph Glaser, a New York theatrical agent and boxing manager; Julius Isaacson, Terrell's former manager and a New York underworld associate; Anthony Accardo, the Chicago crime syndicate's 'Godfather'; Felix Alderisio, Accardo's second-in-command; Gus Alex, the boss of the Chicago crime syndicate's gambling operations; and Gus Zapas, a top Chicago aide to labor leader Jimmy Hoffa. The government wanted to know if Accardo, Alderisio, Alex, Zapas, and perhaps some of their New York affiliates had violated federal gambling and racketeering laws in their attempt to hijack the March 29 promotion. U.S. Attorney Edward Hanrahan sought indictments against anyone who may have used "terror tactics" to tamper with "the arrangements to promote in New York City the ill-fated [Ali–Terrell] fight." The UPI claimed that a crime syndicate would have gotten half of Terrell's $300,000 purse had the fight been held in New York. The key witness was Glickman. If he would detail the processes by which mob involvement in boxing took place, the government would have a chance at indicting the gangsters who may have interfered with the promotion. Witness Isaacson proved to be no help, and Zapas and Alex exercised their Fifth Amendment rights rather than testify. The statements by Brenner, Markson, and Schoenwald were taken on March 30. Glickman told his story on March 31, discussing his entry into the fight game, his associations with boxers, and his relationships with fellow witnesses. After Glickman's testimony, Hanrahan announced that he would postpone further testimony to consider the evidence. He reserved the right to call the witnesses again and ordered federal protection for Glickman. On April 15, Glickman entered the hospital for exhaustion and released himself from the FBI's protective custody, which the government feared signaled a deal between the former manager and the gangsters he had offended. According to unnamed officials working the case, Glickman agreed not to implicate Accardo and Alderisio in exchange for his life. With its star witness suddenly uncooperative, the government wrapped up the investigation. It indicted Gus Alex on April 15. Members of the black press were disappointed by the government's failure to make more of an impact on mob control of professional boxing, while white reporters were silent on the investigation's conclusion. In-person interview with Ernie Terrell, Chicago, IL, July 19, 2002. For descriptions of Terrell's and Glickman's problems in New York, see Ed Stone, "Glickman Denies Terrell Controlled by Underworld," *Chicago's American*, November 19, 1965; AP report, "Ernie Says Charge 'Lie,'" *Atlanta Journal*, November 19, 1965; UPI report, "Deny Terrell License to Fight in New York," *New York World-Telegram and Sun*, January 28, 1966; Jim McCulley, "N.Y. Denies Terrell's Bid For Title Bout With Clay," *New York Daily News*, January 29, 1966; Robert Lipsyte, "State Commission Denies License to Terrell," *New York Times*, January 29, 1966; Lipsyte, "Boxing's Bogeyman's Back"; Dave Nightingale, "Ernie Denies Glickman Ties," *Chicago Daily News*, February 1, 1966; Phil Pepe, "The Terrell Case," *New York World-Telegram and Sun*, February 17, 1966; Jesse Abramson, "Terrell Lost Date By Coincidence," *New York Herald-Tribune*, February 17, 1966. For discussions of the FBI grand jury hearings, see Cannon, "This Mismatch Is For the Title"; AP and UPI report, "Probe on Terrell Death Threat," *San Francisco Examiner*, March 26, 1966; AP report, "U.S. Probes Threat to Terrell's Life," *New York Herald-Tribune*, March 27, 1966; UPI report, "Inquiry Ordered on Boxing Threat," *New York Times*, March 27, 1966; "Who's Who in Federal Probe of Mob's Link to Boxing," *Chicago Daily News*, March 30, 1966; Edmund J. Rooney, "Boxing Probe Opens Here After Last Minute Site Shift," *Chicago Daily News*, March 30, 1966; "Glickman Tells Jury of Mob's Boxing

Links," *Chicago Daily News*, March 31, 1966; Norman Glubok, "I'll Talk, I'm Not Afraid, Says Terrell," *Chicago Daily News*, March 28, 1966; Robert Lipsyte, "Showdown in Boxing," *New York Times*, March 28, 1966; UPI report, "Ring Pilot Gives Extortion Terms," *New York Times*, March 28, 1966; UPI report, "In this Corner—The Mafia," *San Francisco Examiner*, March 28, 1966; Edmund J. Rooney, "Glickman in City—Guarded by FBI," *Chicago Daily News*, March 29, 1966; Combined News Services, "Glickman's Hobby Goes Sour, Business Fails," *St. Louis Post-Dispatch*, March 31, 1966; "Glickman Hospital Stay 'Indefinite,'" *Chicago Daily News*, May 4, 1966; "Fear Mob Promised Glickman Protection to Stop Testimony," *Chicago's American*, April 16, 1966; "Boxing Jury Indictment," *Chicago Daily News*, April 15, 1966. Also see "Terrell 'Intimidation' Exposes Ring Problem," *Pittsburgh Courier*, May 14, 1966.

23. Ali quoted in Phil Pepe, "Uneasy Lies the Head," *New York World-Telegram and Sun*, March 8, 1966; Ali quoted in Milton Gross, "Clay Distressed Now," *Chicago Daily News*, March 8, 1966; Ali quoted in Milton Gross, "Clay Heaviest of Career," *Chicago Daily News*, March 29, 1966; Ali quoted in Earl Ruby, "Ruby's Report," *Louisville Courier-Journal*, March 2, 1966; Larry Merchant, "A Day With Clay," *Philadelphia Daily News*, March 8, 1966; Ali quoted in Robert Lipsyte, "Youngsters Chatter Helps Clay Endure Camp Drudgery," *New York Times*, February 20, 1966; Ali quoted in Robert Lipsyte, "Clay Says He is a Jet Airplane and All the Rest Are Prop Jets," *New York Times*, March 25, 1966.
24. Brady, "Home TV Carries"; AP report, "Clay, Cooper Home TV is Discussed," *San Francisco Chronicle*, April 28, 1966; UPI report, "Clay Bout on Satellite Relay to US," *San Francisco Chronicle*, April 29, 1966; Milton Gross, "Rolling in the Isles," *New York Post*, May 24, 1966; Arthur Veysey, "See Sellout Crowd for Cooper and Clay Battle," *Chicago Tribune*, May 12, 1966; AP report, "Cassius Wants Jones as Next Opponent," *Hartford Courant*, May 23, 1966; Gene Ward, "Clay in 6—Henry's a Bloody Mess," *New York Daily News*, May 22, 1966; Cooper's Share May Remain a Secret," *Irish Times*, May 24, 1966; "Big Fight Finance," *London Daily Express*, May 23, 1966; AP report, "Clay 11–2 Choice to Retain World Heavyweight Crown Over Cooper," *Wichita Eagle and Beacon*, May 15, 1966; John Rodda, "Why Clay is Coming Here," *Manchester Guardian*, April 18, 1966; "Bookies Say It's Clay," *London Daily Mirror*, May 21, 1966; "The Clay Fight May Go on TV," *London Daily Mirror*, May 9, 1966; "British Broadcast is Set Up for Clay-Cooper Title Bout," *New York Times*, May 9, 1966; Ken Irwin, "Big Fight 'Live' on the Radio," *London Daily Mirror*, May 14, 1966; Mike Grade, "Sportlight," *London Daily Mirror*, April 26, 1966; Desmond Hackett, "'Enry's 'Arvest," *London Daily Express*, April 18, 1966; AP report, "Clay, Beatles Rate Same Tax Category," *Wichita Eagle*, May 27, 1966; Eddie Muller, "Shadow Boxing: Clay's Purse Well-Bitten," *San Francisco Examiner*, June 7, 1966; UPI report, "Title Bout May Pay $140,000 to Cooper," *Washington Post*, April 26, 1966.
25. "He's A Mere Mortal," *San Francisco Examiner*, August 5, 1966; Arthur Daley, "A Visit with Brian London," *New York Times*, August 5, 1966; Arthur Daley, "Britain Showing Little Interest," *New York Times*, August 6, 1966; Sydney Hulls, "Frozen London," *London Daily Express*, August 8, 1966; UPI report, "Clay-London Mismatch was Financial Bomb, Too," *Washington Post*, August 10, 1966; AP report, "ABC to Televise Clay Title Bout," *Washington Post*, July 7, 1966; AP report, "Clay on TV," *Louisville Courier-Journal*, July 7, 1966; AP report, "Clay Title Bout on Live TV," *San Francisco Examiner*, July 20, 1966; Milton Gross, "Cassius 203 ½, Karl 194

¾," *New York Post*, September 10, 1966; Sydney Hulls, "Angelo Predicts a K.O. Win," *London Daily Express*, August 4, 1966; Red Fisher, "British Board Should Have Blocked Bout," *Montreal Star*, August 11, 1966; Gene Ward, "Terrell Outpoints Jones, Fans Boo 'Champ' for Fouls," *New York Daily News*, June 29, 1966.

26. "Clay to Get 50 percent for Bout with Mildenberger," *New York Times*, July 10, 1966; Fred Tupper, "Fight Expected to Draw 40,000," *New York Times*, September 10, 1966; Gross, "Cassius 203 ½"; Hugh McIlvaney, "Clay Wins in 12th Round," *London Observer*, September 11, 1966; AP report, "Mildenberger Accepts Sept. 10 As Date for Title Fight With Clay," *Washington Post*, June 25, 1966; AP report, "Clay Stops German in 12th Round," *Washington Post*, September 11, 1966.
27. Al Buck, "Cassius Puts Out the Cat; Terrell Next—In Garden?," *New York Post*, November 15, 1966; "Title Crowd Shatters Indoor Fight Record," *New York Post*, November 15, 1966; "Clay-Williams Bout Is Slated For 24 Metropolitan Theaters," *New York Times*, November 13, 1966; AP/UPI report, "Clay Rates Williams Fifth among Foes," *San Francisco Chronicle*, November 16, 1966; Al Buck, "Cat Can't Win, Odds Insist," *New York Post*, November 14, 1966; AP report, "Clay-Williams to be on Radio Monday," *Newark Star-Ledger*, November 11, 1966; UPI report, "Mutual Radio Carries Clay Bout," *Washington Post*, November 11, 1966; Gene Ward, "Clay 5–1 to Skin a Cat in Title Fight," *New York Daily News*, November 14, 1966; Gene Ward, "Another Clay Pigeon: Cat KO'ed at 1:08 of the 3d," *New York Daily News*, November 15, 1966; "Branford Set to Televise Clay-Williams," *Newark Star-Ledger*, November 13, 1966; Jack Fiske, "A Shuffle, Some Fun, and a Fight," *San Francisco Chronicle*, November 15, 1966; "Clay TV," *San Francisco Chronicle*, November 12, 1966; Brown quoted in Frank Mastro, "TV Viewers Cheer Clay's TKO Victory," *Chicago Tribune*, November 15, 1966; "A Compound Problem Confronts Cassius!," *Los Angeles Herald-Examiner*, November 1, 1966.
28. "Facts on Houston Fight," *New York Times*, February 8, 1967; "Fight Facts, Figures," *Houston Post*, February 8, 1967; "Clay Now Eyes Old Man Folley," *Los Angeles Herald-Examiner*, February 7, 1967; Gerald Eskenazi, "Telecast Highlight: Close-Ups of Terrell's Face," *New York Times*, February 7, 1967; Jesse Abramson, "Acoustical Dud In Garden," *New York World Journal Tribune*, February 7, 1967; Jim McCulley, "Garden TV: A One-Rounder," *New York Daily News*, February 7, 1967; George Bernet, "Ali's Crowd Cheers Hero in Theater," *Newark Star-Ledger*, February 7, 1967; Steve Cady, "30,000 Expected at Houston Fight," *New York Times*, February 6, 1967; "Garden Among 25 Nearby Sites Presenting Title Fight on TV," *New York Times*, February 5, 1967; Advertisement in *Los Angeles Herald-Examiner*, January 22, 1967.
29. Jim McCulley, "Clay Right to Jaw KO's Folley in 7," *New York Daily News*, March 23, 1967; Kay Gardella, "Clay-Folley Bout to Revive Home TV," *New York Daily News*, February 22, 1967; Jim McCulley, "Cassius Pockets $264,838," *New York Daily News*, March 24, 1967.
30. "Champion is Set for 10th Defense," *New York Times*, April 4, 1967; "Clay and Floyd Do It Again on April 25 in Las Vegas," *New York World Journal Tribune*, April 4, 1967; Robert Lipsyte, "After Patterson, the Field Lies Fallow," *New York Times*, April 3, 1967; Joe O'Day, "Clay, Pat Sign for Encore; Ali's Swan Song," *New York Daily News*, April 5, 1967; AP report, "Clay and Patterson Sign for Rematch," *Chicago Tribune*, April 5, 1967; Malitz quoted in Deane McGowen, "Patterson Fight With Clay is Off," *New York Times*, April 13, 1967.

31. Jimmy Cannon, "Clay-Floyd Fight: A Sanctioned Atrocity," *New York World Journal Tribune*, April 5, 1967; Lamb quoted in UPI report, "Won't Police Fight, Vegas Sheriff Says," *Philadelphia Daily News*, April 6, 1967; Laxalt quoted in UPI report, "Nevada Cancels Clay Title Bout," *New York Times*, April 12, 1967; Dooley and Malitz quoted in McGowen, "Patterson Fight"; UPI report, "Clay Title Fight is Counted Out," *New York Times*, April 15, 1967.
32. Gene Ward, "Ward to the Wise," *New York Daily News*, April 20, 1967; Robert Lipsyte, "Boxing's New Era: The Gold Rush in On," *New York Times*, April 30, 1967; Robert Lipsyte, "Patterson Bout Slated July 15," *New York Times*, May 9, 1967; Gene Ward, "Seven Stalking Clay's Title Willingly; Frazier Stalls," *New York Daily News*, May 10, 1967; "'Not Guilty,' Says Clay in Draft Case," *Newark Star-Ledger*, May 9, 1967; UPI report, "Ring Tourney Moves Closer to Reality," *Louisville Courier-Journal and Times*, May 7, 1967; Nicholas Von Hoffman, "Clay Refuses Induction, Stripped of World Title," *Washington Post*, April 29, 1967; Dave Brady, "8 So-So Heavyweights Bounce Into Title Picture," *Washington Post*, April 30, 1967.

9 Operation Breadbasket in Chicago

Between Civil Rights and Black Capitalism

Enrico Beltramini

Operation Breadbasket (OB) originated in 1962 as the economic arm of Martin Luther King, Jr.'s Southern Christian Leadership Conference (SCLC). Its earliest success came in Atlanta but it was toward the end of the decade in Chicago under the leadership of Jesse Jackson that the organization made its strongest gains. Operation Breadbasket was established to fight economic discrimination against African Americans and would become an important part of the black capitalism movement of the late 1960s and early 1970s. Operation Breadbasket moved beyond traditional civil rights platforms of desegregation and voting rights and instead addressed issues such as black employment and access to capital. The story of Operation Breadbasket in Chicago suggests that during the black power era the entrepreneur moved alongside the radical as an iconic image and source of sociocultural change. It also demonstrates how the contemporary black freedom struggle reacted to the American political swing toward conservatism.

Operation Breadbasket was inspired by a program known as "selective patronage" that was popularized in 1958 by Baptist minister Leon Sullivan in Philadelphia. Sullivan engineered boycotts of businesses that would not hire blacks. Sullivan's success in achieving employment gains for African Americans gained media attention from periodicals like the *New York Times* and *Fortune*. King took notice and invited Sullivan to Atlanta for an October 1962 meeting. He hoped that Atlanta's ministers could replicate what Sullivan and his colleagues had done in Philadelphia. OB emerged from that meeting. Its mission was to "negotiate a more equitable employment practice" by area businesses toward African Americans. The organization was successful in Atlanta and in the South and by 1967 had won jobs that brought $25 million a year in new income to the black community. Inspired by these victories, King and the SCLC folded the OB program into its attempt to bring the civil rights movement north to Chicago, where it was planning a comprehensive campaign for black equality. It was in Chicago where OB would rise to prominence under the leadership of Jesse Jackson, an SCLC veteran, Chicago Theological Seminary student, and associate pastor at Fellowship Baptist Church who would become OB's director and spokesman.[1]

King's Chicago Freedom Movement was intended to demonstrate the viability of the civil rights movement outside the South. SCLC announced the campaign in January 1966, which would begin by challenging the city's racial housing discrimination. Because area clergy were not uniformly supportive of the Chicago Freedom Movement, Operation Breadbasket would be a concession to several ministers who wanted to pursue a program under their own supervision. The following month King spoke at the kickoff meeting for Chicago's Operation Breadbasket, whose initial objective was to abolish racist hiring practices by employers in African American neighborhoods. A multicultural and multidenominational collection of 200 clergy attended and it was from this group that the project's leadership emerged. Forty of these religious leaders stayed afterward to meet in committees that would investigate hiring practices in four areas of the food industry: bread, milk, soft drinks, and soup. The committees would survey companies serving the black community and then reconvene to plot a course of action. Jackson became one of the organization's coordinators during this process.[2]

Operation Breadbasket targeted businesses that dealt primarily or exclusively with black clients. It used the organizational strength of the black church for support and as leverage. Ministers helped OB collect employment statistics of businesses operating, vending, or supplying stores in black areas. If it was discovered that black people were underemployed or relegated to non-executive roles, OB opened talks with the management of such companies. If management would not negotiate, the ministers pursued retaliatory action. They organized pickets at stores, boycotts of products of parent companies, and alerted their parishioners to the discriminatory practices of these local businesses. On Sundays, churches became media centers informing Chicago's African American community which stores to avoid.[3]

With the black church behind it, Operation Breadbasket quickly took hold in Chicago. An important part of OB strategy was to target companies that specialized in fresh food, as they were the most vulnerable to boycotts of relatively short periods. The average commercial life of milk, bread, fruit, and vegetables is a few days. The effects of these boycotts therefore happened nearly in real time. Targeted companies quickly felt the sting. As they capitulated, black pastors negotiated with corporate management and signed agreements that pledged expanded employment and promotional opportunities for African Americans in exchange for an end to the protests and a promise to help these companies recover their lost credibility. Importantly, these campaigns showed that the efforts of relatively few people for a relatively short time could make a big impact. In the first fifteen months of its Chicago operation, mostly behind Jackson's leadership, OB created 2,000 new jobs worth $15 million a year in new income to the African American community. King called Operation Breadbasket the "most spectacularly successful program" of his Chicago movement.[4]

OPERATION BREADBASKET AND MARTIN LUTHER KING, JR., 1966–68

Operation Breadbasket's first campaign in Chicago was against Country Delight Dairy, whose representative insulted a group of ministers that had approached him to gather information about the company's recruitment practices. The situation quickly deteriorated and OB called for a consumer boycott of the dairy's products. Shocked, Country Delight Dairy capitulated after less than a week of picketing. The company announced its intention to hire forty-four blacks within thirty days, although it took longer. In its first months of operation, Breadbasket targeted four other dairies: Borden, Wanzer Dairy, Bowman Dairy, and Hawthorn-Mellody. The first three companies negotiated to hire blacks immediately, while Hawthorn-Mellody acknowledged defeat after four days of boycotts and picketing. Jackson reported to SCLC's executive board in July that Operation Breadbasket had completed all five campaigns successfully, bringing a total of 224 jobs with an annual payroll of $1,800,000.[5]

Breadbasket shifted its attention from dairy firms to soft drink bottlers at the end of July 1966. Within days, Jackson was able to conclude agreements with the two giants, Coca-Cola and Pepsi-Cola, both of which committed to employ thirty new black employees each. These successes encouraged OB to extend its goals and expand its operational scope. Instead of merely hitting distributors, Breadbasket directly challenged supermarket chains that summer. It no longer just demanded jobs, but also pressured major companies to extend business ties with the black community. Breadbasket promoted patronage for black-owned businesses as a means of persuading whites to purchase goods and services from black contractors or deposit funds in black-owned banks. OB leaders believed that blacks needed jobs, contracts, and capital to compete in the market.[6]

The strategy change revealed an understanding of the operations of supermarket chains. Supermarkets are similar to dairy stores. In fact they suffer a higher level of vulnerability. This is not so much in the short life of the product—fresh food only represents a small percentage of their portfolio—as in the structure of the business model. The supermarket model is very similar to that of banks; they make profits through cash management. The store collects money from customers now and pays suppliers later. In order to increase liquidity it sometimes has to reduce prices. Lower prices lead to increased sales. It is obvious that if prices are to remain low, then costs (labor in particular) must also be kept low. Supermarket chains therefore try to balance costs and revenue streams to create an uninterrupted daily flow of money. The company can then withdraw a small portion of this as investment capital that will be used to make the company's profit while the remaining part circulates through the daily operation. An abrupt cessation of the flow of revenue in the form of a boycott can be devastating to companies where cash management has the full responsibility to produce profits. Without reliable revenue streams, supermarkets can't pay suppliers, who stop delivering. The store's stock is depleted and customers go elsewhere. The company may sustain for a few days or weeks, depending on its size. The larger the company is, the less effect the boycott has on it. The more cash available, the longer the protest has to last. Breadbasket targeted businesses in industries where the margin of profitability was small. In those situations, even if black customers were only a fraction of the total, they could still determine the success or failure of the firm. OB's strategy tended to capitalize on what Jackson biographer Marshall Frady called "the disproportionate effect of a concentrated minority force applied to the fractions of decisive margin in an otherwise impossible larger equation."[7]

Operation Breadbasket contacted one major supermarket chain after another in Chicago, including the National Team Company, Jewel Foods, A&P, and High Low Food (Hi-Lo), whose fifty supermarkets included fourteen locations in black neighborhoods. King announced the signing of an agreement with High Low Food around Thanksgiving. The agreement targeted jobs, contracts, and capital. It opened to blacks 183 jobs and promotions in several categories and promised to "fully integrate the company's total work force and will integrate each job category within the company." Six black manufacturers were promised that their products would be "given equal display space and will sell at non-prohibitive mark-ups with competitive products." Commercial accounts from several Hi-Lo stores would "be transferred to two Chicago banks, which have direct relationship[s] with the Negro Community." King was especially pleased with this development. In a speech at SCLC's annual conference, he noted: "And I can say to you today that as a result of Operation Breadbasket in Chicago, both of these Negro-operated banks have now more than double their assets, and this has been done in less than a year by the work of Operation Breadbasket." To sum up the situation, High Low Food's top brass agreed to commit its stores to sell certain products in certain ways, to channel funds to certain banks, and to employ and train certain people. This is why an agency like Operation Breadbasket was crucial. It could negotiate and build a relationship with the company's highest-level management, which was in King's mind an opportunity to champion equitable economic race relations. The result was a supermarket chain serving whites and blacks, employing white and black labor, offering products manufactured by white and black entrepreneurs, and channeling funds to banks owned by whites and blacks.[8]

Nevertheless, there were major limitations on this particular strategy. From King's perspective, High Low Food was a vehicle for racial integration, rather than a business focused on making money. The enterprise was interpreted as a social entity, not as a profit-driven one. The agreement lacked any reference to the labor costs of the new hires and their impact on the balance sheet. In fact, if profitability does not increase because of new hiring, then someone else must be fired. The low margins in the supermarket industry produce constant pressure, and because supermarkets are labor intensive, chains keep personnel costs low by standardizing operations at the store level. To inflict a sudden increase in labor and training costs on a supermarket chain could be lethal, as with the Red Rooster chain of food stores, which had to file for bankruptcy after it was targeted by Breadbasket. King also misunderstood the role of management. In 1967, he demanded that his ministers negotiate with top supermarket managers for jobs and then ask them to "set aside profit for the greater good" and promote a whole better world. But management would never really cooperate with this idea because its goal was to maximize profit. The base of Breadbasket's power was limited to gaining a piece of the pie; it was formulated on the idea of an organization of black consumers that was leveraging its purchasing power to influence the management decisions of firms owned by whites.[9]

King felt, however, that over time Operation Breadbasket could bring capitalism closer to his overall vision of the economy as a fair site where people and enterprises pursued mutual purposes. "The fundamental premise of Breadbasket is a simple one," he said at a press conference. "Negroes need not patronize a business which denies them jobs, or advancement, [or] plain courtesy." King saw business as an entity that could offer jobs, advancement, and other social benefits. It had an obligation to return to society in equal measure whatever it took from society. Even the profit motive was subject to these higher aims, so companies should return profits to communities wherever they were generated. "Many retail businesses and consumer-goods industries," King explained, "deplete the ghetto by selling to Negroes without returning to the community any of the profits through fair-hiring practices." If the company generated profits through black customers, those same black customers (at least figuratively) have earned the right to work for the company.[10]

Corporations had a social responsibility in King's mind and were at the heart of a privately funded welfare system. Private-sector firms played a similar role to that of government agencies in the public arena. They should pursue economic justice and ensure the redistribution of wealth. But because they often did the opposite, Operation Breadbasket under King served as a corrective. Boycotts and other protests were meant to "put justice in business." King also believed that unequal distribution of wealth would be addressed not by appealing to courts of law but instead by dealing with people's hearts and values. Therefore, his vision targeted capitalism's most powerful executives. In King's model, ample wealth was available; what was missing was a just distribution of it. From this perspective, the movement and its techniques were means of moral persuasion. King was increasingly embracing a social democratic agenda. In his view, America was enjoying growth and potentially unlimited economic prosperity, and it was a specific responsibility of the federal government to make sure that the distribution of wealth was accomplished in a just and right way. From his perspective, unemployment was a remediable inconvenience, as the economic means were abundant and the possibility to eliminate unemployment was concrete. It was only a matter of political and corporate will. Not coincidentally, King also came to promote the idea of a guaranteed annual income. This guaranteed income would have assigned a role to blacks alongside whites in the creation of national wealth. It would have reduced economic inequalities and assured everyone, blacks and whites, the right to a minimal self-sustenance. This self-support would not only defeat poverty, but also would also ensure the dignity and self-esteem of workers and expand the boundaries of capitalism, creating new consumers. King's 1968 assassination prevented him from pursuing this vision, of course, and Operation Breadbasket under Jesse Jackson would take a different direction.[11]

OPERATION BREADBASKET AND JESSE JACKSON, 1968–71

Under Jesse Jackson, Operation Breadbasket moved to the center of black capitalism in Chicago, where one of the nation's most vibrant black economies existed. Jackson was already OB's national director by the time of King's assassination and had energized the organization's standard repertoire, fighting for jobs for low-income black people by presenting the threat of boycotts of white-owned and white-managed businesses in black neighborhoods. Jackson negotiated for firms to hire African Americans to work in stores located in black areas, deposit money in black-owned banks, and use the services of black contractors, agencies, and advertising firms. There were also key differences between OB under King and under Jackson. Although difficult to quantify, under Jackson the organization had an intensity and energy that had not previously existed. Jackson embodied the cultural moment far more than King had, connecting OB to a much wider range of community organizations. Finally, Jackson was not as critical of capitalism as King was. King wrote, "There are forty million poor people here. And one day we must ask the question, Why are there forty million poor people in America? And when you begin to ask that question, you are raising questions about the economic system, about a broader distribution of wealth. When you ask that question, you begin to question the capitalistic economy." Jackson, on the other hand, openly embraced capitalism's possibilities for black liberation.[12]

Jesse Jackson was significantly influenced by the counterculture of the late 1960s as he was by the growing feeling of the failure of liberalism. His clothing, hairdo, and rhetorical style made clear his connections with the former, but it was the latter that had an enduring influence on his activity as a civil rights leader. Jackson tried to incorporate his generation's concerns about challenging authority and the hierarchical power structure while resenting the generation gap and slow pace of reform, but he also feared the end of the ages of prosperity and expansive government, which were two of the most enduring legacies of the post-World War II economic boom. Jackson agreed with King that government played a crucial role in eliminating economic discrimination, but gifted with a better understanding than King of how the economy worked, he put the issue into context. Jackson particularly believed that the long era of postwar prosperity was done. The Federal Reserve had increased the interest rate to 5.5 percent in 1968, the highest since the Great Depression. Inflation was growing at a rate of 4 percent per year and was becoming a major problem for American households. This was only the beginning of a spectacular, unpredictable change in the economic cycle. Within a couple of years the direct convertibility of dollars to gold was abandoned because of attacks on U.S. currency by international speculators. Two years later, the Yom Kippur War caused America's first energy crisis. Jackson also had to bear in mind that the effects of a failed war in Vietnam and a recession threatened to permanently undermine social cohesion and therefore race relations. Thus he understood the limitations of King's model.[13]

The coalition of liberals, laborites, and minorities who might have promoted an agenda of government-assisted job desegregation no longer existed and King's vision of a full-blown welfare state seemed unlikely with the presidency in Nixon's hands and the Johnson Administration's Great Society programs under attack. There were no longer the forces within the white establishment willing to pay to provide access to well-paying jobs, well-equipped schools, and affordable housing to African Americans. Jackson's leadership of Operation Breadbasket encapsulated this ambivalence—the growing skepticism of young people and minorities toward institutions in general, together with the feeling that an era of possibility for social justice and economic rights was over, combined with fears about the effect of the collapse of liberal America and its welfare programs.[14]

Jackson's attitude incorporated distrust of the federal government and authority in general, but he was also careful in listening to rising voices of despair from the ghetto. More than the desire to end poverty, black families yearned to be consumers in an affluent society. They did not contest capitalism, only their exclusion from it. Jackson believed that African Americans needed economic power, but contemporary political, economic, and cultural realities forced him to balance his appeals for government-funded welfare with an increasing attention to business as a way to open the gates of affluent society to the African American community. Jackson's connections with urban ghetto life guided his vision of black-owned banks, black-owned urban mortgage lending, and small business loans. Jackson understood that black families were isolated from the affluent society and thus wanted to bridge the ghetto economy with American capitalism. Somehow, he thought, money had to be diverted from white corporations, banks, and retailers, and transferred to black businesses. Black-owned banks with the right size of funds and deposits might provide the access of credit that white-owned banks denied. But not only that: a network of home builders, car dealers, publishers, and consumer goods manufacturers was needed to sustain and encourage the black community's entry into the consumer society.

Without a personal call to action, Jackson feared that the black community could become resigned to waiting passively for the promised efforts of the government. Increasingly, he began to incorporate the philosophies of black self-help and economic independence common to African American radicals. Thus Jackson sought to reorient Operation Breadbasket and its operations. What Jackson did was transform Operation Breadbasket into an economic development agency for the emerging urban entrepreneurial black middle class that also demanded public policies for the advancement of the poor people of the ghetto. Unlike King, who never sought to develop minority-owned small businesses, Jackson looked toward entrepreneurship as a key route to African American empowerment. Operation Breadbasket would become a vehicle to procure resources to foster economic growth for black businesses, build job opportunities, and reduce poverty. Operation Breadbasket soon became a cultural force under Jackson, focused around weekly Saturday workshops that drew thousands to hear him preach. His message was that the African American community had to reduce its economic dependence on white liberals and the federal government by increasing its autonomy. Jackson's leadership redefined OB's relationship with whites. What might have seemed an expression of generosity or a private welfare paid by whites became instead a merchant exchange. Jackson would speak of "reciprocity," meaning the need for a relationship between equals. In Jackson's model, the hiring of black workers, use of black firms and contractors, and investment in black banks was framed not in terms of social justice but rather as interdependence, an exchange of goods, services, and monies between equals.[15]

Under Jackson's leadership, OB responded to the economic realities of the time by putting into place a network of interconnections. It convinced white-managed companies to deposit money into black-owned banks. Then it arranged for black-owned banks to grant loans to black entrepreneurs. These entrepreneurs would then hire African Americans. These new employees would then patronize black-owned businesses. Operation Breadbasket under Jackson positioned itself at the center of these processes and brought together different aspects of black capitalism, something King did not. During this period, OB built economic relationships with black nationalists like the Nation of Islam, street gangs like the Blackstone Rangers, and radicals like the Black Panther Party, not to mention the expanding black entrepreneurial class. In 1969, OB launched Black Expo, a successful professional trade fair, to bring black companies and white clients together. This venture and others like it placed Jackson and OB at the crossroads of the emerging black capitalism movement.

Through Operation Breadbasket, Jackson tried to create a common consciousness among differing fragments of black capitalism. For OB to be successful, it had to reach widely. Chicago during the late 1960s and early 1970s was home to a multitude of economic ventures and business initiatives that connected black nationalism, entrepreneurship, and welfare. It hosted an impressive series of programs that promoted economic opportunity to the African American community, especially its growing middle class. Chicago became arguably the national center of black business with the largest and strongest financial base of any African American community in the United States. Jackson catered to the entrepreneurial inclination of young urban African Americans who had a growing desire for business ownership. He also coordinated community boycotts to address economic segregation in large corporations and called upon the federal government to aid the disadvantaged and unemployed people of the slums. Jackson had to merge the tradition of the pastors who led the civil rights movement with the wave of radicals who looked to the economy as the new political terrain of social change and racial pride.

What Jackson did was embrace both protest and production as central tenets of Operation Breadbasket in an attempt to integrate civil rights with black capitalism. He kept alive a welfare approach to poverty while also supporting black capital accumulation. On one hand, he built partnerships with several Chicago trade unions, challenged grocery and supermarket chains to hire more blacks, and supported the local strikes of black hospital workers, teachers, and bus drivers. On the other hand, he celebrated the rise of black capitalism with his annual Black Expo (he also launched Black Christmas and Black Easter campaigns). He organized parties, exhibitions, concerts, and spectacles centered on the idea of blackness as an economic opportunity. Jackson stressed that black money must stay within the African American community. Over time, Jackson's approach changed, moving away from a vision of privately funded welfare to black capitalism. He always maintained a foot in both camps, but gradually shifted Breadbasket's priorities from creating jobs for poor black people to supporting small, black-owned companies.

Not surprisingly, Breadbasket and Jackson eventually parted ways. Breadbasket had liberal origins, and despite its innovations and successes, it still operated under the presumption of a growing economy, enlargement of welfare, and ultimately through Keynesian logic. King always believed that the public sector needed to provide adequate jobs to reduce black poverty and labor exploitation. He felt that the African American community did not have sufficient resources to ensure full employment. OB would have to be an agent or advocate that promoted social justice together with the government as well as economic advancement through privately funded corporate welfare. Jackson took note, however, not only of the exhaustion of the era of economic prosperity, but also the emergence of a conservative political climate. The rising ideology of self-help required the construction of infrastructures that would facilitate the emergence of a black middle class. Jackson broke with SCLC over the organization's decision to relocate

Operation Breadbasket back to Atlanta at the end of 1971 and resigned his position as OB's national director. Shortly thereafter he launched his own economic empowerment organization called Operation PUSH (People United to Save Humanity). PUSH took Breadbasket's place in Chicago and soon became an agent of both black dignity and economic leadership. PUSH was a symbol of the new economic climate (small is beautiful), a move toward black independence, and a vehicle of African American identity and self-expression.[16]

Operation Breadbasket became both the artifact of a charismatic and enigmatic leader, and a victim of changing times—of the civil rights movement, black radicalism and pride, the crisis of the welfare state, the decline of the Great Society and the collapse of the New Deal coalition, and the stirrings of a countercultural capitalism that would come to full maturity only in the following decade. It was a complex period, marked by a sharp deterioration in the economic conditions of the country, which was caught intellectually between orthodox Keynesian ideas and the new sirens of laissez-faire government. The ideological conflict between the government and the market would come to a head during the Reagan presidency and Jackson would be one of the protagonists. But all of the elements of these changes were already present during the late 1960s. Breadbasket mirrored a profound transformation of the collective perception of the economy. Its history marks the passage from politics to economics as a major field of social debate and the transition from civil rights to the surge of a black business class. More succinctly, Breadbasket tells the story of a creative merger between two figures: reformist hero King and entrepreneurial icon Jackson.

NOTES

1. Martin Luther King, Jr., "One Year Later in Chicago," January 1967, Southern Christian Leadership Conference Records 1954–1970 Collection, Operation Breadbasket Folder, Martin Luther King, Jr. Center for Nonviolent Social Change, Atlanta, GA (hereafter cited as "SCLC Records"), Box 26, 670100–001; John D. Pomfret, "Negroes Building Boycott Network," *New York Times*, November 25, 1962; "The Not-Buying Power of Philadelphia's Negroes," *Fortune*, May 11, 1961, 33–35; "SCLC press release," October 23, 1962, SCLC Records, Box 26, 670100–001; Kenneth R. Timmerman, *Shakedown: Exposing the Real Jesse Jackson* (Washington, DC: Regnery Pub., 2002), 24. Also see Leon Howard Sullivan, *Build, Brother, Build* (Philadelphia: Macrae Smith, 1969); Fred C. Bennette, Jr. Collection, Auburn Avenue Research Library, Atlanta, GA, especially Box 002–003–01, folders 5–9, which contain handwritten minutes from Operation Breadbasket meetings during 1964–66; Morehouse College Martin Luther King, Jr., Collection, Robert W. Woodruff Library, Atlanta University Center, especially Series 6: Southern Christian Leadership Conference Organizational Records.
2. Gary Massoni, *Perspectives on Operation Breadbasket*, M.Div. thesis, Chicago Theological Seminary, 1971, 1–10, 194–95; Jackson, Report, May 17, 1966, n. 24, SCLC Records, Box 26, 670100–001; David J. Garrow, *Bearing*

the Cross: Martin Luther King, Jr., and the Southern Christian Leadership Conference (New York: W. Morrow, 1986), esp. 462; Jesse Jackson, "Dr. Martin Luther King: A Recollection," in John Tweedle, *A Lasting Impression* (Columbia: University of South Carolina Press, 1983); *Breadbasket News*, October 1967; *Chicago Tribune*, February 12, 1966; *Chicago Daily News*, February 12, 1966; *Chicago's American*, February 13, 1966; Minutes of Operation Breadbasket Committee, February 28, 1966, SCLC Records, Box 26, 670100–00; FBI 100–106670-NR, November 22, 1965; *Chicago Defender*, February 5, 1966; Alan B. Anderson and George W. Pickering, *Confronting the Color Line: The Broken Promise of the Civil Rights Movement in Chicago* (Athens: University of Georgia Press, 1986), 152; James R. Ralph, *Northern Protest: Martin Luther King, Jr., Chicago, and the Civil Rights Movement* (Cambridge: Harvard University Press, 1993), 68–69.

3. Tom Landess and Richard M. Quinn, *Jesse Jackson & the Politics of Race* (Ottawa: Jameson Books, 1985), 41.
4. Martin Luther King, Jr., "Where Do We Go From Here?," Delivered at the 11th Annual SCLC Convention, August 16, 1967, Atlanta, GA; Martin Luther King, "One Year Later in Chicago," January 1967, SCLC Records, Box 26, 670100–001; SCLC's Operation Breadbasket, "How to Win Jobs and Influence Businessmen," SCLC Records, Box 24, 172:35.
5. Operation Breadbasket was not the first economic rights program in Chicago. Operation Breadbasket built upon momentum that already existed in the city and thus demonstrated that the economic phase of the civil rights movement was happening well before it was particularly termed "black capitalism." In 1929, for example, the *Chicago Whip*, a militant black newspaper, urged its readers "to spend your money where you can work." The threat of boycotts was especially effective during the Great Depression. Operation Breadbasket built upon this tradition. One of Leon Sullivan's precursors was T.R.M. Howard, a wealthy South Side doctor and entrepreneur and a key financial contributor to Breadbasket. Before he moved to Chicago from Mississippi in 1956, Howard was the head of the Regional Council of Negro Leadership, which had successfully organized a boycott against service stations that refused to provide restrooms for blacks. During the summer of 1963, area black ministers led by Howard formed the Clergy Alliance of Chicago and began a boycott of the Bowman Dairy Company. The boycott failed, but the idea of "selective buying" took hold. Chicago was a particularly effective locale for such action because it has always played a pivotal role in the history of African American politics. From Oscar S. De Priest to Barack Obama—through William Dawson, Harold Washington, Jesse Jackson, and Carol Moseley Braun—the city has a unique history of launching the careers of powerful black politicians. Ralph, *Northern Protest*, 67–68; Barbara Reynolds, *Jesse Jackson: America's David* (Washington, DC: JFJ Associates), 113.
6. Massoni, *Perspectives*, 201–13; Gordon Ewen, "The 'Green Power' of Operation Breadbasket," *Commerce*, April 1968, 24–25, 49–54, 64; Anderson and Pickering, *Confronting the Color Line*, 296.
7. Marshall Frady, *Jesse: the Life and Pilgrimage of Jesse Jackson* (New York: Random House,1996), 399.
8. Garrow, *Bearing the Cross*, 538; Martin Luther King, Jr. "Annual Report delivered at the [Eleventh] Anniversary Convention of the Southern Christian Leadership Conference," August 16, 1967, Atlanta, GA, Walter P. Reuther Collection, Walter P. Reuther Library of Labor and Urban Affairs, Archives of Labor History and Urban Affairs, Wayne State University, Box 44, 670816–000.

9. King, "Annual Report"; Thomas F. Jackson, *From Civil Rights to Human Rights: Martin Luther King, Jr., and the Struggle for Economic Justice* (Philadelphia: University of Pennsylvania Press, 2007), 304.
10. Martin Luther King, Jr., "Press conference on Operation Breadbasket," July 11, 1967, Chicago, IL, Martin Luther King, Jr. Papers, 1950–68, Martin Luther King, Jr., Center for Nonviolent Social Change, Inc., Atlanta, GA, 670711-000; King, "Where Do We Go From Here?"
11. King quoted in Dennis B. Fradin, *The Montgomery Bus Boycott* (Tarrytown: Marshall Cavendish Benchmark, 2010), 37; King, "Annual Report".
12. King, "Annual Report"; King, "Where Do We Go From Here?"
13. Jackson, *From Civil Rights*, 303; SCLC press release, "Green Power for Negroes," November 23, 1966, SCLC Records, 122:6; Martin Luther King, Jr, "Address delivered at meeting of Operation Breadbasket at Chicago Theological Seminary," March 25, 1967, Chicago, IL, SCLC Records, 670325-002; Jesse Jackson, "Strategy to End Slums," May 31, 1966, SCLC Records, 139:45; Philip Foner, *Organized Labor and the Black Worker, 1619–1981* (New York: International Publishers, 1982), 365; Reynolds, *Jesse Jackson*, 55; "Rutherford to Jackson," December 11, 1967, SCLC Records; *Atlanta Journal-Constitution*, December 24, 1967; *Penthouse*, April 1973, 78–80ff; Phillip T. Drotning and Wesley W. South, *Up from the Ghetto* (New York: Cowles, 1970), 19–43; Garrow, *Bearing the Cross*, 584–86; Bruce J. Schulman, *The Seventies: The Great Shift in American Culture, Society, and Politics* (New York: Free Press, 2003), 7; Frank Clemente and Frank E. Watkins, *Keep Hope Alive: Jesse Jackson's 1988 Presidential Campaign: A Collection of Major Speeches, Issue Papers, Photographs, and Campaign Analysis* (Washington, DC: Keep Hope Alive PAC, 1989), 33–40.
14. David Llorens, "Apostle of Economics," *Ebony*, August 1967, 78–86.
15. Peniel E. Joseph, *Dark Days, Bright Nights: from Black Power to Barack Obama* (New York: Basic Civitas Books, 2010); In-person conversation with Peniel Joseph, May 2011, Atlanta, GA; In-person interview with Vincent Harding, November 22, 2011, San Francisco, CA; Reynolds, *Jesse Jackson*, 428–34.
16. Reynolds, *Jesse Jackson*, chapter 10; Timmerman, *Shakedown: Exposing the Real Jesse Jackson*, 43–45; Landess and Quinn, *Jesse Jackson*, 34–82; Frady, *Jesse: the Life*, chapter xi; Jackson, *From Civil Rights*, 303.

10 Progress Plaza

Leon Sullivan, Zion Investment Associates, and Black Power in a Philadelphia Shopping Center

Stephanie Dyer

On October 27, 1968, Philadelphia's African American community turned out by the thousands to witness a high-profile symbol of black power: the dedication of Progress Plaza, a state-of-the-art community shopping center erected in the heart of the North Philadelphia ghetto. Progress Plaza was the brainchild of Reverend Leon H. Sullivan, pastor of Zion Baptist Church and an advocate for community economic empowerment. Reverend Sullivan was already well-known through his leadership of the "400 Ministers" in a selective patronage campaign that claimed to have opened employment opportunities at more than 200 businesses in Philadelphia during the early 1960s, as well as his creation of the Opportunities Industrialization Center (OIC) in 1964, a highly successful job-training program for low-income minority workers that spread to 150 cities nationwide.[1]

By the late 1960s, Sullivan expanded his program of community economic empowerment from getting jobs to owning the resources to create them. "You are looking at Black Power, black economic power," Sullivan told his audience of shoppers and community onlookers at Progress Plaza that day. Yet Sullivan's adventures in black capitalism at Progress Plaza, the most successful of his multiple corporate ventures, highlighted the complexities faced by community development advocates seeking to create public-private ventures to make capitalism work for the benefit of the residents of poor, segregated, inner-city neighborhoods. Despite his best intentions, Sullivan's attempt to jumpstart large-scale retail investment in North Philadelphia failed to translate into significant wealth creation for the local community. Ironically, the more Progress Plaza succeeded in distributing goods and services to the heart of the ghetto, the less it rewarded African American entrepreneurship.[2]

In comparison to the Black Panther Party's vanguard embrace of Third World anti-colonial communism as the black power movement's preferred economic model, it is easy to dismiss Progress Plaza and the era's other black capitalist ventures as insignificant and ill-conceived failures. But a number of scholars, including Robert Self, Matthew Countryman, and Guian McKee, have argued that black capitalists like Sullivan should be understood as participants in the contemporary liberal political coalitions that ruled metropolitan areas like Philadelphia. "Rather than an ideological contradiction," Countryman writes, "Sullivan's ability to combine race-based economic self-help with continued support for integration reflected the worldview of many in a black community confronted with persistent racial discrimination." Sullivan understood racism to be connected to the flight of capital from African American communities and thus tried to leverage black political power to convince the liberal establishment to support investment there.[3]

Sullivan believed that the depressed ghetto economy resulted from a lack of private investment capital. Government policies, therefore, would have to stimulate the inner-city economy. Sullivan viewed job creation as only one aspect of the solution. Equally important for him was the flight of African American consumer dollars to non-black businesses that resulted from the underdevelopment of black-owned business. Black workers without black capitalists would merely become consumers dependent on the white economy. Sullivan stated that his "aim [was] to keep some of the money at home instead of seeing it all flow out . . . into the suburbs, making the wealthy wealthier from the earnings of black folks."[4]

Sullivan recognized the symbolic as well as economic value that the missing landmarks of postwar prosperity in North Philadelphia played in the minds of his African American constituency. Of the more than 400,000 new homes in the Greater Philadelphia area since the end of World War II, African American construction companies had built less than 100 of them; moreover, African American residents were relegated to older housing stock in inner-city areas vacated by whites "who took the money and ran like mad to all-white suburbs to escape the black plague," as Sullivan put it. He understood the problem of suburban sprawl as more than just an issue of housing segregation; it was an issue of African Americans missing out on the chance to participate in the booming commercial development opportunities which leapfrogged over their communities to the metropolitan fringe. "On the highways we pass by thousands of motels, shopping centers, and other establishments of all kinds, but never one of consequence that is owned and managed by a black man," he noted in his 1972 memoir/manifesto, *Build, Brother, Build*. Sullivan was determined to capture some of this investment boom for North Philadelphia and was willing to use white capital to do so.[5]

PROGRESS PLAZA AS "TROJAN HORSE": THE PROBLEM OF BLACK POWER USING WHITE CAPITAL

Sullivan began his broad-ranging program of community economic development in 1962 with the founding of the Progress Movement, one of the first community development corporations in the nation. The Movement advocated self-help in order "to develop a base upon which to participate directly in the free enterprise system." Its first campaign was the 10–36 Plan, in which Sullivan asked Zion Baptist parishioners to donate $10 a month for thirty-six months. The first sixteen payments would establish a trust to be used for scholarships and communal aid. Subsequent payments would be channeled into a venture capital company called Zion Investment Associates (ZIA). Two hundred congregants agreed to buy shares in the plan. Within three years, ZIA was able to embark on its first two commercial ventures, both in response to inner-city housing segregation. When one of Sullivan's parishioners reported that she had been denied an apartment in the predominantly white Oak Lane neighborhood of Philadelphia, Sullivan negotiated to purchase the building outright from the owners for $55,000. Buying the apartment building was a highly symbolic act that brought much publicity to the 10–36 Plan throughout Philadelphia and attracted 300 additional subscribers. This influx of capital allowed ZIA to complete construction of another apartment complex, Zion Gardens, which opened in North Philadelphia in 1966. At the groundbreaking, Sullivan anticipated that ZIA would own $15 million in real estate holdings, including shopping centers, by 1975.[6]

ZIA's commercial ambitions grew even larger in 1968 with the construction of Progress Plaza and the establishment of two manufacturing firms: Progress Aerospace Enterprises and Progress Garment Manufacturing Enterprises. Sullivan's goal in pursuing these projects was twofold: to give African Americans (often those who had completed OIC training programs) access to skilled jobs, but even more so to create high-profile companies that would enhance the symbolic as well as economic status of black business in the city. "[Nowhere] was there a single shopping center built and owned by black people anywhere in the Delaware Valley," he wrote. "There was not a single factory, or any industry of any consequence, that employed large numbers of black people or was owned and operated by African Americans." Sullivan wanted nothing less than to open a wedge for black entrepreneurship in major commercial and industrial sectors, including real estate development and aeronautical production—economic strongholds far removed from black capital's traditional niches in insurance, cosmetics, personal services, and funeral homes. Area resident Gregory Lake wrote the *Philadelphia Tribune* to commend Sullivan, "First he opened the way for Negroes to get better jobs. Then he trained Negroes so they could get even better jobs. Now he's building a shopping center so we can spend the money we make at these better jobs at our own supermarket. Baby, that's what I call 'takin' care of business.'"[7]

Sullivan tried to access resources far beyond the means of his own community, which McKee identifies as a black liberal response to the impact of deindustrialization and white flight on Philadelphia's inner-city neighborhoods. Sullivan often stated publicly that full economic integration was the only solution to the problem of racism. "We black folk must become partners at the helm of the national economy," he stated, "for in the final analysis black men will be respected only in proportion to what they produce to strengthen the nation. No one wants a beggar in his living room." While self-help was critical to his philosophy, Sullivan made full use of the resources available to him through the welfare state and its liberal private-sector allies. Indeed, Progress Plaza and ZIA's other businesses could not have begun without the startup capital provided by these sources. Although the 10–36 Plan had attracted numerous individual investors, the program's capitalization amounted to only $250,000 in 1967, far less than the amount needed to develop even the smallest contemporary shopping center.[8]

In promoting his program of black capitalism in the mass media, Sullivan typically described himself first and foremost as a Christian and an American in order to avoid any connection to Black Panther-style radicalism. Sullivan's program received enthusiastic coverage in mainstream publications as diverse as *Ebony*, *US News and World Report*, and *Business Week*, spurring blacks and whites nationwide to subscribe to the 10–36 Plan. One investor from Alaska who read of Sullivan in the conservative *Human Events* magazine wrote, "We honor you for your obviously Americanist approach to the problems which confront our Republic." A white soldier in Vietnam enthusiastically told Sullivan that he "agree[s] with [him] completely that capitalism can and must be shared by both races." Sullivan's vision of African Americans becoming active producers as well as passive consumers, powerful owners as well as lowly workers, and virtuous patriots fighting for the American way relied upon traditional American discourses of self-help, class mobility, and patriotism that would sound familiar and pleasing to white investors from Main Street to Wall Street.[9]

Sullivan's bootstraps rhetoric notwithstanding, Progress Plaza was primarily financed through government support, foundation grants, and commercial financial institutions. Philadelphia's Redevelopment Authority subsidized the project by selling ZIA a four-and-a-half acre cleared site at a prime location on the Broad Street corridor in the Temple University redevelopment zone for the nominal cost of $280,000. This spared ZIA from having to acquire discrete parcels of land and then obtain permits to clear them, not to mention demolition costs. On top of all this, the construction of the shopping center would still cost $1.7 million dollars. The Ford Foundation provided an outright grant in the amount of $400,000 to construct a job-training center for on-site business entrepreneurs and managers plus $700,000 more to run this nonprofit operation. The federal Small Business Administration (SBA) gave $203,000 to support the establishment of job-training programs in business management and entrepreneurial development. Thus throughout the 1970s, the center's managers had their salaries paid for by grants rather than from the revenues of the shopping center itself. Philadelphia National Bank (PNB) gave ZIA a $1.3 million construction loan; it didn't hurt that PNB's head loan officer to the city's black neighborhoods was a Zion Baptist parishioner. Because of PNB's willingness to loan money to ZIA, the Metropolitan Life Insurance Company of

New York, which routinely backed large-scale shopping center projects in both white suburbs and urban downtowns nationwide, agreed to buy the shopping center's long-term mortgage for $1 million.[10]

Although Sullivan was able to integrate his real estate development project into the world of mainstream commercial high finance, he soon found that private-sector funding compromised his ability to make the shopping center a showcase for black capitalism. Sullivan stated in his agreement with the Ford Foundation that the "purpose of ZIA involved putting the black American into the production and distribution of goods and services to the black community and the larger community." This goal, however, often conflicted with commercial lenders' requirements that at least two-thirds of the shopping center's square footage be leased to tenants who received AAA credit ratings from the firm Dun & Bradstreet. Such tenants grossed more than $1 million a year, far beyond the income of the average small business. As a result, only nine of the sixteen initial businesses that signed leases in the Plaza were black-owned. In order to obtain the mortgage from Met Life, ZIA had no choice but to fill seven of the Plaza's vacancies with large white-owned businesses, including Philadelphia National Bank; the Philadelphia Savings Fund Society; Bell Telephone Company; A&P supermarkets; the Jim and Jane Brady retail outlets of the Florsheim Shoes corporation; and the Jr. Hot Shoppes (later renamed Roy Rogers) fast food chain, a division of the Marriott Corporation.[11]

Some in the African American community were put off by the presence of white businesses in what was supposed to be a black shopping center. *Philadelphia Tribune* reporter Joe Hunter called Progress Plaza a "Trojan Horse" that was "black on the outside, white inside." Local shoe store owner William Hardy, who was denied a spot in the center in favor of the Bradys added, "If they think they are going to find Negro businesses with that kind of rating [AAA] they will look for a very long time. Negroes have not had the opportunity to develop their businesses to that extent." Hardy predicted that ZIA would instead encourage white-owned businesses to hire black personnel as fronts. Locals found A&P's presence particularly objectionable. Not only was it white-owned, but shortly after signing its lease in the Plaza it became the target of a nationwide boycott by Jesse Jackson's Operation Breadbasket for its refusal to hire African Americans for anything but menial positions. Many looked dimly on the store's presence in Progress Plaza. "I think blacks want more alternatives other than an A&P setting up shop and taking money out of the community," said local minister Archie Allen, who participated in the boycott.[12]

Hardy's prediction was correct but his interpretation of its meaning was questionable. Progress Plaza leases indeed required that its larger tenants hire African American managers for their branches. ZIA, however, touted this as a victory because it would give "Negroes for the first time . . . an opportunity to manage and learn of the workings of large corporations." This goal dovetailed with the establishment of a managerial training center on the site by Sullivan's OIC. Subsequent press releases from the Plaza's white businesses highlighted these high-profile black hires, especially those who were graduates of the OIC job-training program. A&P particularly touted its black-operated Plaza store in response to the Operation Breadbasket boycott.[13]

Perhaps in response to community criticism, several months after leasing the rest of the center, ZIA struck a deal to bring in one of the very few African American businesses in the nation large enough to earn an AAA credit rating: the North Carolina Mutual Insurance Company. One of the largest life insurance firms serving the African American market, the seventy-year-old company held over $94 million in assets and had 800,000 policyholders across the nation. Based out of Durham and operating largely through traveling sales agents, NC Mutual had been a respected institution in the lives of Philadelphia's African American community for generations. Having a retail outlet of this firm added tremendous prestige value to the Plaza and helped silence critics of its rental policy.[14]

ZIA officials challenged detractors by arguing that its large white tenants created business for smaller tenants and thus facilitated the presence of African American entrepreneurs. They negotiated higher lease rates from established white businesses in order to subsidize lower rents for the nine smaller black-owned stores in the center. On top of higher fixed rental rates, the larger stores were required to pay an additional percentage rental on their gross profits, ranging from 1.5 percent to 5 percent. Percentage leases such as these were standard practice for shopping centers nationwide. ZIA's not demanding percentage rentals from its smaller tenants clearly was intended to help black businesses that could not afford to move into the shopping center otherwise. "Giving the small businessmen a chance represents high risk for us," Sullivan explained. "They'll make it, we hope. But if they go bankrupt we're left holding the bag." In this sense, ZIA found itself trapped between the political goal of fostering black capitalism and its own economic goal of becoming a successful business venture within the existing constraints of the commercial marketplace.[15]

In considering what was best for the long-term viability of the center, ZIA wanted to ensure profitability. Elmer Young, general manager of the Plaza, responded to criticisms that Sullivan had compromised his black capitalist vision by saying that, like any corporation, ZIA had "to answer to our stockholders too." One such stockholder and Zion church member specifically took issue with the idea that the Plaza should be "a mere relocating project for Negro business" and insisted that it must be "a sound investment program, not a speculation." Alfonso Jackson, a ZIA official who would soon take over Young's position, chided area residents for expecting the organization to behave differently than would any other commercial venture. "[A]s Negro stockholders in our FIRST investment venture, Negro or otherwise, we certainly are eager to participate in a successful as well as profitable venture," he wrote. "Just facing the financial facts of American big business, we should be able to understand that such an Afro-American enterprise, emerging for the first time, is dependent and must accept some of the existing principles of business in order to be created." Jackson noted optimistically that once Progress Plaza and similar ventures were established, then they could challenge the conventional wisdom of Wall Street. Until that time, he hoped the community was not "condemning these first group steps of your African American brothers to step across the new frontiers of large scale business."[16]

Sullivan personally responded to his critics at the Plaza's dedication ceremony in October 1968. "I front for no one but God," Sullivan proclaimed. "All of this—all of these buildings are owned by Negroes," he boomed proudly to the assembled masses, noting that "these corporations and chain stores will be paying rent to black people." While touting the Plaza for giving birth to a black landlord class to whom white chain stores were beholden, Sullivan downplayed the negative effects that populating his center with large retailers would have on black entrepreneurial tenants, who would occupy less than half of the Plaza. Once the center opened for business, Sullivan and ZIA would be confronted with the difficulties of preserving even that small sphere of black capitalism.[17]

SMALL BUSINESS VERSUS BIG BUSINESS AT PROGRESS PLAZA

Once the fanfare surrounding Progress Plaza's opening died down, ZIA was confronted with the difficulties of daily operations in the retail business. Some of the tenants and shopping center managers were congregants of Zion Baptist who had no previous experience. They faced a steep learning curve. There was turnover in upper management after only one year of operation when the shopping center's general manager Elmer Young resigned to oversee development of another ZIA shopping center project in San Francisco, which subsequently never materialized. His replacement Alfonso Jackson described himself as "still in the process of learning the ropes" after accepting the position in January 1970. Management consistently had problems collecting rent from small businesses, whose financial status—like those of most small businesses—remained precarious. By 1971, two stores had closed and were replaced with new tenants, another was up for sale, and two shops were past due with the rent.[18]

Progress Plaza failed to turn a profit during its first five years of existence. Even when the shopping center finally made money, ZIA as a whole still finished in the red due to its unprofitable garment manufacturing and aerospace equipment operations. When ZIA opened the 10–36 Plan to an additional 4,000 investors in 1971, it had to file a report with the U.S. Securities and Exchange Commission (SEC). The SEC prospectus associated several risk factors with the company. ZIA admitted that it had not paid dividends to investors so far, nor was there "immediate prospect for their payment."

Moreover, it could give "no assurances . . . respecting . . . future operations or whether they [shares in ZIA] will be profitable." ZIA also admitted that the growth of the company thus far was "to a large extent attributable" to Reverend Sullivan himself rather than the performance of ZIA management. Lacking his charismatic leadership and extensive connections with the white power establishment, ZIA had done little to prove itself a viable competitor in the private marketplace. In compliance with SEC regulations, ZIA had to offer 10–36 Plan subscribers the ability to withdraw from the program due to its poor prospects. It lost 349 shareholders.[19]

When the ZIA Board of Directors initially debated what to make of these losses, it asserted that profitability was a lesser goal than community improvement, stating that "the program was designed as one of faith which has made significant contributions to many [black] lives" in terms of employment, the opening of managerial positions in white firms, and learning how to start businesses. The Board concluded that "If the subscriber is merely a 'faultfinder' perhaps it is for the best that they withdraw now." Yet ZIA continued to appeal to the symbolism of black power to attract new investors—many of them from outside the black community—despite the admittedly high financial risks. "Much publicity has and will surround the SEC filing of this unique, minority-owned investment program," the firm's attorney stated, citing buzz on Wall Street and in the media after a recent appearance by Reverend Sullivan in New York's St. Paul's Cathedral, "Quite a momentum seems to be developing." The 10–36 Plan ultimately attracted 6,000 investors who waited until 1991 to receive their first dividend of $12 per share.[20]

ZIA ultimately found itself trapped between its twin goals of community empowerment and corporate profitability. A 1971 audit by Lucas Tucker and Company pointed to several serious problems, among them a lack of long-range planning, an inability "to find competent Black management" and the "substantial liability" created by investors leaving the 10–36 Plan. For Progress Plaza in particular, the audit criticized ZIA for not "receiving the best price for its space" and noted that rising costs of operating the center "are not recoverable from tenants." The audit recommended that the firm evict all nonprofits from the center and focus more on its bottom line. ZIA would have to move decisively, one way or another, to save Progress Plaza. It would become either a community center with a few low-end shopping options or a state-of-the-art facility that operated according to the sometimes racially biased tenets of capitalism.[21]

Over the next three years ZIA, behind Sullivan's leadership, made changes in the operations of Progress Plaza, moving decisively toward the bottom line as its key pursuit. It did this by bringing in white-owned chain stores and discontinuing the unsustainable favoritism toward its smaller black tenants. Chains like Kinney Shoes, Sherwin-Williams Paints, Charlie's Small Fry (a local children's clothing store chain), and Montgomery Ward all joined the shopping center by 1974 and were charged a higher gross-percentage rental than previous tenants. As a result of this "decisive management action," the center was able to stem losses and for the first time "about break even" for the year. According to ZIA President Frederick Miller, "In previous reports, the Center had as many as 3 tenants with delinquent rent accounts and an uncertain future . . . these operations have been replaced with more viable tenants. . . . Thus, the shopping center is no longer subsidizing rent accounts." ZIA began charging its smaller, black tenants more as well. They would now be assessed additional rents based upon their annual percentage sales. ZIA also increased their per-square-footage rental costs to be more like those paid by the chains. By this time the ZIA had moved explicitly to a policy emphasizing chain stores, with Sullivan telling the board of directors that he now "realiz[ed] that the triple-A ratables will be the major factors in anchoring our center." He resigned himself to the precariousness of black-owned small business, stating that "we can continue to expect small inexperienced entrepreneurs to encounter problems. Some will survive; others won't."[22]

Small businesses could not keep up and by 1978 nearly every black-owned store in Progress Plaza fell behind in its rent payments. As these businesses failed, they were replaced by chain stores. A stationary store was replaced by a Radio Shack. A men's clothing store relocated to a less expensive site in New Jersey and its space in Progress Plaza was taken over by the Bell Telephone store's expansion. Although some ZIA board members expressed their concern that "caution be taken not to deplete minority participation in the Plaza," the fact was that few black-owned businesses could meet the stringent financial requirements to succeed there. Plus, the chain-store-anchored Progress Plaza was ZIA's only profitable venture. Due to the failure of its manufacturing operations, ZIA faced pressure to tighten its terms with the remaining small black tenants in the center and by 1981 was adopting a zero-tolerance policy including late fees for back rent. "The Plaza is 12 years old and we do not need to artificially sustain tenants any longer," management decreed. "[I]f they become disgruntled and move, we will be rid of a 'deadbeat.'" ZIA paid lip service to its adherence to "the original concept . . . that some special rental consideration be given to Minority Businesses," even as it moved to evict some of the center's original black tenants. On the other hand, the chains did well. The Plaza's A&P outlet was one of the most successful in the Greater Philadelphia area, generating annual sales over $6 million. Ironically, it seemed that the center gained more community patronage the more its stores were like those at suburban shopping centers.[23]

Even the goodwill of a black community determined to demonstrate economic empowerment could not keep small shops open for long periods of time. Ducky's Dashery, an original black tenant, was one such case. Ducky Birts owned and operated a men's clothing store in Camden, New Jersey in the 1960s. He was an early supporter of Sullivan's 10–36 Plan, purchasing three shares for himself and his two sons. When he heard about Progress

Plaza, he decided to move his business. "Rev. Sullivan was with the economics, and that's where my head was," Birts recalled, "it was an honor and a pleasure to service my people with first-class merchandise." Ducky's Dashery succeeded initially, especially with ZIA's rent subsidies, but by 1978 flat sales and rent increases had caused Birts to close his shop. He went on to start a women's store on Wadsworth Avenue in a diverse area of the city that was becoming gentrified.[24]

Although Progress Plaza remained marginally successful throughout the 1980s, its positive economic effects on its North Philadelphia neighborhood waned over time. Despite its profitability, the A&P supermarket which anchored the center nearly closed in the late 1970s as part of a corporate restructuring to shutter several smaller, older stores and concentrate on new and expanding markets. Sixty-eight Philadelphia-area outlets were slated for closure, threatening 7,000 jobs. Rather than risk the negative publicity, however, A&P instead elected to work with the United Food and Commercial Workers Union to bring down labor costs in order to make the stores—which were to be rebranded Super Fresh supermarkets—more profitable. The union agreed to an across-the-board pay cut of 15 percent in order to keep jobs at the Progress Plaza store and elsewhere. Although the supermarket workers' wages fell, the supermarket's prices rose. In 1995, an investigative journalist found that Progress Plaza's Super Fresh outlet charged higher prices for basics such as meat and produce than did a comparable chain store in the neighboring white lower-middle income area of Northeast Philadelphia. By the shopping center's 25th anniversary in 1993, only the North Carolina Mutual Life Insurance Company remained of the original ten black tenants, as opposed to three of the original seven white tenants. Five years later, the center picked up another black-owned business, this one a mom-and-pop beauty salon. Many of Progress Plaza's smaller store tenants were replaced by Asian American entrepreneurs.[25]

African American merchants were now far more likely to be found among the ranks of the street vendors who congregated in the parking lot and sidewalks around the Plaza. Although the city did not permit street vending in this location, the ZIA had allowed them to operate there since the 1960s in the spirit of community economic empowerment. Plaza vendor Rasheed Gordon viewed his work as "grassroots economics" and "the only way for people of little means to establish some form of self-employment and participation in the economy." Vendors sold everything from clothing to books and records to personal care products. By the late 1970s, however, Plaza management and some tenants viewed them as a drain. The First Pennsylvania Bank complained that sidewalk vendors were "reducing their sales." Some of the center's small black business tenants also grumbled about the "on-going conflict of similar merchandise being offered by the vendors." Other stores in the Plaza, however, welcomed their presence. The manager of a women's clothing store said, "We have no problems with the vendors. In fact, they bring customers to us. People come here to get specific things from them and happen to look in our windows and come in. . . . They keep the sidewalks clean, they alert us of known shoplifters, and they're very aware of anything suspicious and warn us."[26]

By 1996, ZIA no longer welcomed the vendors and decided to evict them, which led to a public outcry that forced the organization to reconsider its position. Progress Plaza General Manager Mack Washington requested that the city's License & Inspections Department crack down on illegal street vending in the Plaza. Washington told vendors that they would be fined if they did not move. Vendors pointed out the hypocrisy of ZIA's opposition to them, considering the center's small-black-capitalism roots. "We feel that this place was built for African American economic progress," said vendor Mustafa Brown. "Here we are, trying to do business in our own community. We bring money in, and we spend it here. And they're trying to push us out." Brown noted that "to eject us goes against the principles on which this place was founded." Community activists lobbied to change city regulations in order to keep vending alive at Progress Plaza but local politicians warned that racial preferences could not become the basis for choosing who would be allowed to operate. Ward leader Shirley Kitchen said, "We can't just say to the Asians, 'Just get out,' because they deserve to be there, too. We don't want to start with hard feelings." Ultimately, ZIA abandoned its unpopular anti-vending plan.[27]

TRYING TO REPLICATE THE PROGRESS PLAZA PARADIGM

Progress Plaza quickly found adherents among white conservatives who embraced black capitalism as an alternative to the social programs that proliferated in President Lyndon B. Johnson's Great Society. Richard Nixon made black capitalism a part of his 1968 presidential campaign platform, promising to enact programs to give African Americans "a piece of the economic action." Nixon was so taken with the idea of the Plaza that he made it a campaign stop. Before a miniscule crowd of twenty people (compared to the thousands who rallied to his support in the Philadelphia suburbs later that same day), Nixon congratulated Sullivan on the center's opening and pledged to provide financial support for similar black-led commercial real estate ventures. Once he was elected, Nixon delivered on these promises. He renewed the Johnson Administration's support for Sullivan's OIC and pushed the SBA to grant the Zion Non-Profit Charitable Trust $650,000 to establish the Progress Development Services Corporation (PDSC), a consulting firm designed to help black community groups nationwide start their own commercial development projects modeled on the public/private funding structure of Progress Plaza.[28]

Although public support for this idea was strong, private aversions arose, particularly from white financial institutions and store owners who lacked confidence in the ghetto as a burgeoning market. An International Council of Shopping Centers (ICSC) program subsidized by the SBA failed to build any black-owned centers due to a lack of interest from the chain store tenants needed to obtain financing. Consequently, the ICSC program abandoned its original black ownership goal to focus merely on placing African Americans into management positions in white-owned shopping centers, as had happened in Progress Plaza. The PDSC program initially planned to open six black-owned shopping centers a year but by 1972 had only two—one in Harrisburg and one in Phoenix. "If you're a black guy building in a black area, the triple-AAA stores don't even want to talk to you," PDSC administrator James Swann reported. In both Harrisburg and Phoenix, the PDSC could not find a supermarket chain willing to anchor the centers, so it instead helped local black entrepreneurs found their own grocery stores. On the heels of the urban riots of the 1960s, which caused many of the small white retailers who had traditionally served the ghetto to abandon it for good, it was hard to persuade larger chain stores, many of which had never had stores in the inner city, that it was to their benefit to invest in these neighborhoods. White capitalists were unwilling to risk their bottom line in order to engage in social experimentation. An unnamed chain store executive told the *Washington Post* that "People in our company still have scars" from the riots, and feared a "get whitey" attitude they saw as pervasive in black neighborhoods. Public subsidies were not enough. Without private capital and grassroots support, these inner-city operations would not survive. Sullivan and the PDSC program wound up developing only a handful of black-owned shopping centers throughout the 1970s, including the Haddington Shopping Plaza in the West Philadelphia ghetto.[29]

Sullivan, the PDSC, and the ZIA failed to replicate their initial success when they tried to develop the Strawberry Square shopping center in 1979 in the low-income Strawberry Mansion area of North Philadelphia. Even in the shadow of Progress Plaza, the Strawberry Square project could not attract any AAA-rated supermarket. As the project stalled, the City of Philadelphia stepped in to offer generous subsidies to get it started. The city promised to pay 90 percent of the rents on Strawberry Square's smaller stores and even found a local supermarket to anchor the site. Without a chain supermarket, however, developers claimed that they could not obtain commercial financing, and by 1982 PDSC and ZIA had pulled out of the Strawberry Mansion project altogether, leaving other community groups to try to get it off the ground. It seems that the ZIA decided that no degree of initial public subsidy would be sufficient to ensure a successful shopping center without chain tenants over the long haul.[30]

There were still those in the ZIA, however, who refused to accept this doctrine. They became the backbone of a new community group bent on completing the Strawberry Square project. ZIA member Reverend Thomas Ritter believed that "independent black ownership has more meaning toward development of a middle class and jobs" than simply bringing chain stores to the ghetto. He left ZIA and founded his own nonprofit organization to revive the Strawberry Square project. Returning to the original goals of the PDSC that favored black entrepreneurship over the credit-worthiness of chain stores, Ritter partnered with commercial developer Robert Gassel and received strong public support for the project. Ritter obtained a $2.5 million construction loan from the Philadelphia Savings Fund Society (PSFS), backed by a $2.2 million loan guarantee from the City of Philadelphia, as well as smaller loans from Philadelphia National Bank, the Philadelphia Industrial Development Corporation, and the Philadelphia Citywide Development Corporation. His 65,000-square-foot center integrated street vendors who paid a nominal rent. And rather than lease to a white-owned supermarket, he arranged for a worker-owned cooperative supermarket to take over the center's anchor site. Seventy-five area workers gave between $2,500 and $5,000 each to found the co-op and paid the Philadelphia Association of Cooperative Enterprises (PACE) $1.5 million to train them to manage a grocery store. The supermarket was called O&O, which stood for Owned and Operated.[31]

Within two years of Strawberry Square's 1985 opening, however, O&O faced bankruptcy. The anchor store proved unprofitable and was unable to generate sufficient foot traffic to funnel customers to the rest of the stores in the shopping center. Although conceding that the store was badly managed, the O&O board of directors blamed its failure on the poor training its owner-workers received from PACE and claimed that city officials who had oversight of the center's operations should have intervened sooner. PACE blamed the intrusion of neighborhood activists. Neighborhood activists blamed the co-op for overstaffing the store and thereby cutting into profits. City officials pointed the finger at the basic cooperative structure of the supermarket, which lacked the expertise of "private sector owners with experience." Regardless of the cause of O&O's miserable performance, Ritter was "caught between a rock and a hard place," and reluctantly evicted O&O. Reeling from the absence of an anchor tenant, Strawberry Square defaulted on its major construction loan in 1989, causing the City of Philadelphia to have to pay $2.2 million to PSFS. Only when the shopping center finally obtained a chain supermarket in 1991 to replace O&O was it able to recover financially and repay the city.[32]

Progress Plaza officials faced a huge challenge in 1998 after A&P made good on its longstanding threat to leave when it declined to renew the lease on its Super Fresh supermarket. Citing the small store size—it was 17,300-square-feet in an era when 60,000-square-feet was considered state-of-the-art—A&P gave ZIA less than one week's notice that it would be closing. ZIA scrambled to find a replacement. The major regional chains passed. Only the Raspino/Wargo Corporation, which operated two Super Foodtown supermarkets in the West Philadelphia ghetto, indicated some interest. But Super Foodtown stores were non-union, thus Super Fresh employees could only be rehired with lower wages and fewer benefits. Moreover, A&P would only guarantee the jobs of managers and senior store employees by reassigning them to other outlets, sometimes at a much lower salary and rank. Thus the closing of the store would be a hard hit to its sixty unionized employees. The United Food and Commercial Union Local 1776 obtained a court injunction preventing A&P from shuttering the store on such short notice and then transferring the lease to Raspino/Wargo, citing a Philadelphia ordinance that required firms to give the city sixty days' notice before closing, as well as the union's contractual right of first refusal to purchase and operate the store. Union lawyer Nancy B.G. Lassen framed the union's case as standing up for the residents of the North Philadelphia ghetto: "we in the union can take care of ourselves. . . . But what are you going to do about the community? We're hoping the city will wake up and smell the roses and get involved in this matter." The union's actions forced ZIA into a precarious position. It needed to have a supermarket in Progress Plaza, regardless of wages and employee benefits. But the anchor site in the shopping center would remain inactive while ZIA was tied up in the court battle between A&P and the union.[33]

Once this snafu was resolved, however, the aging shopping center was in a great position to revitalize its business with the planned development of Jump Street USA, a $50 million retail and entertainment complex slated for the site of an old movie theater directly across Broad Street from the Plaza. After Leon Sullivan's death in 2001, the ZIA Board of Directors sought to partner with established shopping center developers Kravco—owners of the nationally-known King of Prussia suburban mega-mall—to transform the Plaza into a vibrant, mixed-use space including lofts, offices, restaurants, and rehabilitated storefronts. But when Kravco was acquired by national shopping mall developers Simon Property Group it backed out of the deal. ZIA again turned to public sector resources, this time a $500,000 grant from a Pennsylvania state initiative to bring grocery stores to depressed communities. "You can't build communities without access to healthy and affordable food," said Pennsylvania Secretary of Community and Economic Development Dennis Yablonsky. Sullivan's program of community economic empowerment had been trumped by the urgent need to maintain basic public health in North Philadelphia by facilitating community access to a commercial supermarket.[34]

ZIA also set up a new nonprofit trust to pursue funding for redevelopment, which in some ways echoed its original strategy of the 1960s. The trust's mission, however, was quite different than the original vision for Progress Plaza. Rather than to promote black capitalism, the trust revived the center in order to remedy fundamental problems that had emerged in North Philadelphia, namely public health concerns. ZIA partnered with a local nonprofit dedicated to bringing grocery stores into impoverished urban communities. But even with such help, it was difficult to attract a supermarket chain to the center because the anchor site was too small. The trust would need to triple the size of its supermarket space in order to attract a viable tenant. With the financial support of the nonprofit, as well as donations from other organizations and the City of Philadelphia, the trust was able to raise $20 million to redevelop the supermarket space and the rest of Progress Plaza. By then the trust's black capitalist goals were significantly less ambitious than in the 1960s, simply looking to hire construction workers from the community rather than insisting on black entrepreneurship.[35]

Progress Plaza's history demonstrates that the same plasticity which made black power such a popular concept during the 1960s and 1970s left it open for diverse and contradictory interpretations and uses in later years. For Progress Plaza's African American neighbors, workers, and consumers, the shopping center itself could be a symbol of communal pride—proof that the capitalist engine of the postwar economy churned in the ghetto, too. Yet in terms of promoting black capitalism, Progress Plaza arguably had a negative impact on the community, bringing white-controlled big business into the heart of the ghetto in ways that compromised black entrepreneurship. Sullivan's bid for black empowerment raised the bar for inclusion in the neighborhood's premiere commercial center beyond the means of most small local businesses, displaced African American tenants and vendors, and increased African American patronage of white-owned businesses. At Progress Plaza, much of the capital flowed out of the community into the pockets of white chain store owners and the white-owned banks that financed its development. Ultimately, Progress Plaza did achieve Sullivan's goal of bringing the mainstream capitalist economy into the black community. But it failed to make black capitalism the equal of white capitalism, leaving it open for exploitation in ways that resonated more with the colonialist critique of black power radicals like the Black Panther Party than a believer in American capitalism like Sullivan would ever want to admit.

NOTES

1. "Negro Community Dedicates $1.7 Million Progress Plaza," *Evening Bulletin*, October 28, 1968; "Dr. Leon Sullivan Hits 'Front Man' Charge in Progress Plaza Speech, *Philadelphia Tribune*, October 29, 1968.
2. Sullivan quoted in "Negro Community Dedicates."
3. Robert Weems and Lewis Randolph, *Business in Black and White: American Presidents and Black Entrepreneurs in the Twentieth Century* (New York: NYU Press, 2009); Robert O. Self, *American Babylon: Race and the Struggle for Postwar Oakland* (Princeton: Princeton University Press, 2004); Matthew Countryman, *Up South: Civil Rights and Black Power in Philadelphia* (Philadelphia: University of Pennsylvania Press, 2005), 110; Guian McKee, *The Problem of Jobs: Liberalism, Race, and Deindustrialization in Philadelphia* (Chicago: University of Chicago Press, 2008).
4. Leon Sullivan, *Build, Brother, Build* (Philadelphia: Macrae Smith, 1969), 162.
5. Sullivan, *Build*, 162–66.
6. Sullivan, *Build*, 169–70; "ZIA Agreement with Ford Foundation," March 31, 1971, Opportunities Industrialization Centers of America Records, Temple

University Urban Archives, (hereafter cited as "TUUA OICA"), Box 73, Folder 27; "Break Ground Sunday for Zion Baptist Group's Apt. Project," *Philadelphia Tribune*, July 17, 1965; "Zion Baptist Church Investment Group in Another Step Forward," *Philadelphia Tribune*, September 25, 1965.

7. Sullivan, *Build*, 166–67; Gregory Lake, "3 Cheers for Rev Sullivan," *Philadelphia Tribune*, February 18, 1967.
8. McKee, *Problem of Jobs*, 182–210; Sullivan, *Build*, 162.
9. "Black Church Launches Space Factory," *Ebony*, November 1968, 42; "Black Capitalism at Work: What's Happening in Philadelphia," *US News & World Report*, February 17, 1969, 64; *Business Week* article from November 2, 1968 cited in letter from Roy E. Platt to Leon Sullivan, November 15, 1968; Collin A. Niver to Leon Sullivan, December 17, 1968; SSG James C. Reesman to Leon Sullivan, March 8, 1969. Last three sources all from TUUA OICA, Box 75, Folder 2.
10. Elmer Young, Jr., "Zion Gardens Not for Poor Only," *Philadelphia Tribune*, August 1, 1967; "ZIA Agreement with Ford Foundation"; "Negro-Operated Shopping Center Gets $400,000," *Philadelphia Tribune*, April 15, 1967; "'School' for Negro Businessmen Comes with $400,000 Grant," *Philadelphia Tribune*, July 29, 1967; "Negro Project to Get Money of Ford Fund," *Philadelphia Bulletin*, September 29, 1968; "17 New Stores Owned by Negroes, Received Loans from SBA Setup," *Philadelphia Tribune*, February 4, 1969; "Negroes to Open a Shopping Center," *New York Times*, September 29, 1968; J. Lester Blocker, "The Story of Progress Plaza," *Banking*, August 1969, 41, 78.
11. "ZIA Agreement with Ford Foundation"; Joe Hunter, "Progress Plaza Shopping Center Said to Shun Negro Business," *Philadelphia Tribune*, November 14, 1967; "Negro-Owned Shopping Center Set to Open with Six White Companies," *Philadelphia Bulletin*, September 16, 1968.
12. Hardy quoted in "Progress Plaza Shopping Center Said to Shun Negro Business"; Allen quoted in "Operation Breadbasket Picketing A&P Stores," *Philadelphia Tribune*, October 8, 1968.
13. "Negroes to Own 50% of Shops, Progress Plaza Planners Say," *Philadelphia Tribune*, November 18, 1967; "The 1st Penna Bank Manager in Progress Plaza Lauds Company," *Philadelphia Tribune*, November 30, 1968; "Savings Fund Society Branch Manager in Progress Plaza 'Sure' of Success," *Philadelphia Tribune*, November 30, 1968; "A&P Supermarket in Progress Plaza Has Everything You Need," *Philadelphia Tribune*, November 19, 1968.
14. "NC Mutual Signs Progress Plaza Lease," *Philadelphia Tribune*, April 23, 1968. Also see Walter B. Weare, *Black Business in the New South: A Social History of the NC Mutual Life Insurance Company* (Durham: Duke University Press, 1993).
15. Sullivan quoted in "Negro-Owned Shopping Center Set to Open with Six White Companies."
16. Young quoted in "Negroes to Open a Shopping Center"; Jackson quoted in B. Taylor, "Progress Plaza Must Return Profit," *Philadelphia Tribune*, December 2, 1967; Unnamed ZIA stockholder quoted in A.J. Jackson, "A Progress Plaza Stockholder Defends 'Exclusive' Leases," *Philadelphia Tribune*, December 2, 1967.
17. Sullivan quoted in "Dr. Leon Sullivan Hits 'Front Man' Charge."
18. "Progress Plaza Head Resigns to Take Post on West Coast," *Philadelphia Tribune*, January 20, 1970; ZIA Board of Directors Meeting Minutes, February 2, 1970, TUUA OICA, Box 72, Folder "ZIA Board of Directors Meeting Minutes 1970–73"; Report of Progress Plaza Shopping Center, July 27, 1971, TUUA OICA, Box 74, Folder 19.

19. "ZIA Agreement with Ford Foundation."
20. ZIA Board of Directors Meeting Minutes, October 12, 1971 and January 12, 1972, TUUA OICA, Box 72, Folder "ZIA Board of Directors Meeting Minutes 1970–73." ZIA attorney quoted in October 12, 1971 minutes; Vincent Thompson, "Sullivan celebrates 'a dream fulfilled," *Philadelphia Tribune*, August 24, 1993.
21. Lucas, Tucker and Co, "ZIA Inc and Subsidiaries summary findings," December 31, 1971, TUUA OICA, Box 73, Folder 34.
22. Frederick Miller letter to ZIA Board of Directors, December 19, 1973, TUUA OICA, Box 72; Frederick Miller letter to ZIA Board of Directors, September 17, 1975, TUUA OICA, Box 73, Folder 38; Frederick Miller letter to ZIA Board of Directors, January 21, 1976, TUUA OICA, Box 72; ZIA Board of Directors meeting minutes, October 26, 1976, TUUA OICA, Box 72.
23. "Progress Investment Associates, Inc. Operations Analysis," January 1, 1977, TUUA OICA, Box 72.
24. Thompson, "Sullivan celebrates"; Birts quoted in Herbert Lowe, "Progress Plaza to Mark 30 Years in Business," *Philadelphia Inquirer*, September 21, 1998.
25. Lowe, "Progress Plaza to Mark"; Sherry Stone, "Prices, Quality, and Variety Differ in Philly Grocery Stores," *Philadelphia Tribune*, August 4, 1995.
26. All quotes from Marjorie Valbrun, "Vendors balk at eviction orders," *Philadelphia Inquirer*, April 1, 1996.
27. Frederick Miller letters to ZIA Board, May 31 and November 17, 1976, TUUA OICA, Box 72; Progress Investment Associates Board of Directors meeting, December 18, 1979 and January 23, 1980, TUUA OICA, Box 72; Brown and Kitchen quoted in Valbrun, "Vendors balk at eviction orders".
28. Nixon quoted in Robert Semple, Jr., "Nixon Visits Negro Slum and Warns White Suburbs," *New York Times*, September 22, 1968; Burt Schorr, "Shattered Dreams," *Wall Street Journal*, May 1, 1972.
29. Swann and unnamed executive quoted in Schorr, "Shattered Dreams."
30. Linn Washington, "Spring Start for Strawberry Square," *Philadelphia Daily News*, January 31, 1984.
31. Leslie Scism, "Churches Constructing Shopping Centers," *New York Times*, July 14, 1991; Ritter quoted in Maida Odom, "Seeking Cause for Grocery's Woes," *Philadelphia Inquirer*, March 30, 1987.
32. Ritter quoted in Odom, "Seeking Cause for Grocery's Woes."
33. Herbert Lowe, North Phila Supermarket to close," *Philadelphia Inquirer*, August 21, 1998; Richard G. Barnes, "North Phila Super Fresh will remain open for two months," *Philadelphia Tribune*, August 21, 1998; Lassen quoted in Herbert Lowe, "Judge to rule on store's closing," *Philadelphia Inquirer*, August 22, 1998.
34. Lowe, "Judge to rule on store's closing"; Progress Investment Associates board of directors meeting, November 18, 1977, TUUA OICA, Box 72; ZIA board of directors meeting minutes, April 21 and May 19, 1981, TUUA OICA, Box 73; Vincent Thompson, "Sullivan celebrates 'a dream fulfilled,'" *Philadelphia Tribune*, August 24, 1993; "Vendors Balk at Eviction Orders"; Vernon Clark, "Redevelopment Plan in North Philadelphia Dropped," *Philadelphia Inquirer*, January 2, 2004; Dennis Yablonsky quoted in Anthony S. Twyman, "500,000 for Progress Plaza Effort," *Philadelphia Inquirer*, August 10, 2005.
35. Twyman, "500,000 for Progress."

11 Black Power on the Factory Floor

Kieran W. Taylor

Under the banner of black power, African American activists undertook an ambitious array of cultural, political, and economic initiatives during the late 1960s and early 1970s. These efforts, built upon prior civil rights victories and the era's rising spirit of militancy, had an enormous impact. More than 1,000 newly elected African Americans took office. African American studies programs sprung up at colleges and high schools across the nation. Black entrepreneurs, working with government officials, reflected the contemporary shift toward African American economic growth by launching a series of banking and business enterprises. The most ambitious of these projects was a 5,000-acre planned community in North Carolina called Soul City, which was funded by the U.S. Department of Housing and Urban Development.[1]

Black activists also concentrated on transforming the American workplace. Sometimes these efforts emerged when rank-and-file workers responded to grievances and injustices on the job. Other times, they were part of radical campaigns to establish a socialist movement in the United States. The 1964 Civil Rights Act gave black workers new tools to challenge racist employment practices that relegated them to low-paying menial positions, excluded them from trades, and exposed them to brutality and dangerous conditions. The expansion of the public and service sectors during this era opened up thousands of jobs to African Americans, making the workplace an important site of struggle. A series of events—the 1968 Memphis sanitation workers' strike, the formation of all-black union caucuses, and a wave of wildcat strikes by black autoworkers—fused civil rights activism with organized labor campaigns, signaling the revival of a tradition that had been driven into remission by Cold War anticommunism.[2]

New Jersey autoworker Wilbur Haddock's path to activism typified the newfound determination by rank-and-file workers to extend the black freedom struggle to the shop floor. Haddock, who played college football and later fought in the Korean War, began working at the Ford Motor Company's Mahwah facility thirty miles north of his Newark home in the late 1950s. Mahwah was one of the company's largest and most productive assembly plants. Nearly half of Mahwah's workforce was African American, but discriminatory housing practices and public transportation routes forced half of them to carpool from Newark, Harlem, and the Bronx. During these long drives, Haddock and his coworkers discussed how black workers were concentrated in the body shop, where they were treated unfairly by white foremen and denied access to higher-paying positions.[3]

There had been labor disputes at Mahwah for years and a national strike closed the plant for two months in 1967, but when Haddock and his colleagues took their concerns to the United Auto Workers (UAW) they found the union to be unresponsive. So they brought their case to local civil rights organizations, including the Bronx chapter of the Congress of Racial Equality (CORE), and learned that such racial discrimination was widespread. Partnerships with other worker groups confirmed that the problems were not unique to Mahwah.[4]

Haddock and his coworkers formed the United Black Brothers (UBB) to represent African American concerns, but doing so presented challenges in bridging the generation gap within Mahwah's black workforce. At first they embraced a black power style—dungarees, boots, afros, leather jackets with political pins—that appealed to younger workers. They eventually realized, however, that they were alienating potential allies, especially older workers, so they decided to cut their hair and adopt a less confrontational image. This pragmatism, although it cost them some support, indicated the organization's efforts to unify Mahwah's African American workforce.[5]

UBB led several hundred black workers in an April 1969 walkout after a colleague was fired by a supervisor who called him a racist epithet. The organization demanded that the UAW allow it to represent African American workers in negotiations with Ford. Although logistically and strategically unprepared for a strike, UBB's connections to radical organizations sustained it. Area members of the Black Panther Party and Students for a Democratic Society lent critical resources and logistical advice, providing supplies and developing systems for feeding picketers, distributing groceries to strikers, and helping them apply for unemployment benefits.[6]

The protest disrupted production for a week and resulted in worker gains. Ford transferred the white supervisor from Mahwah and hired African Americans in departments that had been closed to them. It also fired Haddock and others it perceived to be ringleaders, in part to disrupt the momentum that UBB had achieved. But the organization proved strong over the next year, and under sustained pressure from UBB, Ford reinstated Haddock and the fired strikers with their seniority intact.[7]

MARY MOULTRIE, WILLIAM SAUNDERS, AND THE CHARLESTON HOSPITAL STRIKE

When five black nurses' aides were fired in 1967 following a conflict with their white supervisor, Mary Moultrie approached activist William Saunders to help her organize a campaign that would put an end to the discrimination that she and her black coworkers faced at the Medical College of South Carolina Hospital. Saunders and Moultrie began meeting regularly with low-wage healthcare workers and it soon became clear that their grievances went far beyond the latest incident. As Moultrie reminisced years later, "It was a lot of discrimination, heavy workload, nurses referring to blacks as 'monkey grunts,' and all sorts of things that you either have to tolerate it or you're fired."[8]

Saunders' biography was vital to his activism. Raised near Charleston on Johns Island, he grew up steeped in Gullah culture, which drew from African and Afro-Caribbean sources to forge a unique language and identity. Gullah people were rural and mostly poor—looked down upon not only by whites but also blacks. Marked as an islander by his clothes and speech, the young Saunders knew the importance of race, class, and ethnicity. After being wounded during the Korean War, Saunders returned home in 1954, finished high school, and joined the Johns Island Progressive Club, which had been founded a few years earlier by Esau Jenkins, a successful farmer and community leader.

The Progressive Club was a kind of one-stop shop for black political activity on Johns Island. It was a school for citizenship and voter education, a recreation center, and a cooperatively run grocery store. Saunders became involved in voter registration drives. His affiliation with Jenkins and the Progressive Club also connected him to a national network of activists and associations, including the Student Nonviolent Coordinating Committee (SNCC), the Highlander Folk School, and the Southern Christian Leadership Conference (SCLC), which by the early 1960s had adopted the Johns Island model for educating civic activists across the South. Mary Moultrie also had a history of activism tied to Esau Jenkins. As a teenager she had worked in a restaurant he owned, where she became involved in his voter-registration campaigns.[9]

Saunders had drifted ideologically from Jenkins by the end of the decade. Saunders believed that SCLC nonviolence was counterproductive, arguing that it took from blacks the option of self-defense and the threat of retaliation. He opposed school integration, thinking that it would hurt more African Americans than it would help, because black teachers and administrators would be the first ones to be let go once schools were integrated. These positions infuriated mainstream African American leaders, who petitioned against Saunders's election to the board of the federally funded Office of Economic Opportunity, an antipoverty agency.[10]

Mary Moultrie had spent much of the 1960s employed as a unionized nurse in a New York hospital, but forming a union was neither her goal nor Saunders' when they convened the hospital worker meetings. The labor movement had not been a major force in Charleston since its peak in the 1940s and both were aware that talk of a union could scare potential allies and bring about a ferocious reaction from the hospital and the government.

Furthermore, whereas Moultrie's union experience left her confident in their effectiveness, Saunders's attitude toward unions might be characterized as suspicious. "We were not looking for a union; we were looking for a hospital workers' association, because we saw unions at that time being almost as bad as management," he recalled. "But we wanted an association, and our argument was strong then and it is strong today, is that the doctors had an association, the nurses had an association, why the hell couldn't the workers have an association?"[11]

The hospital workers' group gained momentum when they returned the fired nurses' aides to work by petitioning the federal Department of Health, Education, and Welfare under the 1964 Civil Rights Act. Attendance at their meetings increased and over the next year Saunders and Moultrie helped black hospital workers identify their issues and take action. "They had to be the ones to recognize that they had a problem," Saunders said. "When these nurses stood up, that was the problem. And we were able to settle the problem for them—back on the job, back in, the whole thing, but we were able to say to them also, 'Now, what about the other people in the hospital that don't have enough nerve that you have?'" The core group then recruited additional workers who registered their own complaints. The pay scale offered many African American employees less than the federal minimum wage. Some were forced to take lunch breaks in the boiler room.[12]

The unity of the Charleston workers attracted attention from outside the city, even as hospital officials ignored their concerns. Looking to expand its base beyond New York City, Drug and Hospital Workers Local 1199 sent key organizers to Charleston in late 1968. Despite his wariness of unions, Saunders welcomed Local 1199's assistance. He was aware of its strong reputation for organizing low-wage and non-white workers in New York, as well as its early support of the civil rights struggle. Moreover, Saunders, Moultrie, and other activists recognized that their negotiations with the Medical College were at a standstill and that they would need more pressure to force the hospital to bargain.

Amidst rising tensions between labor and management, hospital administrators dismissed twelve union supporters, including Moultrie, on March 18, 1969. These women had participated in a brief takeover of the hospital president's office and were then fired for tardiness. The following day, 450 Medical College Hospital workers walked off the job demanding the reinstatement of the activists and an end to discrimination. The strikers, almost all of whom were women, were soon joined on the picket lines by another sixty women from the Charleston County Hospital. SCLC organizers came to Charleston to mobilize African American church and community support and to coordinate strategy on the ground.

The mood grew tense in Charleston. Protests disrupted tourism and a boycott of an important shopping corridor put additional pressure on the city's power structure to encourage the hospital to settle. Such marches defied court orders, leading to the mass arrests of workers, their family members, and students, some not yet in their teens. In defiance of an official curfew, strike organizers held nighttime demonstrations and the historic city took on the appearance of a war zone as the National Guard moved in to prevent wider disruption. Facing the constant threat of extralegal violence, Mary Moultrie moved out of her home for her and her family's safety, sleeping on a cot at the union hall under the watchful eyes of armed young people from a local street gang.[13]

When the strike surpassed 100 days, hospital officials agreed to the workers' key demands. The hospital rehired strike leaders, established a new grievance procedure, and provided modest pay increases. In addition to the heat they were under in Charleston, hospital administrators had faced pressure from state politicians in Columbia to avoid bloodshed by bringing about a settlement. Federal officials had also threatened to pull hospital training grants due to discriminatory practices. The union, too, was under pressure to settle. Local 1199 leaders in New York believed that the strike was draining valuable resources from their base and that there was little hope that the fledgling Charleston local would ever contribute much to the union's coffers. The union surrendered on the central issue of official recognition, although it maintained a presence in Charleston under Moultrie's leadership for several months after the strike.[14]

The strike left an ambivalent legacy. The embrace of Local 1199 had been pragmatic. The union was a useful mechanism for drawing attention to the workers' plight and marshaling resources they had not been able to access. After the strike, however, they felt abandoned by Local 1199, which failed to provide them with the necessary training, resources, or personnel to sustain a union local. Saunders also criticized Local 1199 for pulling Moultrie and other key leaders from Charleston during the strike to assist with other union organizing drives. Moultrie had proven to be an effective speaker and she served 1199 as a potent symbol of the continuing fight for African American equality in the South. Although she became central to its expansion strategy, her travels distanced her from the struggle in Charleston, as well as from her coworkers and friends.[15]

JAMES FORMAN, GENERAL BAKER, ED WHITFIELD, AND RAYMOND EURQUHART: BLACK RADICALS TURN TO THE WORKING CLASS

After a decade of ceaseless political activity, James Forman spent much of the fall of 1969 reflecting on his leadership of SNCC, the organization for whom he had served as executive secretary through much of its heyday. During an extended visit to Atlanta he recorded more than twenty-five hours of an oral history intended to summarize the lessons of the previous decade and guide the black freedom movement's strategy for the 1970s. A research trip to Martinique in December offered additional opportunities to reflect, and it was from there that he wrote to colleagues of his growing conviction that the black working class would be the key agent of change during the next phase of the movement. Deeply impressed by a series of strikes and protests by black autoworkers in Detroit, Forman observed that African Americans were disproportionately represented in jobs that were "strategically situated near the centers of mass production," thus giving them the ability to disrupt the economy—a power they might leverage for political gains. According to Forman, these black workers had mostly been ignored by SNCC, whose civil rights reform agenda had "resulted in the middle class of the black community entrenching itself further." Forman pledged to address these errors in the months ahead by "uniting workers, students, farmers, and street brothers into a disciplined, centralized, mass political party or workers organization."[16]

The ferment created by thousands of rank-and-file black workers like Wilbur Haddock and Mary Moultrie signaled to activists that the workplace would be a significant site for organizing in the 1970s. Black radicals had been frustrated with the pace and scope of liberal reform and were disheartened by the growing fractiousness of the movement. Major rifts threated to disunite organizations like SNCC, the Black Panther Party, and CORE. Searching for new ideas and strategies, black radicals looked to African, Asian, and Latin American liberation movements for inspiration, embracing Marxist ideologies to guide their activities. Some took jobs in factories in order to foment rebellions from below against employers and racist labor leaders alike. Others joined trade union bureaucracies and carved out organizing positions that provided varying degrees of support and political independence. Some of those who made this turn to the working class hoped merely to push the labor movement's politics in a more explicitly antiracist and progressive direction. Others aimed to establish an alternative communist party in the United States and gravitated toward organizations that were part of the New Communist Movement of the 1970s.[17]

It would be hard to overstate the significance of the Detroit wildcat strikes in directing the African American Left's attention to the potential for working-class activism. In May of 1968, less than a year after the devastating Detroit Rebellion and a month after Martin Luther King, Jr.'s assassination, a series of seemingly spontaneous strikes at the eight-story Dodge Main plant led to the formation of the Dodge Revolutionary Union Movement (DRUM), a militant organization of black workers. DRUM demanded an end to job discrimination and unsafe working conditions. It also took aim at the UAW, which despite its official support of the mainstream civil rights movement had done little to challenge the industry's racist employment practices and kept African Americans out of union leadership positions. Within a few months, black workers formed Revolutionary Union Movements at other Detroit-area auto plants and employers, such as Blue Cross and Blue Shield, United Parcel Service, Henry Ford Hospital, and the *Detroit News*.[18]

By 1969, local black radicals created an umbrella group—the League of Revolutionary Black Workers—to coordinate factory-based organizing efforts, defend members against reprisals, extend their presence in the community, and connect to groups of black workers in other cities. Propelled by a boundless sense of energy and imagination, League members ran candidates for union office, battled police brutality, advocated local control of schools, and provided legal counsel to defendants in several high-profile political trials. They also launched a publishing house, a film production company, and a study group for whites who wished to support the League.[19]

Radical activists around the nation discovered the League through *Finally Got the News*, a 1970 cinéma vérité film that featured movement leaders in startling and intimate black-and-white footage of production and picket lines. The League was also featured in the pages of periodicals *The Movement*, *Radical America*, and *Guardian*. In its March 1969 edition, *Guardian* devoted a special section to Detroit's "black worker insurgency." Its correspondent declared that the city's "black workers movement is the most important revolutionary action in the country" and that "all the elements are here. The vanguard is here. The workers are here. The guts of monopoly capitalism's production are here. And the conditions are worsening in Detroit's auto plants."[20]

At the center of the black worker protests was a small group of young African American intellectuals who had spent several years attempting to forge an alliance of workers, students, and radical activists. At one time or another, they had each worked in various Detroit-area industries to either earn a living or to make political inroads with the working class. Among them, General Gordon Baker, Jr. provided a key link to black autoworkers. At the end of 1961, Baker, the son and grandson of autoworkers, moved across town to be closer to Highland Park Community College, where he was a student. Sharing a love of partying, politics, and jazz, Baker and two roommates dubbed themselves the Young Turks. They participated in anti-discrimination protests, discussed articles from *Muhammad Speaks* (distributed on campus by the Nation of Islam), and listened to "Radio Free Dixie," a mix of political commentary and black music broadcast from Cuba by North Carolina political exile Robert F. Williams.[21]

After hearing Malcolm X address a February 1962 police brutality protest rally at Olympia Stadium, Baker joined the African Nationalist Pioneer Movement, an offshoot of Marcus Garvey's Universal Negro Improvement Association. He helped run the organization's Detroit bookstore and its various study groups fueled his interest in African American history, culture, and politics. Baker was drawn to the Pioneer Movement's militant style and analysis of racism but grew increasingly frustrated by a contradiction he saw between their fiery rhetoric and feeble practice. After nationalist friends failed to support him when he organized a protest to challenge his draft notice, Baker came to regard them as "weekend militants who wanted to sit up and talk black shit on Saturday and Sunday and go kiss ass all week."[22]

Baker's critique of nationalism reflected a tension within the black liberation movement. Radical black activists, including those who were oriented toward working-class politics, often dismissed cultural nationalism as an updated version of Booker T. Washington's racial uplift philosophy with its emphasis on self-improvement and self-help. They also accused cultural nationalists of failing to confront the racism and poverty that most African Americans faced on a daily basis.[23]

The ideological lines on the left were porous, and incendiary rhetoric often obscured nuance. Inspired by the African liberation struggles, most black activists supported some version of Pan-Africanism—a belief in the shared fate of the African Diaspora's oppressed people. Black activists of all kinds also embraced cultural nationalism. Even as the Black Panther Party, for example, launched bitter polemics against cultural nationalists, sometimes even engaging them in deadly confrontations, it also carried out its own program focused on African American history and cultural pride; Panther berets and leather jackets helped define the era's style. The Panthers painted California-based cultural nationalist organization US as apolitical, but in fact US pursued a top-down political strategy through which it sought to influence the internal practices of black organizations and forge working coalitions among them.[24]

These contradictions and complexities notwithstanding, many African American labor radicals considered cultural nationalism a threat to their efforts to build a black workers' movement and feared it would divert young African Americans from class struggle. Founders of DRUM and the League contended that their early organizing efforts were undermined by cultural nationalists who harassed one of their colleagues for being married to a white woman and opposed their reprinting of articles and speeches by non-black revolutionaries like Che Guevara and Ho Chi Minh. In this regard, Baker proved important. His longstanding relationships with nationalists inoculated DRUM and the League from the worst attacks. As Baker recalled:

> I probably would've been snubbed at and not thought much of, probably would've been attacked by some of them. But I always had a hedge amongst them that nobody else had but me. Even later on during the League and stuff. Nationalists wouldn't move on me and such because I came out of that. It was probably unique, and I didn't realize it was kind of important until I get to looking, when you start looking back.[25]

It was not until Baker transferred to Wayne State University in 1963 that he began to identify a group of black radicals who were more inclined toward direct action and organizing the working class than were cultural nationalists. To protest the Detroit City Council's refusal to pass a fair-housing ordinance, Baker and several comrades in a newly formed student group named Uhuru (Swahili for "freedom") disrupted a municipal ceremony staged to attract the 1968 Summer Olympics to the Motor City. A few months later, in defiance of a U.S. State Department ban on travel to Cuba, Baker and three other Uhuru members were among eighty-four students who traveled to Havana, where they spent time with Robert F. Williams and met Che Guevara and other revolutionaries from around the world. Cuba's "revolutionary laboratory" was revelatory and Baker's conversations with diverse anti-colonial activists pushed him toward multinational Marxism-Leninism. "I just had to go stay in a hotel a couple of days just trying to regroup," he recalled. "Everything you thought you used to know was gone out the window."[26]

Direct contact with anti-colonial activists led many black nationalists to embrace a "Third World Marxism," that attempted to join together colonized workers in the struggle against imperialism and racism. In the summer of 1970, Cornell University student Ed Whitfield relocated to Greensboro, North Carolina to teach math and science at Malcolm X Liberation University, which had been organized as an alternative to white schools. Sharing the Pan-Africanism of the school's founders, Whitfield, a former campus activist and NAACP youth leader in Arkansas, taught African history and culture and encouraged students to develop practical skills like tailoring, architecture, and teaching that would allow them to serve newly liberated African nations. But Whitfield's views shifted as he met African students and deepened his understanding of African politics. A stint in Liberia working on a land development project convinced him that Liberians had less need for "highly skilled ideologues" from North Carolina than for American capital. A group of African students from the Pan-African Student Organization in the Americas further challenged Whitfield's reflexive hostility to Marxism. "Many of us had somewhat dismissed Marxist analysis as being white," he remembered. "But here are these clearly African, more African than we, clearly revolutionaries who were making use of an analysis to make sense out of things that otherwise didn't make any sense." With a new outlook that organizing workers on the job and in their neighborhoods was the key to re-energizing the black movement, Whitfield and many of his political associates took jobs in tobacco plants and textile mills while laying the groundwork for a national organization of black radicals.[27]

Another black North Carolina native, Raymond Eurquhart, developed his commitment to organizing workers in the improbable setting of a U.S. Air Force base in England. His efforts to fight Air Force discrimination while active as an airman connected him to radical antiwar students from Cambridge University and leaders of the London-based Black Panther Movement—a collective of East Indian nationalists and Marxists unaffiliated with the American group of the same name. The Panthers included Trinidadian writer Darcus Howe and Howe's uncle C.L.R. James, the anti-colonialist writer and activist. Howe, James, and their colleagues piqued Eurquhart's developing interest in nationalist politics, anti-imperialism, Marxism, African culture, and the labor movement. The group staged poetry readings, watched radical films and theater productions, and attended courses on capitalism. Anti-colonialists from across the globe came to the Panthers to gain support and publicity for their causes. Eurquhart met dissident Iraqi, Iranian, and Pakistani intellectuals and learned about South Africa's anti-Apartheid movement and the Algerian struggle for independence. The Panthers also supported striking British miners and, following James's lead, made special efforts to ally with trade unionists. When he returned home in 1972 to Durham, Eurquhart joined a socialist organization that planned to organize the city's workers by strategically placing its members in the tobacco factories, communications industry, and at Duke University. His assignment was the American Tobacco Company, where he worked for the next thirteen years.[28]

DRUM, THE LEAGUE OF REVOLUTIONARY BLACK WORKERS, AND BLACK WORKERS CONGRESS

As African American radicals immersed themselves in the worlds of workers, they learned that their success or failure often rested on events and social forces beyond their control. For nearly three years Baker had distributed copies of his provocative newsletter, *Vanguard*, to indifferent coworkers on the line at the Dodge Main plant. After the Detroit Rebellion in July of 1967, however, they began to take notice. Many of them, including Baker, had been among the 7,000 people swept up in mass arrests by the National Guard, Michigan State Troopers, the Detroit Police Department, and the U.S. Army's 82nd Airborne Division, which had joined forces to squelch the rebellion. As these detainees returned to work, their rage spilled onto the factory floor. Some fashioned the bullet casings that had littered the streets into necklaces, which they wore as symbols of resistance. "People came back in that plant with their hair grown out, and fifty caliber bullets around their neck, and it was a sight to see," Baker recalled, "They weren't taking any more shit." This anger and determination would fuel the wildcat strikes and the establishment of DRUM the following year.[29]

The health of the economy also affected an organizer's ability to engage coworkers and motivate them to take action. Low unemployment rates and steady economic growth near the turn of the decade had encouraged militancy; American workers had set records for strikes in 1969–70. But after the recession of 1973–74, workplace organizing proved difficult. Insecure about their employment in an increasingly volatile economy, workers became less willing to engage in protest activity. The Left, including black radicals, misjudged the historical moment and assumed that rising misery would necessarily translate into dissent and popular demands for change. It did not. Workers' responses to economic crises were diffuse and inchoate. They were as inclined to blame themselves, or to direct their anger at new coworkers or Asian competition, as they were to confront their employers and political leaders. This misreading of working-class responses to economic dislocation widened the distance between radicals who believed that a revolution was imminent and workers who were desperate to hold on to their jobs.

Employers began to push back against workplace radicals. Supervisors and security personnel partnered with law enforcement—and sometimes union leaders—to identify and weed them out. As new entrants into the labor force, many of the factory-based radicals were also among the first fired when layoffs hit. They became isolated from their coworkers, forced into the difficult position of advocating from the outside. Baker, for example, was dismissed from Dodge and blacklisted from the Chrysler Corporation for his role in the Detroit wildcat strikes. After Wilbur Haddock's firing during the 1969 Mahwah strike, he returned to work and ran unsuccessfully for union president while continuing to provide leadership to African American workers. A second dismissal in 1973, however, was permanent, and that separation from his base of support proved impossible to surmount; the group in the plant slowly drifted apart and Haddock was forced to channel his political work into community-based causes.[30]

When unemployment and inflation rose during the 1970s, dozens of black and white leftists arrived in Detroit with high hopes of taking part in the "American Petrograd"—where workers and their intellectual allies would make revolution. Most of the activists at the core of DRUM and the League of Revolutionary Black Workers, however, had been routed from the plants. Even more disappointingly to the newcomers, the League was in the midst of a bitter dispute over strategy and the use of resources. Baker and his supporters believed that the League's increasingly diversified activities had undermined its factory organizing. They welcomed the looming split in the League as an opportunity to consolidate their work around the "organization of black workers" and to "remedy the erroneous tendency . . . to consider it only a part of our general activities." Mike Hamlin, John Watson, and other League leaders resigned from the group and defended their efforts to expand and diversify the group's programs. Hamlin had worked especially hard to recruit allies from the black middle class, white radicals, and supporters outside of the city. They provided new resources and served as a shield for black members in Detroit who faced continual attacks by employers, law enforcement, and the UAW.[31]

As the League moved toward an irreparable split, James Forman relocated to Detroit in June of 1971 at the invitation of Hamlin and Watson, who hoped to draw upon Forman's extensive network of activists to help them develop the Black Workers Congress. Built upon the momentum and reputation of the League, the Black Workers Congress was launched at the end of 1970 as a vehicle through which radical workers in other cities might form their own revolutionary union movements. As Hamlin explained, "it wasn't enough simply to organize a Dodge and an Eldon [Gear and Axle plant], but . . . we had to move long term. We had to think in terms of protracted struggle and organize black workers across the country and across industry." Although initially structured as a broad-based coordinating body joining various black, Asian, and Latino groups that shared the League's worker orientation, the Black Workers Congress soon emphasized its role as an intermediary organization through which its leaders hoped to establish a new communist party.[32]

Specifically, Hamlin and Watson charged Forman with providing political education classes that combined intensive criticism of each member's daily practice with the study of Marx, Lenin, Mao, and other revolutionary theoreticians. The classes aimed to forge unity across the Congress's twenty or so centers of activity that ranged from the General Motors Revolutionary Movement in Atlanta to the Harriet Tubman Bookstore in Los Angeles. Congress leaders also hoped that the classes would steel members for the long struggle, while combating a tendency on the left toward undertaking spontaneous protest activity without having first built a base of support. Hamlin, Watson, and Forman agreed that this had been a fundamental weakness of SNCC, the Detroit movement, and the Black Panther Party, in which Forman had briefly served as Minister of Foreign Affairs. As Hamlin later observed, the achievements of DRUM and the League initially required "some pretty reckless folks" to stand outside the factory gates, facing harassment and intimidation from "reactionary workers" and the police. But these "undisciplined elements in the organization" soon became a liability, and the League's leaders failed to reign in "outrageous acts" committed by some of its members. Thus, political education classes served to direct that volatile element of the movement toward building black worker power, as well as to weed out those whose behavior might prove problematic.[33]

For many workers and activists alike the political education classes could be alienating or tedious, especially after working long hours at a factory. In a frank self-assessment, one recruit admitted that her "development is the lowest of all comrades in the district," because of her inability to find study time. She explained that after attending three mandatory meetings a week, each of which "requires reviewing notes and preparing," and working a full day, she had no time to attend her own union meeting. Many of these activists were lost to the movement, as career pursuits, the demands of parenting, and maintaining relationships took precedent over political work. But when grounded in the workers' experiences and facilitated with sensitivity to their varying levels of formal education, the classes could be empowering. For some, the intensive training they received through the Black Workers Congress and its political-education program provided both an ideological framework for understanding the world and valuable organizer training that they would continue to draw upon long after the Congress's demise. After moving beyond his dismissal of Marx and Engels as Europeans, Vietnam veteran and metal worker Wendell Jean Pierre realized "that the conditions of the workers they were so vividly describing were like those at the Kaiser Plant. And, the workers had nothing but their labor for sale in a country where money meant everything." Pierre also began to connect his experiences as a black Marine to working in the "pot room" at Kaiser Aluminum, where most of the black workers toiled under white supervision and the temperature remained at 120 degrees "just like Vietnam."[34]

Many of the same organizational tensions that had stymied the Detroit movement also plagued the Black Workers Congress. National leaders' grandiose projections of the Congress as the vanguard of an impending black-led revolution bore little connection to the realities of local organizing. Reports from the regional groups reflected a variety of activities, which although far from glamorous typified the nuts and bolts of movement building. Members of the Georgia Organizing Committee met with striking black workers at Allied Food to discuss how they might support their two-month-old strike and followed up by arranging for local television coverage, assisting workers in developing a strike newsletter, and arranging for local students to boycott the company's distributors. Working at Owens-Illinois, another Congress member reported that "the lines have been speeded up so that the women pack a great deal of defective bottles," and that their requests for more line help have been ignored. The Congress had also convened a group of black workers and white radicals to coordinate "how we want to move in the next union meeting—what things we want to bring up and some plans to try to mobilize more workers to support particular ideas."[35]

But as the unfriendly political terrain of the 1970s made organizing at the local level more challenging, leaders became overwhelmed and sometimes turned on one another. An internal report describing work at the Hampton-Newport News project reflects some of those difficulties. A Marxist-Leninist study group there that included both students and production workers soon decided to "function independently, but in coalition with each other." The radicals at Hampton Institute engaged in protests, "but failed to do any significant rank and file organizing" and were "repressed and disciplined by the administration" without much student opposition. The factory-based cadre was divided between those who favored spontaneous disruptive action and those who hoped to work within the existing trade union structure, "which when coupled with an overall reluctance to begin to engage in any level of practical activity, caused the group to become totally internalized—and after six sporadic months, non-functional."[36]

As the highest profile figure within the Black Workers Congress, James Forman received much of the blame for its unraveling. He was maligned for his excessive travel, tendencies toward self-promotion, and his inability to connect to local organizers and workers. Increasingly, the group's national leaders, including Forman, placed a premium on theories that bore little correlation to conditions on the ground. As in many of the subsequent efforts to build a new communist party, the demands of party building and the emphasis on recruiting "advanced workers"—too often meaning other young radical intellectuals—conflicted with the need to develop a mass program that was meaningful to working people. By the spring of 1973, Forman was forced out of the Black Workers Congress. The following year the organization changed its name to the Workers Congress. It continued for several years before disbanding. Most Congress activists continued to pursue local efforts, often through emerging communist organizations or unions.

The post-1960s effort to organize a labor-based radical movement failed and the American working-class suffered tremendous losses during the 1970s and 1980s. Industrial jobs disappeared and real wages fell as unionization rates dropped to historic lows—a function of both structural changes in the economy and the ascendance of reactionary politics. But even as the economy worsened and the Left fragmented, activists continued to advance the "slow and respectful work" of organizing black workers.[37]

Using a false name and social security number, General Baker was hired at Ford's massive River Rouge facility in 1973, where he worked for nearly thirty years and continued his shop-floor activism. A new factory and a different era demanded an organizing strategy that relied more on working through the union to demand better working conditions and less on spontaneous disruptions that fed off worker anger. "The movement had ebbed," Baker recalled, and unlike his old local, UAW Local 3 at Dodge Main, the members of Local 600 had a long history of militancy, especially in the blast furnace and coke ovens where Baker worked. "They weren't rough because of me. It was rough to begin with. I mean the conditions and shit we worked in just made them rough and militant." Baker was even elected union president shortly before River Rouge was shut down in the late 1980s.[38]

Mike Hamlin found his own niche at the labor movement's periphery as a social worker specializing in crisis management and workplace violence. In his office and on the shop floor, Hamlin counseled hundreds of Detroit workers coping with the effects of deindustrialization and the brutality of industrial labor. "I'm the person they call in when there has been some violence at a factory: a shooting, a knifing, threats that neither management nor the union can deal with," Hamlin observed. "I may have seen more of this kind of strife than anyone in the country." Ed Whitfield and Ray Eurquhart were shop-floor activists in tobacco plants in Greensboro and Durham, respectively, and participated in efforts to build a national communist movement. When manufacturing plants closed in North Carolina, both shifted to community-based organizing. Eurquhart also remained active in the labor movement as a union leader representing Durham's municipal employees.[39]

Following the Charleston strike, Mary Moultrie worked for nearly thirty years as a program organizer for the St. Julian Devine Community Center. As an employee of the City of Charleston, Moultrie was careful to maintain a low political profile, but she regularly counseled former coworkers who complained of many of the old problems at the hospital. Moultrie and her associates also provided encouragement and supervision to hundreds of neighborhood children. Those deep bonds continue to bear fruit.

In their recent return to the labor movement, Moultrie and William Saunders advised a group of Charleston sanitation workers who reported that the city had subjected them to unnecessary danger and abusive supervision. In a storefront union office, Moultrie and Saunders listened to the workers describe the latest injuries and insults they endured on the job. As always, Moultrie and Saunders echoed back to the workers what they heard, suggested appropriate responses, and slowly developed within them their capacities to fight for themselves.[40]

NOTES

1. For an overview of such activity, see Jeanne F. Theoharis and Komozi Woodard, eds., *Freedom North: Black Freedom Struggles Outside the South, 1940–1980* (New York: Palgrave Macmillan, 2003); Judson L. Jeffries, ed., *Black Power in the Belly of the Beast* (Champaign: University of Illinois Press, 2006); Peniel Joseph, ed., *The Black Power Movement: Rethinking the Civil Rights-Black Power Era* (New York: Routledge, 2006). For analysis of Soul City, see Devin Fergus, *Liberalism, Black Power and the Making of American Politics: 1965–1980* (Athens: University of Georgia Press, 2009), 196–231.
2. Nancy MacLean, *Freedom is Not Enough: The Opening of the American Workplace* (Cambridge: Harvard University Press, 2006); Paul Johnston, *Success While Others Fail: Social Movement Unionism and the Public Workplace* (Ithaca and New York: ILR Press, 1994). Regarding the rise of black labor protest in the late 1960s, see Damon Stetson, "Negro Members are Challenging Union Leaders," *New York Times*, June 29, 1969; Michael Honey, *Going Down Jericho Road: The Memphis Strike, Martin Luther King's Jr.'s Last Campaign* (New York: W.W. Norton and Company, 2007); Dan Georgakas and Marvin Surkin, *Detroit: I Do Mind Dying*, 2nd ed. (Cambridge: South End Press, [1975] 1998); David Goldberg and Trevor Griffey, eds., *Black Power at Work: Community Control, Affirmative Action, and the Construction Industry* (Ithaca: Cornell University Press, 2010). On civil rights unionism and its Cold War demise, see Robert Rodgers Korstad, *Civil Rights Unionism: Tobacco Workers and the Struggle for Democracy in the Mid-Twentieth Century South* (Chapel Hill: University of North Carolina Press, 2003); Michael Honey, *Black Workers Remember: An Oral History of Segregation, Unionism, and the Freedom Struggle* (Berkeley: University of California Press, 1999); Ellen Schrecker, *Many are the Crimes: McCarthyism in America* (New York: Little, Brown and Company, 1998).
3. David K. Shipler, "Housing Bias in the Suburbs is Blamed for Labor Shortages There," *New York Times*, April 13, 1970; John Darnton, "Slum-to-Suburb Commuting for High Pay has its Perils," *New York Times*, July 19, 1970; "Conversation: Wilbur Haddock on the United Black Brothers," *Souls* 2:2 (Spring 2000): 27–33.
4. "Ford Workers Quit," *New York Times*, September 6, 1961; "Ford Mahwah Plant Halted by Walkout," *New York Times*, November 28, 1962; "Production at Ford, Halted by Strike, Resume," *New York Times*, November 7, 1967; "Conversation: Wilbur Haddock," 27–33.
5. "Conversation: Wilbur Haddock," 30–31. Also see Wilbur Haddock, "Black Workers Lead the Way," *The Black Scholar* 5:3 (November 1973): 43–48.
6. Walter H. Waggoner, "Ford Plant Shut in Racial Dispute," *New York Times*, April 29, 1969; Damon Stetson, "Negroes at Ford's Jersey Plant Continue

Strike," *New York Times*, April 30, 1969; "Ford Operations Normal in Jersey," *New York Times*, May 1, 1969; "Conversation: Wilbur Haddock," 28–29.

7. Haddock, "Black Workers Lead the Way," 43–48.
8. In-person interview with Mary Moultrie, William Saunders, and Rosetta Simmons, March 5, 2009, Charleston, SC. Transcript available in the Citadel Oral History Program Collection, The Citadel Archives and Museum, Charleston, SC. For a more detailed narrative and analysis of the hospital workers' strike, see Leon Fink and Brian Greenberg, *Upheaval in the Quiet Zone: A History of Hospital Workers' Union, Local 1199* (Urbana: University of Illinois Press, 1989); Leon Fink, "Union Power, Soul Power: The Story of 1199 and Labor's Search for A Southern Strategy," *Southern Changes* 5:2 (March–April 1983): 9–20.
9. In-person interview William Saunders (conducted with Jennifer Dixon), June 17, 2008, North Charleston, SC. Transcript in The Southern Oral History Program Collection, Number 4007, Southern Historical Collection, Wilson Library, University of North Carolina at Chapel Hill (hereafter cited as "SHC"); William C. Saunders, "Sea Islands: Then and Now," *Journal of Black Studies* 10:4 (June 1980): 481—92.
10. Moultrie, Saunders, and Simmons interview; Fink and Greenberg, *Upheaval*.
11. Saunders interview; Fink and Greenburg, *Upheaval*.
12. William Saunders, interview by Leon Fink, March 1, 1980, Charleston, South Carolina, in the Hospital Workers Papers, Avery Research Center, College of Charleston, Charleston, SC.
13. Moultrie, telephone conversation with the author, July 17, 2012.
14. Moe Foner, interview by Robert Master, October 3, 1985, Columbia University Oral History Research Office Collection.
15. Saunders, interview by Fink; Moultrie, Saunders, and Simmons interview. Local 1199 also developed a documentary film about the Charleston struggle that was used as a recruiting tool. *I Am Somebody*, directed by Madeline Anderson, with Ralph Abernathy, 30 min. (Onyx Productions, 1970).
16. James Forman to Donald P. Stone and Flora Stone, December 21, 1969, Forman Papers Manuscript Division, Library of Congress, Washington, DC (hereafter cited as "Forman Papers"), Box 118, Folder 15. The letter was later published in Forman's memoir. See James Forman, *The Political Thought of James Forman* (Detroit: Black Star, 1970), 187–88. On Forman's activities that fall, see James Forman, Diaries 1969, Forman Papers, Box 1, Folder 10.
17. The New Communists took their inspiration from the Chinese Revolution and the postwar anti-colonial movements. New Communists rejected the Soviet-aligned Communist Party USA, alleging the party had made its peace with capitalism. For more on the New Communist movement, see Max Elbaum, *Revolution in the Air: Sixties Radicals Turn to Lenin, Mao, and Che* (New York: Verso, 2002); Robin D.G. Kelley and Elizabeth Esch, "Black Like Mao: Red China and Black Revolution," *Souls* 1:4 (Fall 1999): 6–41.
18. Sidney Fine, *Violence in the Model City: The Cavanaugh Administration, Race Relations and the Detroit Riot of 1967* (Ann Arbor: University of Michigan Press, 1988); Heather Ann Thompson, *Whose Detroit? Politics, Labor, and Race in a Modern American City* (Ithaca: Cornell University Press, 2001); Nelson Lichtenstein, *Walter Reuther: The Most Dangerous Man in Detroit* (Champaign: University of Illinois Press, 1997).
19. Georgakas and Surkin, *Detroit: I Do Mind Dying*; James A. Geschwender, *Class, Race, and Worker Insurgency: The League of Revolutionary Black Workers* (Boston: Cambridge University Press, 1977); Thompson, *Whose*

Detroit?; Ernest Allen, "Dying From the Inside: the Decline of the League of Revolutionary Black Workers," in Dick Cluster, ed., *They Should Have Served that Cup of Coffee* (Boston: South End Press, 1979), 71–109.

20. *Finally Got the News*, produced and directed by Stewart Bird, Rene Lichtman, and Peter Gessner, 55 min. ([1970] 2003); Robert Dudnick, "Black Workers on the March: Special Supplement on Black Worker Insurgency in Detroit," *Guardian*, March 8, 1969.
21. In-person interview with General Baker, May 24, 2004, Highland Park, MI. Transcript available in SHC. For more on Robert F. Williams, see Timothy B. Tyson, *Radio Free Dixie: Robert F. Williams and the Roots of Black Power* (Chapel Hill: University of North Carolina Press, 2001).
22. Baker interview.
23. James Forman, Explanation of the Congress Manifesto, January 3, 1971, Forman Papers, Box 62, Folder 4.
24. Scot Brown, *Fighting for US: Maulana Karenga, the US Organization, and Black Cultural Nationalism* (New York: NYU Press, 2003).
25. Baker interview; In-person interview with Mike Hamlin, June 19, 2004, Detroit, MI. Transcript available in SHC.
26. Baker interview.
27. In-person interview with Ed Whitfield, November 14, 2002, Greensboro, NC. Transcript available in SHC. On Malcolm X Liberation University (MXLU), see Fergus, *Liberalism, Black Power*, 54–90. Whitfield's experiences paralleled those of MXLU's cofounder, Owusu Sadauki, who reported on his political conversion while behind enemy lines in Mozambique in 1971 in a series of articles published in *African World*. Many of Sadauki's close associates followed him in spearheading the short-lived Revolutionary Workers League. See Elbaum, *Revolution in the Air*, 199–200; Sally Bermanzohn, *Through Survivors' Eyes: From the Sixties to the Greensboro Massacre* (Nashville: Vanderbilt University Press, 2003), 128.
28. In-person interviews with Raymond Eurquhart, March 9, 2002 and March 24, 2002, Durham, NC. Transcripts available in SHC.
29. Baker interview.
30. Haddock remained active in Newark politics and taught courses in the public policy program at St. Peter's College in Jersey City until his 2003 death. See "Wilbur Haddock of Newark, Professor of Public Policy, 68," *Newark Star-Ledger*, February 24, 2003.
31. See League of Revolutionary Black Workers, "On Splits," [July 1971] and "John Williams, Rufus Burke, and Clint Marbury to Brothers and Sisters," [August 1971]. Both documents from Kenneth V. and Sheila M. Cockrel Collection, Walter P. Reuther Library of Labor and Urban Affairs, Detroit, MI (hereafter cited as "Cockrel Collection"), Box 7, Folder 9; Mike Hamlin, John Watson, and Kenneth Cockrel, "The Split in the League of Revolutionary Black Workers: Three Lines and Three Headquarters," [June 1971], Box 1, Folder 19, Detroit Revolutionary Movements Collection, Walter P. Reuther Library of Labor and Urban Affairs, Detroit, MI.
32. Mike Hamlin, "Toward the Organizing of Revolutionary Union Movements," May 1–2, 1971, Cockrel Collection, Box 4, Folder 14.
33. James Forman Diary, January 12, 1971, Forman Papers, Box 1, Folder 14; Mike Hamlin, "Toward the Organizing of Revolutionary Union Movements," May 1–2, 1971, Cockrel Collection, Box 4, Folder 14. For more on the activities and the demise of the Black Workers Congress, see Georgakas and Surkin, *Detroit: I Do Mind Dying*, 131–50 and Geschwender, *Class, Race, and Worker Insurgency*, 203–204; Hamlin interview.

34. Unnamed recruit quoted in Hat, "Monthly Report," October 1974, Forman Papers, Box 66, Folder 11; Wendell Jean Pierre to All Vietnamese People, June 23, 1971, Forman Papers, Box 63, Folder 12.
35. Georgia Organizing Committee of the International Black Workers Congress, Monthly Report, January 1971, Forman Papers, Box 65, Folder 12; Unnamed Congress member quoted in Owens Illinois Analysis, September 1973, Forman Papers, Box 66, Folder 10.
36. Black Workers Congress Southern Region, Southern Regional Report, February 18, 1972, Forman Papers, Box 66, Folder 1.
37. Charles M. Payne, *I've Got the Light of Freedom: The Organizing Tradition and the Mississippi Freedom Struggle* (Berkeley: University of California Press, 1995), 236–64.
38. Baker interview.
39. Georgakas and Surkin, *Detroit: I Do Mind Dying*, 230; Eurquardt interviews; Whitfield interview.
40. Kieran Taylor, "Charleston Sanitation Workers Fight for Union Recognition," July 15, 2009, http://labornotes.org/node/2329 [accessed October 3, 2011].

12 Acquiring "A Piece of the Action"

The Rise and Fall of the Black Capitalism Movement

Ibram H. Rogers

In the spring of 1968, Americans debated how to address what was perceived to be an urban crisis. Rebellions in major cities ("race riots" in the contemporary parlance) and longstanding structural inequalities had driven many communities to desperation. Candidates in the upcoming presidential election had to tackle the issue and earn black votes in order to win the nation's highest office. Republican hopeful Richard Nixon and his team of advisors called their response "black capitalism," a strategy that provided financial and professional aid from government agencies and other enterprises to develop black-owned urban businesses. Nixon shrewdly framed his initiative as a positive manifestation of black power. On the campaign trail, he argued that most militants were not separatists, but instead wanted to "be included in . . . to have a share of the wealth and a piece of the action." Nixon asserted that the federal government's focus should be "oriented toward more black ownership, for from this can flow the rest—black pride, black jobs, black opportunity, and yes, black power, in the best, the [most] constructive sense of that often misapplied term."[1]

This chapter explores the national black capitalism movement between 1965–74 that was galvanized by a combination of grassroots action and the support of the Nixon Administration. Black power first leaped into the American political mainstream as a result of urban rebellions in the mid-1960s and Stokely Carmichael's popularization of the slogan during a 1966 march. African Americans from a wide range of perspectives forged social movements that became known collectively as the black power movement. One of these efforts, the black capitalism movement, stimulated a groundswell of black business activity, rejuvenated "buy black" campaigns, prompted governmental, black organizational, and white corporate support for black business, and urged for community-owned enterprises and an independent black economy. This mass movement began in 1965 but would ultimately rise and fall in tandem with Nixon.

ORIGINS OF THE BLACK CAPITALISM MOVEMENT

The black capitalism movement was rooted structurally in the chronic marginalization and undercapitalization of black businesses that were unable to provide much community employment. The 1966 *Negro Handbook* noted that there had been for decades "a gradual and steady erosion of the position of the Negro business community." Marcus Garvey's Universal Negro Improvement Association filled the void left by failing black enterprises following World War I and Elijah Muhammad's Nation of Islam served the same purpose after World War II. Muhammad had counseled his followers to establish businesses and employ African Americans. Malcolm X, a leading voice within the organization, traveled the country championing black economic nationalism, although he would reject capitalism in his later years.[2]

Whereas much of the era's activism concentrated on increasing black employment, resulting in the Labor Department's encouraging whites to hire African Americans and the 1964 Civil Rights Act's outlawing of job discrimination, the contemporary black capitalism movement focused on increasing the number of black business owners. The federal Economic Opportunity Act established the Office of Economic Opportunity that facilitated the Economic Opportunity Loan (EOL) Program charged with providing business loans and technical assistance to the inner-city poor. The EOL Program, as part of President Lyndon B. Johnson's War on Poverty, went into effect in 1965. At first it was plagued by a high rate of loan defaults because the criteria (to qualify you had to have limited business experience and low income) almost assured that businesses would fold. Within a year, however, the federal Small Business Association (SBA) took over the reins of EOL, changed the criteria, and made practically all of its loans to African Americans until 1968.[3]

As these federal initiatives developed, a number of grassroots organizations promoting black capitalism also formed. With $2,000, the National Economic Growth and Reconstruction Organization (NEGRO) was born in New York City with Dr. Thomas W. Matthew, who left his lucrative job as a neurosurgeon, as its first president. First acquiring a small hospital in 1965, three years later NEGRO controlled $3 million in assets and helped to employ more than 500 black workers. NEGRO, according to Matthew, was a "constructive form of black power." Another organization called Freedom, Independence, God, Honor, and Today (FIGHT) formed in Rochester in 1965 with $100,000 in start-up funds gathered by local churches. Its success led to the creation of the Rochester Business Opportunities Corporation, which pooled community resources to promote, finance, and offer technical assistance to black-owned and -operated firms. In 1968, Rochester residents formed a related organization, FIGHT-ON, to manufacture vacuum cleaners and electrical transformers. The Watts Labor Community Action Committee became the nation's largest antipoverty conglomerate, owning companies that provided jobs and services for locals. In 1966, professional football star Jim Brown announced his retirement from the sport and his intention to lead the newly formed Negro Industrial and Economic Union to provide loans for black entrepreneurs. Established in Cleveland, it quickly went national and was renamed the

Black Economic Union (BEU). The BEU became arguably the black capitalism movement's premier organization.[4]

Organizations that had been a part of the mainstream civil rights struggle for black political power, including the Congress of Racial Equality (CORE), began to focus instead on economic development. At CORE's 1966 conference, Harlem chapter head Roy Innis presented a twelve-page report detailing how he had recently helped form the Harlem Commonwealth Council Inc. (HCC) with a $50,000 grant from Columbia University. Innis's proposal became CORE's guiding policy. By the late 1970s, the HCC was a $32-million corporation controlling all of the commercial real estate on 125th Street at the center of Harlem. CORE activists also attended the first National Conference on Black Power, where resolutions were passed to support black capitalism through "buy black" campaigns, neighborhood credit unions, and a venture fund. Religious leader Dr. Nathan Wright, Jr. chaired the 1967 conference. In his book, *Black Power and Urban Unrest*, Wright termed the Marxist expression of black power a "painful excess." As Nixon would, Wright equated responsible black power with black capitalism. By no means, however, did all (and probably not even most) black power activists buy into black capitalism. One older conference attendee declared, "I don't want to be exploited by a black man any more than I want to be exploited by a white man."[5]

Government agencies and white-led corporations also reflected the shift toward black capitalism. Congress increased the SBA budget to $2.65 billion in 1967 and required the agency to give half of its loans to people (including whites) in urban areas. Also that year, approximately 1,200 business, labor, religious, civil rights, and government leaders formed the Washington, DC-based National Urban Coalition. One of its main objectives was to alleviate the urban crisis by supporting black capitalism. Henry Ford II, chairman of the Ford Motor Company, and David Rockefeller, president of Chase Manhattan Bank, were two of the many powerful corporate players that joined. Ford was also instrumental in creating the National Alliance of Businessmen, which was funded by the Department of Labor, to train poor urban residents for jobs needed in the local workforce.[6]

MAINSTREAMING THE BLACK CAPITALISM MOVEMENT

"Black capitalism" became a key issue in the 1968 presidential election between Nixon and his Democratic challenger Vice President Hubert Humphrey. Urban rebellions and rising black militancy forced the candidates to address the inequalities that led to the crises in the cities. In 1968, blacks owned 2 percent of the companies in Watts, approximately 15 percent in Harlem, and 3 percent of all industry nationally. The solution was "black capitalism," which Nixon had originally defined as being initiated mostly by the private sector, but with some government support as well. New York

Governor Nelson Rockefeller summarized the Republican position when he said that black capitalism "is a necessity . . . and industry should bear the financial responsibility of such a program." The smoke clearing from five straight years of urban rioting had led to an unprecedented opportunity for black buyers to acquire properties from white merchants in the inner city. According to the *Wall Street Journal*, the rebellions convinced "influential white businessmen and bankers, along with Federal officials, that black business ownership is essential to help defuse the racial enmity crackling across the nation." SBA had already increased its lending to blacks and Latinos from 222 loans worth $4.2 million in 1967 to 325 loans totaling $7.6 million in 1968. To foil the Republicans further, the Johnson Administration, with Humphrey and SBA head Howard J. Samuels in the spotlight, announced its own black capitalism plan called "Project Own." Several black opinion makers came out in support of "Project Own," including syndicated columnist William Raspberry and the Urban League's Whitney Young. With his opponent promising increased federal subsidies, Nixon was compelled to pledge further federal government support if he were to win key African American votes. He packaged his revised black capitalism pitch and sent it to black radio stations, which earned him increased black support.[7]

Contemporary organizations drew strategic inspiration from black capitalism. CORE formally embraced black capitalism at its 1967 annual convention. The organization was also at the center of a group that drafted the Community Self-Determination Bill, which was introduced in Congress in 1968 to produce federally chartered community development corporations that would own all of the businesses in designated neighborhoods. The bill did not pass, although a number of prominent black capitalists lobbied for it. Using a $230,000 government grant, in 1968 African American bankers formed the National Bankers Association, an outgrowth of the National Negro Bankers Association founded in 1926. Officials from the National Business League, founded by Booker T. Washington and by then in its sixty-eighth year with fifty local chapters, called upon the two presidential candidates and the business community to pledge $1.5 billion toward local development corporations. Black power activists, including black capitalists, gathered in 1968 for the National Conference on Black Power. Enclosed in the conference invitation was a speech by the president of the Clairol hair care supplies company, who said he understood black power as "ownership of apartments, ownership of homes, ownership of businesses." Black capitalists used the conference to promote their cause, although many attendees were resistant.[8]

African American organizations steered the black capitalism movement in 1968 even as white industrialists and the two major political parties tried to grab the wheel. The National Urban Coalition set up two corporations—one providing venture capital for blacks and another giving them technical and managerial assistance. B. Green & Company, a major Baltimore wholesale enterprise, helped black grocers acquire inner-city supermarkets from white owners. The venture capital was provided by the newly formed and Ford Foundation-funded Council for Equal Business Opportunity (CEBO). By September 1968, the Ford Foundation was investing heavily in urban black America, including North Philadelphia's Progress Plaza, a brand-new shopping mall, built by activist Reverend Leon H. Sullivan's black investment organization. "You are looking at Black Power!" Sullivan proclaimed at the mall's opening. In a short time, CEBO became a national organization headquartered in Washington, DC with branches in ten cities providing managerial training and project assistance. Meanwhile, Floyd McKissick, who had been replaced by Roy Innis as CORE's national director, opened a black capitalist firm, McKissick Enterprises, in Harlem.[9]

As the presidential election approached, some black capitalists and prominent black athletes, including basketball legend Wilt Chamberlain, baseball pioneer Jackie Robinson, and football icon Jim Brown, went against the black tide and backed Nixon on his way to a narrow victory. As black capitalists reached out to Nixon, he reached back. He met with a contingent of high-profile black businessmen in San Diego, the most vocal of whom was NEGRO's Dr. Matthew. Nixon appointed Robert J. Brown, the former cop turned public-relations mogul turned businessman, as his special assistant on civil rights (or better yet black capitalism). In December 1968, Howard Samuels, with Nixon's approval, announced the creation of the National Advisory Council on Black Economic Development, composed of African Americans from more than forty organizations.[10]

Even as anti-capitalists and anti-nationalists criticized it, the black capitalism movement gained momentum in the months following Nixon's election. A black doll manufacturing company was launched in Los Angeles. Muhammad Ali opened the nation's first Champburger Quick Service restaurant in Miami. James Brown and Mahalia Jackson each started their own national food chain. Jesse Jackson facilitated a buy-black "Black Christmas" in Chicago. Boston's only black-owned and -operated movie house opened, as did Harlem's sole brokerage office. After purchasing 1,810 acres of land in Warren County, North Carolina, McKissick Enterprises announced its plans for "Soul City" that winter. The planned city would provide jobs and housing for 18,000 blacks through a marriage of industry, commerce, and residence. Soul City was the first all-black community built from scratch in the twentieth century. It received a $14 million grant in 1972 from the federal Department of Housing and Urban Development. By the late 1970s, however, the federal government withdrew funding, and the project never reached McKissick's ambitious goal of independent economic sustainability.[11]

ZENITH OF THE BLACK CAPITALISM MOVEMENT

Before his inauguration, Nixon pledged to "do more for the Negro than any president has ever done." The chief White House overture to black capitalism was the establishment of the Office of Minority Business Enterprise (OMBE) within the Department of Commerce. Nixon signed OMBE into existence (along with a National Advisory Council for Minority Enterprise) through Executive Order 11458 on March 5, 1969. To forestall Congressional resistance, OMBE had a narrow mandate. Its job was to coordinate the 116 public-enterprise programs that were divided among twenty-one federal agencies in ways that would stimulate black access to capital. "Our aim is to open that route to potentially successful persons who have not had access to it before," Nixon said in a statement. Nixon tabbed Commerce Secretary Maurice H. Stans as the leader of the federal effort to aid black capitalism. Known as a strict conservative, Stans accepted the charge because he sensed its vote-getting potential. But OMBE struggled from the beginning due to meager funding, public cynicism, bureaucratic tension, and its limited power. It secured a mere two grants for non-white businesses in its first few months of existence.[12]

Even as federal efforts stalled, the black capitalism movement continued to thrive from the bottom up in 1969. The number of African Americans seeking to establish their own businesses in South Central Los Angeles doubled over the course of a year. Black economists joined organizational heads to found the Caucus of Black Economists. The nation's first black-owned computer analysis firm opened. Youth Pride Inc., led by former Student Nonviolent Coordinating Committee (SNCC) leader and future Washington, DC mayor Marion Barry, ran a landscaping enterprise, five gas stations, a maintenance company, and a fifty-five-unit apartment complex. By the middle of the 1970s, however, Pride fell into the red due to the recession, mishandling of funds, and swift expansion.[13]

There was a debate within the black capitalism movement about the roles of white entrepreneurs and the federal government. Atheneum published the widely praised *Black Capitalism: Strategy for Business in the Ghetto* by Theodore Cross, the editor and publisher of *Banker's Magazine*, who urged the government and corporate America to invest heavily in urban black America. On the other side of the black capitalist ideological pole, Roy Innis offered an essay titled, "Separatist Economics: A New Social Contract." New York City economist Dunbar S. McLaurin introduced the Ghetto Economic Development and Industrialization Plan (GHEDIPLAN). Arguing that black entrepreneurs needed more than capital and training, McLaurin urged the federal government to pursue strategies that gave African Americans control of their economy.[14]

The success of the black capitalism movement exposed it to criticism from both blacks and whites on the left and right. The black community's most booming critiques came out of the National Black Economic Development Conference in April 1969. More than six hundred people attended, including black Marxist James Boggs, who circulated a position paper titled, "The Myth and Irrationality of Black Capitalism." Also at the conference, SNCC's James Forman presented the "Black Manifesto," a scathing indictment of

U.S. capitalism. The delegates approved the manifesto and passed resolutions rejecting black capitalism and championing cooperative economics. Economist Andrew Brimmer, the first African American on the Federal Reserve Board, became one of the movement's chief detractors. The anti-nationalist wrote about "The Trouble with Black Capitalism"—the tenuous predicament of small businesses and dismal state of African American purchasing power—in the press. Congress held widely publicized hearings on black capitalism, interrogating Nixon aides. Dissent in the SBA's new Office of Minority Entrepreneurship became national news when Phillip Pruitt, the acting assistant director, resigned on July 11, 1969, publicly rebuking Nixon for failing to back black capitalism. Although the SBA released a progress report stating that "minority" loans had jumped from 1,676 worth $29.9 million in 1968 to a record high of 4,120 worth $93.6 million the following year, critics of the black capitalism movement would not relent. The *New York Times* called Nixon's programs "deeply disappointing." The most devastating grassroots critique came from Robert Allen's book, *Black Awakening in Capitalist America.* "The corporatists are attempting with considerable success to co-opt the black power movement," he wrote. "Their strategy is to equate black power with black capitalism.[15]

The cultural sensibilities of the black power movement were conducive to black capitalism. Contemporary slogans like "black is beautiful" and "buy black" reflected an increased public appetite for black businesses and products. Black capitalists, whether they depended on government funding or private investment, had unprecedented opportunities in 1969. An impressive project that received national attention was a black-owned shopping plaza built on a nine-acre strip in Memphis. A black-owned clothing manufacturer opened in Harlem. White entrepreneurs also invested heavily in such ventures, like the thriving Terry Manufacturing Company in Roanoke, Alabama, a black-owned clothing company making about $1 million a year. The Winston Mutual Life Insurance Company, with offices in six cities and a fifty-year history, opened a new $750,000 headquarters in North Carolina. The federal government allocated an increasing number of contracts to black businesses. The SBA took the lead in the procurement initiative, proposing to award $38 million and $100 million in contracts to small, non-white-owned businesses in 1970 and 1971, respectively. By January 1970, thirty firms had received special government orders under this program.[16]

The increased number of black-owned corporations that received start-up funds from the federal government and white entrepreneurs raised questions about who was in control of the black capitalism movement and what was its purpose. The Nixon Administration asserted that the government and corporate America should spearhead black capitalism. After a meeting between the president and his fifty-eight-member advisory council for minority enterprise, Commerce Secretary Stans announced the creation of Project Enterprise, the first large-scale federal program to fund black capitalism directly. Corporations could pledge at least $150,000 to sponsor a federally-backed Minority Enterprise Small Business Investment Company (MESBIC). Stans told reporters, "We believe this new program for capitalization and business assistance will encourage many thousands of our minority group members to seek 'a piece of the action,'" and set a goal of 100 MESBICs by June 1970. Still, black capitalists were divided as to the best route for African Americans to get "a piece of the action." As the *New York Amsterdam News* editorialized, "Take any 20 so-called black leaders or a like number of white bleeding hearts and ask for a decent formula for black capitalism and you will get 20 different answers."[17]

Even with this increased investment in black business, there was growing concern about the movement's viability and widespread criticism by African Americans of the Nixon Administration's involvement. A poll released in January 1970 indicated that most of the nation's 444 black elected officials condemned Nixon's handling of black capitalism. At times it seemed that the administration's values were at odds with those that informed the movement's black power perspective. Cooperative black ownership of community institutions was a key element of the movement, but Stans insisted that OMBE provide aid exclusively to entrepreneurs. Three disgruntled OMBE staffers resigned as a result of this ideological impasse. The failure of a widely touted group of black-owned and -controlled food stands in Atlanta, established by Georgia legislator Julian Bond and financed by a local white civil rights leader, prompted the *New Pittsburgh Courier* to call black capitalism a "delusion" and the *Chicago Defender* to refer to it as a "mere dream." Monthly Review Press published Earl Ofari Hutchinson's critical book *The Myth of Black Capitalism*. Black feminists such as Kay Lindsey asserted that the movement's strivings to "encourage the acquisition of property among Blacks via Black Capitalism . . . would probably serve to further intensify the stranglehold on women as property." A recession beginning in 1970 also presented challenges, wreaking havoc on black auto dealers. Three years prior, black capitalists proposed replacing urban white dealerships with black ones, because at the time only one of the nation's 28,000 new-car lots was black-owned. Although the number had grown to twenty-nine, only two of them turned a profit. Black banks also suffered, but a speech by Andrew Brimmer prompted a public response from the black National Bankers Association in early 1971 that resulted in a dramatic comeback. From 1970–73, the total assets of black-owned banks surged from $400 million to more than $1 billion and the number of "minority-owned" banks doubled.[18]

The recession and the swirling opinions about the movement did not slow black capitalism, which neared its zenith in 1970. The insurance and securities brokerages of retired NFL star Bobby Mitchell were booming. A group of Baltimore African American businessmen set a precedent when they assumed total control of a federally insured $4 million housing project. An astounding thirteen black consumer magazines began publishing that year, including *Essence*. Magazines like *Black Business Digest*, which lasted until 1973, and *Black Enterprise*, which served as the voice of the movement, reflected the spirit of the times. African American economists founded *The Review of Black Political Economy*. Three kinds of black firms experienced massive growth—consulting firms that designed government programs for poor African Americans, public relations firms that taught white corporations how to market to black consumers, and employment agencies that helped white offices find suitable black employees. Hair care manufacturer Johnson Products rode the cultural demand for its Afro-Sheen product line to become the first black enterprise to be listed on the American Stock Exchange. The following year, financial firm Daniels & Bell Inc. became the first-ever black member of the New York Stock Exchange. Willie Daniels, its president, called it a "major and significant breakthrough in efforts to further black capitalism." Major growth occurred in the South, where the majority of black insurance companies (thirty of thirty-seven), savings and loan associations (twenty-three of forty), and banks (fourteen of twenty) were based. These enterprises accounted for total assets exceeding $500 million, prompting *Ebony* to refer to the region as "the promised land" for black capitalism, while *Black Enterprise* reported that a "minor greenback revolution" was taking place there. An economic symposium in the summer of 1971 estimated that the black economy was primed for substantial growth.[19]

The Nixon Administration, encouraged by the growing number of black mayors and elected officials, not to mention the rapidly approaching 1972 presidential election and criticism that it was not keeping its election promises to blacks, strove in record fashion in 1970 to place contracts into the hands of black firms. A *Black Enterprise* reporter referred to the trend as the "silver lining . . . in the storm-clouds" of the contemporary recession. Stans stated in November 1970 that the federal government planned to buy $100 million in goods and services from "minority" enterprises by June 30, 1971, after purchasing $9 million in fiscal 1969 and $22 million in fiscal 1970. The SBA assured the OMBE that 500 franchise commitments would go to non-white entrepreneurs.[20]

Meanwhile, community development programs funded by the Office of Economic Opportunity were well received in cities like Cleveland, Brooklyn, and Detroit. Such action was necessary in the face of the government's inability to meet its targets for black capitalism. A *New York Times* report claimed that the "Nixon Administration's plan to produce more minority capitalists . . . has fallen far short of its goals." Indeed, merely nine companies had funded MESBICs, a fraction of Stans' goal of 100. In a Congressional address in October 1971, Nixon proposed a twenty-fold increase in federal aid for non-white businesses. "We will not realize the full potential of our nation until neither race nor nationality is any longer an obstacle to full participation in the American marketplace," he said. Nixon also signed an executive order to increase the OMBE's flexibility. A U.S. Census Bureau survey in 1971 revealed that the black capitalism movement had done little to exacerbate deeply rooted economic inequalities. Although non-whites accounted for 17 percent of the population, their business receipts were 0.7 percent of the total. Non-whites owned about 2 percent of all American enterprises, totaling approximately 150,000 firms, usually small retail stores and service operations with fewer than five employees.[21]

With the 1972 presidential election looming, the black capitalism movement reached a crossroads between those who supported the Nixon Administration's initiatives and those who sought new directions. Sargent Shriver, the Democratic candidate for vice president, blamed the president for putting the nation's black community in "a depression of major proportion." The Congressional Black Caucus assembled politicians, business leaders, and economists who debated proposals for a ten-year economic program for black America. Richard F. America, an African American economist, called for a 10 percent transfer of all Fortune 500 companies to blacks and provided "a new rationale for income redistribution." The black capitalism movement was well represented at that year's National Black Political Convention. Economist Robert Browne wrote about the "economic basis for reparations to black America." Browne was also a part of the team of black economists mobilized by Jesse Jackson that drafted an "economic bill of rights" that demanded a redistribution of wealth and a guaranteed minimum income for American families. A significant portion of the black capitalism movement was now redirecting its energies toward a hybrid model that not only included free enterprise and entrepreneurship, but also redistributions of wealth and stronger welfare programs. But there were also those African Americans who did well under Nixon, and they supported his re-election campaign. Entrepreneurs who received government contracts were especially loyal, as were some black celebrities. *Jet* published pictures of Sammy Davis, Jr. embracing Nixon at the Republican National Convention, prompting the greatest response (mostly negative) the magazine had ever had on any topic. As federal agency grants and loans to non-white enterprises peaked in 1973 at $670 million, however, there were growing numbers of observers who pointed to the emerging black middle class as evidence of Nixon's success. Although not all black capitalists believed this, there was new optimism brewing for black business owners who had survived the recession and were now bolstered by record government support and a newly consolidated OMBE. The wig company owned by Naomi Sims, the first black superstar model, grossed $5 million that year. *Black Enterprise* profiled the nation's top 100 black businesses; the feature included a letter from Nixon, who wrote, "their accomplishments prove that we are making progress." At the top of the list was Berry Gordy's Motown Industries and second was the Johnson Publishing Company. For the next decade, Motown was the most successful black enterprise in the nation, with annual sales topping $50 million.[22]

DECLINE OF THE BLACK CAPITALISM MOVEMENT

The decline of the black capitalism movement paralleled the rapid fall of Richard Nixon. In 1973, the Senate Watergate Committee investigated White House corruption on many fronts, including its dealings with black entrepreneurs. It found that applicants for federal grants and contracts, like the chair of the Watts Labor Community Action Committee, had been required to endorse the president. Congress partnered with the Department of Justice to launch a series of investigations into OMBE and SBA projects in more than thirty cities. The OMBE was decentralized and reorganized, which some black capitalists saw as the beginning of the end of the movement. Fearing the collapse of their projects, a coalition of groups that included the National Business League and the Congressional Black Caucus, began to lobby the federal government to save black capitalism. Although individual entrepreneurs were spared, the black capitalism *movement* was no more by 1974. The intoxicating black power luster of self-determination, black pride, and self-love had dulled. And just as Nixon's endorsement of black capitalism injected a profound energy into the movement in 1968, the Watergate scandal and the president's estrangement from the American people sapped it of its energy.[23]

Nixon's resignation combined with a severe recession in 1974 to cripple the black capitalism movement. OMBE's budget stagnated at $52 million, meaning it could no longer fund new projects. Programs to increase the ranks of black MBAs faltered as education costs rose and financial aid grants shrunk. Black entrepreneurs continued to receive federal support, but no longer did the government serve as a galvanizing force for a mass capitalist movement. Black economists and business leaders second-guessed the wisdom of catering exclusively to African American customers. Andrew Brimmer suggested that talented blacks take their skills to more stable white corporations. John H. Johnson, head of Johnson Publishing, warned that a black businessman must "never limit himself to serving black consumers alone." In the wake of stagnant federal aid, diminishing markets, a credit squeeze, inflation, and soaring black unemployment, these ideas proved alluring to many who once constituted the black capitalism movement. As black power sensibilities lost their currency, what was left of the black consumer market became increasingly attracted to products from white-owned corporations. "The net result," according to historian Manning Marable, "was the increased marginalization of the Black entrepreneur."[24]

In less than a decade the vital black entrepreneur had been relegated. Black capitalists had received from black nationalists a popular mandate to lead the fight for economic self-determination and more black employers as the black freedom struggle turned away from the demands for more black employees that characterized the civil rights movement. They founded groups like NEGRO and FIGHT, provided jobs for African Americans, and demanded funding from the government. Although the government responded, beginning with the Johnson Administration's creation of the EOL program in 1965 and continuing through Nixon's resignation, it must be remembered that politicians were usually motivated for different reasons than black capitalists were. Whereas many black capitalists saw the movement as fundamental to African American liberation, politicians were merely trying to assuage the urban crisis that had resulted in five consecutive years of rioting. Ultimately, federal intervention into black capitalism was seen by many as repressive, resulting in supporters disowning the movement as government control increased. The unparalleled outpouring of federal aid produced a legion of individual black capitalists. Some used their economic power to support the Nixon Administration, enrich only themselves, and oppose the popular mandate that called for community control and ownership. Others were socially responsible, consciously *black* capitalists who used their businesses to empower their communities. The incredible upsurge from 1965–74 of new black businesses and development corporations was accompanied by a very high failure rate. Many of the period's new creations did not survive for long. Ultimately, therefore, the legacy of the black capitalism movement is mixed. Legends of success matched tragedies of failure during this period of unprecedented black economic activity.

NOTES

1. Dean Kotlowski, "Black Power—Nixon Style: The Nixon Administration and Minority Business Enterprise," *Business History Review* 72:3 (Autumn 1998): 413–14; Nixon quoted in Robert E. Weems and Lewis A. Randolph, *Business in Black and White: American Presidents & Black Entrepreneurs in the Twentieth Century* (New York: NYU Press, 2009), 115.
2. *The Negro Handbook* (Chicago: Johnson Publishing Co., 1966), 215. For the Nation of Islam's ideas on black economic nationalism, see Malcolm X, "The Ballot or the Bullet," in George Breitman, ed., *Malcolm X Speaks: Selected Speeches and Statements* (New York: Merit Publishers, 1965), 38–39.
3. Juliet E.K. Walker, *The History of Black Business in America: Capitalism, Race, Entrepreneurship* (New York: Macmillan, 1998), 269.
4. Matthew quoted in Charles E. Brown, "How Negro-Owned Bus Co. Is Changing Watts," *Jet*, January 4, 1968, 46–48; William L. Van Deburg, *New Day in Babylon: The Black Power Movement and American Culture, 1965–1975* (Chicago: University of Chicago Press, 1992), 116–17; Edward H. Jones, *Blacks in Business* (New York: Grosset & Dunlap, 1971), 168–69; "A Growing Operation," *Los Angeles Times*, January 17, 1971; "Brown To Help Negro Economy," *Baltimore Sun*, July 15, 1966; Robert L. Allen, *Black Awakening in Capitalist America* (Garden City: Doubleday, 1969), 128–29.
5. James Dowdy, "Harlem Commonwealth Council: A Business Success Story," *Review of Black Political Economy* 10:1 (Fall 1979): 59–60; Nathan Wright, Jr., *Black Power and Urban Unrest: Creative Possibilities* (New York: Hawthorn, 1967), 14; Unnamed conference attendee quoted in Allen, *Black Awakening in Capitalist America*, 134.
6. Kotlowski, "Black Power—Nixon Style," 416; Allen, *Black Awakening in Capitalist America*, 180–81.

7. Editorial page, "Aiding Black Capitalism," *New York Times*, October 14, 1968; Rockefeller quoted in "Rocky Endorses Black Power," *Chicago Defender*, August 7, 1968; George Davis, "Giving Capitalism Black Roots," *Washington Post*, May 11, 1969; Robert B. Semple, Jr., "Nixon Preparing to Court 7 or 8 Industrial States," *New York Times*, June 21, 1968; James Yuenger, "Hubert Backs Black Business," *Chicago Tribune*, July 21, 1968; Weems and Randolph, *Business in Black and White*, 87–103; Burt Schorr, "'Black Capitalism,'" *Wall Street Journal*, August 13, 1968; Jim Hoagland, "'Black Capitalism' a Paradox," *Washington Post*, May 13, 1968; "Says Black Leaders Back Nixon's Plan," *Chicago Defender*, July 11, 1968; Donald Janson, "Nixon Discerns a New Coalition," *New York Times*, May 17, 1968.
8. Weems and Randolph, *Business in Black and White*, 134; "Bi-Partisan Unit Maps 'Black Capitalism' Bill," *Chicago Defender*, December 21, 1968; Rowland Evans, Jr. and Robert D. Novak, *Nixon in the White House: The Frustration of Power* (New York: Random House, 1971), 137; "NBA Part Financial Renaissance," *Baltimore Afro-American*, April 18, 1970; "$1,500,000,000 Aid Asked For 'Black Capital,'" *Philadelphia Tribune*, September 14, 1968; unnamed Clairol president quoted in Allen, *Black Awakening in Capitalist America*, 138; Matthew J. Countryman, *Up South: Civil Rights and Black Power in Philadelphia* (Philadelphia: University of Pennsylvania Press, 2006), 206–207.
9. "Aiding Black Capitalism"; Schorr, "'Black Capitalism'"; Robert J. Samuelson, "Equal Business Opportunity Group Meeting With Success," *Washington Post*, March 6, 1969; Philip Greer, "Ford Foundation $10M for Social Projects," *Boston Globe*, September 30, 1968; Sullivan quoted in Countryman, *Up South*, 115–17; Clayton Willis, "McKissick Moves in a New Direction," *New York Amsterdam News*, October 5, 1968.
10. "Wilt to Work With Nixon," *Philadelphia Tribune*, September 7, 1968; Thomas J. Sugrue, *Sweet Land of Liberty: The Forgotten Struggle for Civil Rights in the North* (New York: Random House, 2008), 443; Robert B. Semple, Jr., "Nixon's Meeting With Negroes Stirs a Dispute," *New York Times*, August 18, 1968; Gloria Wolford, "Robert Brown, Black Businessman, Is Nixon's Appointee," *Chicago Defender*, December 10, 1968; "Black Council Will Advise On Business," *New York Amsterdam News*, January 4, 1969.
11. Jean Murphy, "Toymakers Turn On Black Self-Esteem," *Los Angeles Times*, May 15, 1970; "Muhammad Ali's Champburgers," *Chicago Defender*, December 31, 1968; "'Soul' Singer Forms Fast Food Restaurant Chain," *New Pittsburgh Courier*, January 25, 1969; Jack Nelson, "Negro Must Own At Least 50%," *Los Angeles Times*, February 3, 1969; "Negroes Tell Plans for a 'Black Yule,'" *Chicago Tribune*, November 26, 1968; "4 Community Groups Merge in Lawndale," *Chicago Defender*, December 18, 1968; "Public Housing Tenants Take Over Gas Station," *Chicago Tribune*, February 9, 1969; George McKinnon, "MOVIES: Black-owned cinema year old," *Boston Globe*, February 6, 1970; Robert E. Dallos, "Former Shoeshine Boy Attempts to Bring Wall Street to Harlem," *Los Angeles Times*, February 2, 1969; Christopher Strain, "Soul City, North Carolina: Black Power, Utopia, and the African American Dream," *Journal of African American History* 89:1 (Winter 2004): 57–74.
12. Nixon quoted in Robert B. Semple, Jr., "Nixon is Reported to Pledge Gains in Negro Benefits," *New York Times*, January 14, 1969; Kotlowski, "Black Power—Nixon Style," 420–24; Nixon quoted in Ethel L. Payne, "President Nixon Creates Minorities' Business Unit," *Chicago Defender*, March 6, 1969; Robert J. Samuelson, "Small Business Unit Director Named," *Washington Post*, March 14, 1969.

13. Jack Jones, "Problems for Blacks in Business Listed," *Los Angeles Times*, May 19, 1969; George Davis, "Giving Capitalism Black Roots," *Washington Post*, May 11, 1969; Frank McRae, "Black Computer Office Opens," *Washington Post*, March 10, 1969; Peter Baestrup, "Enterprise Points With Pride to Slum Projects," *Los Angeles Times*, March 27, 1969; Jonetta Rose Barras, *The Last of the Black Emperors: The Hollow Comeback of Marion Barry in the New Age of Black Leaders* (Baltimore: Bancroft Press, 1998), 125.
14. "'Strategy For Business in the Ghetto' Praised," *Chicago Defender*, May 31, 1969; Dunbar S. McLaurin and Cyril D. Tyson, "The GHEDIPLAN for Economic Development," in William F. Haddad and G. Douglas Pugh, eds., *Black Economic Development* (Englewood Cliffs: Prentice Hall, 1969), 126–37.
15. Andrew Brimmer, "The Trouble With Black Capitalism," *Nation's Business*, May 1969, 78–79; Gayraud S. Wilmore, *Black Religion and Black Radicalism: An Interpretation of the Religious History of Afro-American People* (Maryknoll: Orbis Books, 1989), 275–78; James Farmer, "The Black Manifesto," in Gayraud S. Wilmore and James H. Cone, eds., *Black Theology: A Documentary History, 1966–1979* (Maryknoll: Orbis Books, 1979), 84; Robert E. Weems, Jr. and Lewis A. Randolph, "The National Response to Richard M. Nixon's Black Capitalism Initiative: The Success of Domestic Détente," *Journal of Black Studies* 32:1 (September 2001): 69; "3 of Nixon's Aides Face Senate Quiz on 'Black Capitalism,'" *Chicago Defender*, June 12, 1969; "600,000 Nonwhite Firms Needed, Says SBA Head," *Washington Post*, July 1, 1969; Robert J. Samuelson, "Record Loans by SBA," *Washington Post*, July 15, 1969; Rowland Evans and Robert Novak, "Negro Aide's Departure From SBA May Signal New Day for the Agency," *Washington Post*, July 17, 1969; Editorial page, "Black Capitalism," *New York Times*, August 24, 1969; Allen, *Black Awakening in Capitalist America*, 14–15.
16. "Memphis Gets Black-Owned Store Plaza," *Washington Post*, August 23, 1969; "Dress Factory Opens Uptown," *New York Amsterdam News*, August 9, 1969; Douglas W. Cray, "After Banquets, Alabama Negroes Get Down to All-Black Textile Business," *New York Times*, November 2, 1969; Naomi McLean, "N.C. Life Insurance Company Opens $750,000 headquarters," *Baltimore Afro-American*, December 13, 1969; Kotlowski, "Black Power—Nixon Style," 430–32; Burt Schorr, "Too High a Price?," *Wall Street Journal*, January 8, 1970.
17. Stans quoted in Paul Delaney, "Negro Business is Assured of Aid," *New York Times*, November 7, 1969; Editorial page, "Whither Black Capitalism?," *New York Amsterdam News*, August 30, 1969.
18. "Officials Say Nixon Shows Little Concern for People," *Baltimore Afro-American*, January 31, 1970; Rowland Evans and Robert Novak, "Stans Likely To Prevail In Dispute Over Black Capitalism Ideology," *Washington Post*, January 1, 1970; Jon Nordheimer, "Black Atlanta Venture Backfires on Liberals," *New York Times*, June 15, 1970; Alfred Baker Lewis, "Charges Black Capitalism a Delusion," *New Pittsburgh Courier*, September 19, 1970; Editorial page, "Is Black Capitalism A Mere Dream," *Chicago Defender*, September 19, 1970; Earl Ofari Hutchinson, *The Myth of Black Capitalism* (New York: Monthly Review Press, 1970); Kay Lindsey, "The Black Woman as a Woman," in Toni Cade Bambara, ed., *The Black Woman: An Anthology* (New York: Mentor, 1970), 105; "Black Bank Association Hits Critic," *Chicago Tribune*, January 8, 1971; Kotlowski, "Black Power—Nixon Style," 436–37.
19. "Mitchell Eyes Big Business," *Chicago Defender*, January 5, 1970; "Black Businessmen In Control of $3,880,000 Housing Unit," *Baltimore Afro-*

American, February 28, 1970; Jannette Dates and William Barlow, *Split Image: African Americans in the Mass Media* (Washington, DC: Howard University Press, 1993), 404–405; "Publisher's Preface to the Inaugural Issue," *Review of Black Political Economy* 1:1 (Spring/Summer 1970): iii; Saul Friedman, "Race Relations Is Their Business," *New York Times*, October 25, 1970; Walker, *History of Black Business in America*, 306; Daniels quoted in "First Negro-Controlled Firm Gets Big Board Membership," *Baltimore Sun*, June 25, 1971; Simeon Booker, "Black Business is Tops in South," *Ebony*, August 1971, 56–58; "The Economy: A Recession for Blacks?," *Black Enterprise*, September 1970, 47–48; "'State of the Black Economy,'" *Chicago Defender*, June 7, 1971.

20. "The Economy: A Recession for Blacks?," 47–48; Stans quoted in "$100 Million to be Spent on Small Business," *Balti smore Afro-American*, November 28, 1970.
21. "U.S. 'Black Capitalism' Effort Gathers Steam," *Baltimore Afro-American*, April 4, 1970; Joseph R. Slevin, "Minority Program Gets Off Ground," *Washington Post*, April 5, 1970; Paul Delaney, "U.S. Minority Aid Faulted in Study," *New York Times*, August 17, 1970; LaBarbara Bowman, "Poverty Agencies Quarrel Over Black Capitalism Plan," *Washington Post*, August 8, 1970; Paul Delaney, "Black Capitalism Program Falling Far Short of Goals," *New York Times*, June 29, 1970; Nixon quoted in "$63 Million to Aid Minority Business," *Atlanta Daily World*, October 15, 1971; William Chapman, "Receipts of Minorities' Businesses Found Less Than 1% of U.S. Total," *Washington Post*, August 25, 1971.
22. Shriver quoted in "Shriver Sees Blacks in Major Depression," *New York Times*, October 7, 1972; "The National Black Enterprise Conference: A Step Toward Developing a 10-Year Economic Program," *Black Enterprise*, April 1972, 34–37; Richard America, "A New Rational for Income Redistribution," *Review of Black Political Economy* 2:2 (Winter 1972): 3–21; Richard America, "What Do You People Want?," in Ronald W. Bailey, ed., *Black Business Enterprise: Historical and Contemporary Perspectives* (New York: Basic Books, 1971); Peniel Joseph, *Waiting 'Til the Midnight Hour: A Narrative History of Black Power in America* (New York: Henry Holt, 2006), 276–79; Robert S. Browne, "The Economic Basis for Reparations to Black America," *Review of Black Political Economy* 2:2 (Winter 1972): 67–80; "An Economic Bill of Rights," *Review of Black Political Economy* 3:1 (Fall 1972): vii–41; "Blacks for Nixon," *New Republic*, October 7, 1972, 8–9; Paul Delaney, "Black Supports of President Under Fire," *New York Times*, October 17, 1972; "Interagency Report on the Federal Minority Development Programs," Executive Office of the President, Office of Management and Budget, Department of Commerce, Small Business Administration, March 1976, I, Paul C. Leach Papers, Box 28, Minority Business Folder, Ford Presidential Library, Ann Arbor, MI; Karl D. Gregory, "Brief Report of the State of the Black Economy," *Review of Black Political Economy* 3:3 (Spring 1973): 3–16; Ben J. Wattenberg and Richard M. Scammon, "Black Progress and Liberal Rhetoric," *Commentary*, April 1973, 35–44; Walker, *History of Black Business in America*, 301, 305; "A Letter From President Nixon," *Black Enterprise*, June 1973, 3.
23. Kotlowski, "Black Power—Nixon Style," 440; "OMBE Reorganization Seen Endangering Minority Enterprise," *Philadelphia Tribune*, September 1, 1973; Paul Delaney, "Minorities Seek to Aid to Business," *New York Times*, November 20, 1973.
24. "Blacks' M.B.A. Struggle," *New York Times*, January 6, 1974; Paul Delaney, "Minority Budget Stirs Complaints," *New York Times*, January 25, 1974;

Thaddeus H. Spratlen, "Inflation and the Presidential Economic Summit: Issues and Implications from a Black Perspective," *Review of Black Political Economy* 5:2 (Winter 1975): 143–57; John H. Johnson, "Not Enough Black Capitalists," *New York Times*, April 21, 1974; Manning Marable, *How Capitalism Underdeveloped Black America* (Boston: South End Press, 1983), 164.

13 Soul City, North Carolina and the Business of Black Power

Christopher B. Strain

On January 13, 1969, in the office of the U.S. Secretary of Agriculture in Washington, DC, Floyd McKissick announced his intention to build a city in Warren County, North Carolina. Soul City was to be a multiracial, multicultural development for underprivileged and disadvantaged persons; newspapermen quickly deemed it a "black-built" town. As McKissick, former national director of the Congress of Racial Equality (CORE), explained, "White men have built other cities. We want this city to reflect the many cultures, the many nations that exist in American society. . . . Soul City will be an attempt to move into the future, a future where black people welcome white people as equals." Area newspapers told the tale, reflecting the rise and fall of McKissick's idea. Early headlines during the period 1969–73 used words such as "hopeful," "dream," "praise," "thrive," "endorse," and "hail" to describe the project, but headlines after 1975 used words such as "tangled" and "criticized" to convey the town's problems. The excitement of Soul City's early years gave way to critics, circling like buzzards in the air of optimism that enveloped the experimental town. When Soul City's pioneers stumbled, political heavies such as Representative L.H. Fountain and Senator Jesse Helms were ready to swoop in and pick them apart, claiming that the project was doomed from the start to fail. Soul City's founder was a man of relentless vision, but forces would conspire to prevent that vision from becoming the harmonious community he imagined.[1]

McKissick sought to create a model community and his American Dream involved a communitarian vision far different from the traditional quest for individual success and material gain. "Soul City is going to be . . . a city place of truth which ought to have a high tower with a beacon of light to let the world know it's there and a place where man can develop himself to what he wants to be." This echo of John Winthrop's "city upon a hill" was set not in seventeenth-century Massachusetts but in the Piedmont region of twentieth-century North Carolina. It was utopian in the sense that it was visionary: as the city took shape, rising from the Carolina mud, it carried with it all of the tensions and fears of America's torrid racial past, even as it set the stage for a brighter future. Born out of the chaos and hope of the 1960s, Soul City prefaced the New Urbanist trend of the 1980s and 1990s; furthermore, it represented the first sustainable black community built from scratch in the twentieth century, with assistance from the federal government. It was unique among twentieth-century alternative communities with regard to its idealistic initiative, its detailed planning, its massive funding, and its ostensible failure. The scope of Soul City as a 1970s-era utopia is without parallel, and the story of how McKissick's dream city materialized—and failed to materialize—represents not only a dramatic combination of black power and communitarianism but also an untold and largely unknown chapter in the African American quest for inclusion in the American Dream.[2]

Floyd B. McKissick led a life of activism. Born on March 9, 1922, in Asheville, North Carolina, he was attending Morehouse College in 1941 when the Japanese bombed Pearl Harbor. McKissick promptly quit school and enlisted in the U.S. Army. Upon returning from Europe, he completed his studies at North Carolina Central University and in 1951 became the first black man to attend the University of North Carolina Law School. An accomplished attorney, McKissick led the fight to eliminate the trespass statutes used to thwart nonviolent direct-action campaigns by civil rights activists. In 1963 he was elected national chairman of the Congress of Racial Equality (CORE). In 1966 he succeeded James Farmer as national director, serving two years. His book *Three-Fifths of a Man* (1969) was one of the most powerful works to come out of the civil rights era. It captured the disillusionment following Martin Luther King, Jr.'s assassination and boldly called for socialistic reform and biracial unity in the United States alongside black empowerment.[3]

Soul City was as much a city-sized projection of McKissick's persona and his beliefs as it was a new business proposition. Developed by Floyd B. McKissick Enterprises, Incorporated, Soul City would be located on a 5,180-acre site, fifty miles north of the Raleigh/Durham/Chapel Hill area in a rural, economically depressed part of the Piedmont. Ads claimed that it would be "the only freestanding (not associated with an existing city) new town in the making," as well as "the largest and most innovative project ever undertaken by a minority-owned developer." The city was intended not only to stem the outward migration of rural blacks but also to entice urban residents from slums and ghettoes back to the countryside. It offered an alternative to metropolitan blight and decay.[4]

McKissick found an answer to the problems of urban America in black economic empowerment. For many African Americans the appeal of black power lay in its excitement and energy. Stokely Carmichael, who wrote one of the definitive explanations of black power in the late 1960s, advised that the average person "wanted to build something of his own, something that he builds with his own hands." McKissick explained in *Three-Fifths of a Man*, "Economic power is the first prerequisite for political power. Unless the Black man attains economic independence, any 'political independence' will be an illusion. White intimidation and control, especially in the ghettos and the rural South, will continue as long as the Blacks are economically dependent."[5]

The idea for Soul City gestated slowly. As a soldier overseas, McKissick had seen Europeans rebuilding their war-torn cities. Seeing the architects and engineers and city planners working in conjunction with the U.S. Army and "thinking in terms of people," it dawned on him "how few Black people were actually involved in new construction trades or new city planning or regional planning and construction [in the United States]." The massive effort to rebuild Europe also impressed upon McKissick that proper planning plus government commitment was a winning formula for such endeavors. Upon returning to the United States, he discussed the idea of an alternative city with one of his law professors, but deferred his dream until resigning from the directorship of CORE. He incorporated McKissick Enterprises on August 23, 1968 to "develop business ideas and to form additional enterprises by corporate or other forms of business structures in the building of a Black economy."[6]

According to press releases, organizations contributing to the project also included: the Soul City Company, general partners in the development; the Soul City Foundation, Inc., responsible for "social planning" for the new community; the Warren Regional Planning Corporation, developing minority business opportunities in the area; HealthCo, Inc., a "health care delivery system" designed to serve both the existing residents of Warren County and the new residents of Soul City; the Soul City Investment Corporation, designed to carry out investment ventures in the development; the Soul City Sanitary District, "the first unit of local government at Soul City," empowered to build and operate water and public health utilities while levying taxes and issuing bonds to support these utilities; and the Soul City Utilities Company, a public corporation set up to construct the water and sewage facilities.[7]

Funding for Soul City was to come from private sources and banking interests for land acquisition and preliminary staffing while the federal government would also contract specific projects. Bonds were issued under a $14 million U.S. Department of Housing and Urban Development (HUD) guarantee made possible under Title VII of the Urban Growth and New Communities Act of 1968 (as amended in 1970) certifying the "inherent economic feasibility of the project." Soul City, according to its planners, was "not a begging proposition" because it could, and would, "pay for itself."[8]

At the end of its development period, estimated to be between twenty and thirty years (McKissick told one investor that Soul City would be completed "by the end of this century"), the city would have a population of 50,000 people, supported by 24,200 "basic and dependent" jobs. It would have eight "residential clusters (villages)," each with its own elementary school as well as an "Activity Center" providing convenience services and community facilities. Soul City would also have an educational park that would offer "academic, skill development, and adult educational programs" for all individuals "above elementary level." The city would boast a man-made lake, parks, and recreational facilities comprising one-third of the total development acreage. It would have a plaza serving the whole community with shopping, "municipal structures," and a tourist complex with hotel/motel facilities, office space, meeting rooms, and—anticipating the flood of people who would want to come and visit—souvenir and gift shops. The centerpiece of this plan was to be an "Afro-American trade center," which would serve "as a link to African culture and industry." Finally, Soul City would have an industrial park, separate from the residential areas.[9]

The long tradition of African American town development offered McKissick reason to be hopeful. In the nineteenth century many free blacks organized communities where they could receive vocational and liberal arts training, serve apprenticeships, support themselves, and become self-reliant. Before the Civil War there was Brooklyn, Illinois, founded by Free Frank. Communities such as Nashoba, Tennessee, and the Port Royal Experiment on South Carolina's Sea Islands initially flourished, but ultimately proved unsustainable. After Reconstruction, black "Exodusters" migrated to Kansas, where they founded the town of Nicodemus. Mound Bayou, Mississippi; Boley, Oklahoma; and Promiseland, South Carolina followed.[10]

In the mid-twentieth century black separatists dreamed of repatriated lands within the United States where African Americans could stake their claim. Leaders of the Detroit-based Republic of New Africa (RNA) hoped to "liberate" territory in South Carolina, Georgia, Alabama, Mississippi, and Louisiana to create a separate black state. Such plans, however, were grounded more in theory than in reality, because government-subsidized start-up payments of land and $400 billion in reparations were not forthcoming. More instructive from McKissick's point of view was Columbia, Maryland, which became a model in city planning after its inception in 1963. Built from the ground up, Columbia aimed to avoid urban sprawl through mixed-use zoning; residential and recreational development would balance commercial and industrial development in what planners hoped would become an alternative to hodge-podge growth. The first residents moved into Columbia in 1967 and over the course of the next decade it thrived. Blending the nationalist consciousness of nineteenth-century black communal experiments with the thoughtful planning of Columbia, the creators of Soul City aimed to work within the system to achieve what the RNA could not achieve outside the system: a sustainable black community executed within a traditional capitalist framework.[11]

THE MAKING OF SOUL CITY

Warren County was an interesting choice for McKissick's experiment in city building. Named after a Massachusetts doctor who died fighting for American independence at Bunker Hill, Warren County is contiguous with the North Carolina–Virginia border, atop the crazy-quilt pattern of North Carolina's northeastern counties. When McKissick conceptualized Soul

City in 1969, the county was about two-thirds African American and one-third white, with a few Native Americans. With small farms dotting the area where tobacco once ruled, the county seemed to have an air of past grandeur. Second-growth oaks and pines flourished where ancient hardwoods once stood. Jack-in-the-pulpit, dogtooth violets, and Turk's cap lilies bloomed early in the spring season of wildflowers; St. John's wort, once considered a charm against evil spirits, also grew there. Place names such as Old Bethlehem, Dewberry, Greenback, and Lickskillet celebrated the county's rustic heritage. The grand Jones Spring Hotel, where politicians, planters, and gamblers thronged in the mid-nineteenth century, stood deserted and dilapidated. Robert E. Lee's daughter lay buried in a nearby cemetery, and local whites seemed to take pride in the county's Confederate heritage: a billboard at the county line welcomed visitors to "Klan Country."[12]

McKissick's choice of Warren County was strategic. In his view, the mixed ethnic and demographic makeup of the county—predominantly black, rural, and poor—favored an endeavor like Soul City. In 1969, the per capita income in Warren County was $1,638 with 6,500 people out of a total population of 15,810 living "below low income level." At $3,465, the median *family* income for African Americans was less than the national *per capita* income of $3,705. Farming was less viable than it once was; as Bernard Thompson, the white administrator of the nonprofit Soul City Foundation, put it, "the tractor has done away with the mule, and the cotton pickers [machines] have done away with the cotton pickers [laborers]." Children who grew up in Warren County were leaving in search of opportunities in Richmond, Norfolk, Washington, New York, Atlanta, Nashville, and Louisville. They left behind a demographic group that was older and poorer. Pulpwood manufacturers, which traditionally required little labor while draining an area's natural resources, employed the largest number of industrial workers. People in Warren County needed work, and with a high-school dropout rate of 44.7 percent, the region ranked behind the state average in all areas of educational achievement by its population. It was ripe for expanding industries.[13]

The area also had natural resources and infrastructure that made it attractive for industrial development, which no doubt figured into McKissick's plans. Just a few miles to the north was Kerr Reservoir, with enough water to support a sizable city. Interstate Highway 85 (I-85) was one mile to the west of the proposed site, I-95 was fifteen miles to the east, and a major railway, the Seaboard Coastline Railroad, cut through the property. It was near the Raleigh–Durham–Chapel Hill area and its airport. Close to so many good universities, Soul City would enjoy technical support from the research and development facilities associated with the region.

Some Warren County whites balked initially at the idea of Soul City. Two aspects of the proposed community bothered them. First, its socially progressive interracialism challenged local mores. Although North Carolina was more progressive than most neighboring states, many residents still sometimes met anything outside the norm with suspicion if not open hostility, and Soul City—a deliberately multiracial community in the heart of "Klan Country"—was certainly outside the norm. Second, it was a black enterprise conceptualized and engineered by African Americans. Not unlike other white southerners, white North Carolinians living in the Piedmont region sometimes interpreted such initiative by their black brethren not as healthfully ambitious but as dangerously "uppity." The former owner of the land for Soul City received so many menacing phone calls in the days after the sale that he left town for a brief cooling-off period.[14]

Local officials seemed surprised by the announcement of Soul City's coming to their area and took a wait-and-see attitude. W.A. Miles, mayor of Warrenton, said the news came as a "complete surprise," while Frank W. Reams, executive director of the Warren County Industrial Development Commission, heard of the plan "on the radio." Amos L. Capps, chairman of the Warren County Commission, said, "This could either be the worst thing that has happened, or the best, a real shot in the arm." Anticipating white fear, McKissick stressed that the community would be neither segregated nor separatist. "How do we know integration won't work?" he asked. "No one has really tried it yet. Soul City will enable blacks and whites to come together as equals."[15]

McKissick recognized industry as the essential ingredient in Soul City's success. "We need more industry in new towns," he stated. "Soul City's economic base must be oriented entirely to manufacturing." Soul City would raise the standard of living for the residents of Warren County, who would stay at home rather than migrating in search of work—"that is, if industry really gets involved to the benefit of the people, the new community and, of course, industry itself." Soultech I, the city's first industrial complex, would be one of the first four physical constructions at Soul City.[16]

McKissick moved in early 1973 from his comfortable home in New York into a trailer on the edge of a cornfield, on the site of what would become Soul City, within view of an antebellum mansion, a barn, and several ramshackle outhouses. McKissick was behind his anticipated timetable. "Everything requires negotiation," he admitted that summer. "Even industry that's interested in a site has to send in a team and you have to go back and prepare a report. But we're very, very close now."[17]

Undeniably, progress was being made. The Economic Development Administration of the U.S. Department of Commerce, the Army Corps of Engineers, and the nearby towns of Henderson and Oxford were all working with Soul City to develop a $9 million regional system that would pipe water through twenty miles of lines to all three towns. Planners were exploring innovative ideas, including recreational facilities such as the 160-acre "Afro Park." They also considered—three years *before* the creation of Habitat for Humanity—"sweat equity" home financing in which the future owner would provide his or her own labor to defray construction costs. Further expansion depended on the successful financing of a $14 million bond issue by the Soul City developers, but in the interim the community grew slowly and steadily. The inaugural issue of the *Soul City News* in late summer of 1973 included a photo of puppies playing, with the caption, "Population Increases to 33."[18]

North Carolina Governor James E. Holhouser was a strong Soul City advocate. He indicated his support for the new community in a letter to U.S. Department of Housing and Urban Development Undersecretary Floyd Hyde. "We are moving to get this project underway, as we deem [it] innovative, creative, and important to the economic development of our region," he wrote. Holhouser gave more than just lip service to Soul City; the state of North Carolina committed $1.7 million in investment capital to the venture. Soul City represented to Holhouser "one of the few positive projects in the nation today seeking to bring all of our people together" in an organized effort to "solve the problems which they face as well as those problems which face the nation as a whole." In endorsing the new town, he implied that Soul City might help to ameliorate the problems of racism, poverty, and urban violence that plagued the nation. Speaking at the city's November 9, 1973 official groundbreaking ceremony, Governor Holhouser declared it "a moment of historic proportions" during which "the eyes of the nation" were on Soul City and its "pioneers." Soul City was "far more than just another city," it was nothing short of "a tribute to man's ability to dream new dreams and to put those dreams to work."[19]

A few months later in January 1974, Soul City consisted of a skein of muddy roads, a health service, and a jumble of mobile homes that housed forty of the fifty fulltime staff: architects, planners, health and social workers, financial experts, and educational and job-training personnel. It also included a Head Start and a daycare center. Evidence of progress was abundant. The old billboard welcoming visitors to "Klan Country" still remained, but new state highway signs also announced Soul City's presence. Bulldozers and trucks were cutting and paving roads and workers were laying water and sewer lines. Construction began on Soultech I: a huge concrete, steel, and gray-glass structure encompassing 40,000 square feet of manufacturing space and 12,000 square feet of office space. Most of Soul City's tangible progress was in its exhaustive planning with shelves of statistical projections, volumes of fund-raising materials, and mountains of drafts and architectural renderings. The ratio of backlogged job applicants was about 60 percent black to 40 percent white, reflecting a truly biracial mix. Announcing the Soul City Company's completed sale of $5 million of bonds on Wall Street, McKissick declared on March 19 that Soul City "is on its way." And it was.[20]

Residents started arriving in 1974. Janice Crump, her husband, and their three children left a comfortable life in Atlanta to move into a trailer at Soul City that year. She was a Delta Airlines reservationist; her husband, a homebuilder. "We were real pioneers," she recalled five years later. They had come because they saw "more than the fields and the dirt roads and the mud." They saw "a promise of what it could be." Other early arrivals came from cities like Cleveland, Detroit, Houston, and New York and many of them worked on the Soul City Company staff.[21]

Street names reflected the racial pride and optimism of the new venture. The main street of Soul City was named Opportunity Boulevard. Some street names recalled local trees and birds, but many byways, most of which were never cut or paved, indicated a preference for heroes of black history: Nat Turner Street, Charles Howard Road, John Brown Drive, Harpers Ferry Lane, Christopher Adda Trail, Thomas Payne Pathway, Toussaint L'Overture Avenue, Henry Highland Garnet Boulevard, Frederick Douglass Street, David Walker Road, Dred Scott Drive, Harriet Tubman Lane, George White Avenue, and Sojourner Truth Trail.[22]

Brochures, pamphlets, and celebrity endorsements promoted to prospective residents the possibility of a better life. One advertisement assured potential residents that Soul City was "the first city in the world that's built around your family." It was a city designed "to fit into people's plans." The close proximity to employment ensured that "you'll spend time enjoying yourself instead of commuting." House prices reasonably ranged from $25,000 to $70,000, with townhouses starting at $20,000. Veterans Administration, Federal Housing Administration, and conventional financing would ease home ownership. Water, sewer, power, and telephone lines were in place underground, "where they won't be an eyesore." Schools, parks, medical care, and dental care were all at hand. "You'll find almost everything you could ask for in Soul City. And anything you won't find right here isn't far away," promised one brochure. In a letter signed "Country Preacher," Reverend Jesse Jackson pledged his support to Soul City, which he was certain would "become a reality." McKissick also tried to enlist heavyweight boxing champion Muhammad Ali as a Soul City investor and spokesperson.[23]

One advertisement proclaimed Soul City "The Bold Alternative" and "the responsive community." It would "provide economic opportunities for thousands of people who have been denied them in the past." The new town, "truly representative of the innovative spirit which built America," would anchor "an open society in which all people regardless of race, color, or economic status will not only be welcome but also find opportunities for self-development and freedom." Those who would participate "stand now at the threshold of a bold new venture in community development—of mission high," the brochure announced, inviting brave men and women to join. Together, the citizens of Soul City "will meet the challenge of America." It sounded almost too good to be true.[24]

McKissick aligned himself with the Nixon Administration during this period. Although in 1970 he had called President Richard M. Nixon "one of the nation's leading proponents of law and order—fascist style," just two years later he contributed to the Nixon campaign, raised funds for

Nixon, headed a national committee to persuade blacks to vote for Nixon, and served on the Committee to Re-elect the President's Black Executives Advisory Committee. Although many of his civil rights allies were stunned by this about-face, McKissick had his reasons. For one, there was no Republican party organized in Warren County, so its formation provided a convenient vehicle to challenge white Democrats at township and county commission meetings. The party in control in Washington also had the power to appoint census takers and poll watchers, which would be key positions in a new, developing community like Soul City. McKissick warned, however, against anyone's taking his support for granted. "I don't want anyone to feel he has my vote in his hip pocket," he explained. "I believe if I go to one party and can't establish what I want, then I have the freedom to go to the other party."[25]

McKissick's new political alliance greatly increased the effectiveness of his fundraising efforts. Soul City gained the support of the U.S. Department of Housing and Urban Development, which backed a $14 million federal bond to finance the project's initial development phases in the summer of 1972. Supporting Nixon, whose investments in black entrepreneurship attempted to attract African American voters, also fit with McKissick's philosophical notion that economics is the basis of American politics. McKissick's black critics charged him with allying himself too closely with the white political structure, but he defended his actions by claiming "if blacks are ever to be liberated, they must adopt a philosophy of sophistication, competence, and strategy." Whether McKissick "sold out" or not was debatable, but if he did, he certainly held out for the highest bidder. "He has learned where the money is and he's going out and getting it," one reporter noted in June 1973. "Skeptics there unquestionably are," he added, "but with the kind of money McKissick has corralled so far, they are keeping their skepticism to themselves at the moment." The HUD bond breathed life into the project, and propelled the town from the drawing boards and architectural renderings into reality.[26]

RESISTANCE TO SOUL CITY

McKissick's political swing to the right, however, failed to shield him from the backlash that federal support for the project engendered. Even as McKissick sent friendly correspondence to Senator Jesse Helms the politician asserted that "I should make clear that I do not favor the expenditure of taxpayers' funds on the project known as 'Soul City.'" Helms also threatened to audit the project "in order that all citizens may have complete facts on which to base their judgment of this type of federal spending of their tax money." McKissick tried fruitlessly to convert Helms to the cause, even visiting the Senator's Washington office, where he was denied access. Repeated invitations for Helms to visit Soul City went unanswered.[27]

Soul City's slow progress empowered its political opponents. More than $5 million in federal funds had been spent on Soul City by spring of 1975, but there were still few visible signs of success: no shops, no homes, and no industry. Premature rumors of Soul City's demise circulated, particularly in Raleigh's *News and Observer.* Senator Helms and Representative Fountain smelled blood and closed in for the kill. They called for an investigation of HealthCo, the federally funded health care facility at Soul City, which quickly became a lightning rod for controversy. Critics charged that HealthCo was "a two-house trailer enterprise in a non-populated city," staffed by workers drawing "unrealistic (i.e. exorbitant)" salaries. Taxpayers' dollars "were going down the clinic drain" in Soul City. The clinic galvanized Helms's and others' faultfinding.[28]

Political attacks on Soul City ensued. An investigation by the U.S. General Accounting Office effectively shut it down for eighteen months until the government finally lumbered to the conclusion that the project was legitimate and had clean finances. Three further audits called for by the project's Congressional critics yielded the same conclusion. Instead of championing Soul City for withstanding such harassment, the press chronicled a slow downward spiral as Soul City failed to materialize on schedule. Suggestions of nepotism and financial mismanagement took their toll. After the audits, news reports on Soul City began to highlight the enterprise's problems more than its achievements.[29]

McKissick resented media criticism of Soul City when it became personal. One particularly damning article in the *Wall Street Journal* accused him of leading an extravagant lifestyle, symbolized by his large home. "Why should anyone care how I spend my own money?" he retorted angrily. "That big house is partly to create land values . . . partly to put up our important visitors. We don't have no hotel here." Criticized for naming the Magnolia-Ernest Recreational Complex pool after his parents, he replied, "Who the hell else should I name it after?"[30]

When it became apparent that Soul City was more than just a pipedream, and that it was in fact in the process of becoming a reality, and when it became apparent that big money was involved, critics and political enemies became much more serious about challenging the enterprise. Two factors, both of which came ironically at the height of the town's success, marked the beginning of the end for Soul City. First, Soul City came about when politicians like Fountain and Helms wanted to establish credibility with their constituencies by undercutting the civil rights movement as it branched into new arenas. Second, tensions between state politicians and HUD, a federal agency, reflected the ongoing conflicts over states' rights in the South.

The HUD financing proved Faustian. It invited criticism. McKissick had to counter the perception that he was being given a handout. "Nobody is giving Soul City any 5 million," he stressed. "All HUD is saying is that if we go broke, they'll guarantee our bond obligations to the investors, and I can guarantee to you that we're not going to go broke." But this guarantee unintentionally served as a kind of license to fail. By providing a built-in bailout mechanism, HUD may have dulled the hunger and raw ambition that had made Soul City successful up to that point.[31]

HUD opted in 1979 to discontinue the new town as a Title VII development, meaning that there would be no more federal money for Soul City. The board of the HUD-affiliated New Community Development Corporation voted to phase out Soul City by acquiring the project's assets from the Soul City Corporation. "It's like cutting off a man's hand and then condemning him because he can't pick up anything," McKissick complained. "People have invested their lives in this place, much more than their money," he added. "That's what just kills me . . . we just can't let it die." The media piled on. *Newsweek* declared that the project was "far short of its goal" and "may be in danger of collapse." A local op-ed piece called the venture "little more than a fantastic dream" and "an outstanding example of government waste of public funds." The HUD report absolved McKissick of any wrongdoing, adding that Soul City's apparent failure "in no way reflects adversely on the capabilities of the developer."[32]

The North Carolina Black Leadership Caucus coordinated a "Save Soul City" campaign that petitioned President Jimmy Carter with over 1,500 signatures of support, but negative press continued to keep potential investors away while the city withered. There were some initial signs of life; Perdue, Inc., one of the nation's largest poultry companies, built a 500-acre operation in Warren County in 1979 that would remain active for decades. By the late 1980s, however, Soul City was dead to all but those living there, although some residents never conceded defeat. One woman challenged a newspaper article that declared Soul City had "all but faded away." In a letter to the *Raleigh News and Observer*, Elvira J. Kirkland wrote, "Your reporter should have investigated more thoroughly before conveying her conclusions about Soul City in the article of June 26." She asked, "Can a community that has acquired so many assets be fading away?" She cited the community's health center, volunteer fire station, preschool, recreational facilities, senior citizens' development, and other achievements as evidence of the project's vitality. But there could be no denying that Soul City never lived up to expectations. In the early 1970s, an environmental impact statement prepared by HUD estimated that about 18,000 jobs and 14,750 households would be created in Soul City over the last three decades of the twentieth century, predicting a city of 44,000 by the year 2005. It was not to pass: unofficial census data showed 80 black residents and 15 white residents in 1977, 105 blacks and 15 whites in 1979, and in the 1980s and 1990s these numbers dwindled.[33]

There are two main reasons why Soul City did not succeed: it failed to attract industry and its major benefactor, the federal government, wavered in its financial support. Some of the political opposition to Soul City was fueled by racism, but McKissick has also been criticized for his management of the operation. The economic recession of the 1970s must also be considered; it made a venture like Soul City much more difficult to realize than when it was conceived years earlier.[34]

It was a big mistake to plan the success of a city built in a rural area on attracting industry without having any advance guarantees. Warren County may have been a poor choice that affected Soul City's outcome negatively. It was an impoverished locale in a southern state long controlled by rural elites. Its proximity to Durham and Chapel Hill may have looked good in the brochures but there were few real connections, geographic proximity notwithstanding. For the vast majority of residents in Warren County, these centers of research and higher learning offered little. Locating Soul City there made its development as an industrial city of 50,000 people an uphill struggle under the best of circumstances, especially because the developers had no commitments by any large manufacturers. Furthermore, Warren County held little allure for the young black professionals who might have been interested by the promise of Soul City. Had Soul City been placed closer to Durham and Raleigh, it might have attracted more interest not only from these individuals but also from manufacturers; however, putting Soul City closer to major cities would have made land acquisition much more difficult and expensive.

It would be overly simplistic to argue that Soul City, like countless other black ventures, fell prey to the calculated efforts of political and cultural forces hostile to its success, although such efforts did occur. McKissick asked in 1979, "I wonder what we really could have accomplished had I the ongoing assistance of Senator [Robert] Morgan, Senator Helms, and Representative Fountain." Soul City's supporters were certain that racial prejudice was part of the calculus that made it fail, and certainly it motivated the likes of Helms, but was it the main factor in the federal government's abandoning the project? If all parties involved agreed that it would take twenty to thirty years to develop this project, then why did the federal government stop funding it after only seven years? President Jimmy Carter's national urban policy sought economic development through grants, loan guarantees, and interest subsidies available to private firms. When HUD withdrew, Carter was establishing an urban policy based primarily on self-help instead of federal support, which dovetailed with Soul City's long-term vision. For several possible reasons, however, including the Congressional rejection of a National Development Bank, Soul City's too-slow rate of progress, and the persistent economic downturn, the Carter Administration somehow lost faith in the venture and abruptly withdrew its support.[35]

Media often reported the shortcomings of Soul City instead of its successes largely because the venture's accomplishments fell short of the grandiose expectations that everyone—believers, skeptics, and especially Floyd McKissick himself—put on the plan. McKissick positioned Soul City as nothing short of the uplift of the race, a venture shaped by black power and a new emphasis on black economic self-determination. "This is the civil rights movement of the 1970s," he declared. McKissick perhaps contradictorily viewed Soul City as a necessary experiment in biracial community while sometimes describing it as a black venture, although he also described it as a multiracial endeavor. He was fond of quoting bluesman Huddie Ledbetter, better known as "Lead Belly," who sang:

> We're in the same boat brother,
> We're in the same boat brother,
> And if you shake one end, you gonna rock the other
> It's the same boat brother.

An idealist, McKissick knew it took cooperation across racial lines to build a city. He wore the moniker of "dreamer" proudly because he understood that it took big dreams to make a place such as Soul City work; but, in the end, dreams were not enough to make Soul City thrive in the way he hoped it would. Did hubris play a role? That is, did McKissick pursue the *national* groundwork for this project while neglecting to lay the *local* foundation, by forgetting to develop the necessary connections with government officials in Oxford, Henderson, and Warren County? In short, was Soul City a viable plan, blocked by political forces aligned against it, or is it the story of a dreamer who lacked the business and political skills to turn his vision into reality? The questions related to Soul City's demise merit further investigation and some recent studies have begun this task.[36]

As the civil rights movement grew beyond desegregation and voting rights, it became apparent that American democracy and society required even deeper reform to address racial inequalities. To realize fully the promise of the civil rights movement, African American economic empowerment needed to accompany social and political equality. Without the former, the latter carried little meaning. New black communities could serve as vehicles for this empowerment. Soul City represented the sense that black citizens were collectively creating a space to realize their own tailored version of the American Dream; it *was* the new civil rights movement of the 1970s, as McKissick claimed. As a model of city planning, it foreshadowed the trend in design to create unified, mixed-use, urban spaces that include multicultural neighborhoods and that cater to families of differing economic backgrounds. New Urbanism, as this trend is called, continues to define the cutting edge of city planning in the twenty-first century as architects and developers find new ways to unify industry and residential living while combating suburban sprawl.[37]

To call Soul City a novel concept would be to undervalue the role African Americans historically played in building America's towns and cities. "Soul City is not a new idea," McKissick explained. "We've been running cities for years. On the plantations the work was done by blacks—the black engineers, black cooks, the black blacksmith, the black carpenter, and the black roofer—they all controlled the destiny of the white man." But if Soul City represented a continuation of African American industriousness, rather than a novel expression of it, then that industriousness found an unprecedented expression in this "black-built" town. Soul City was unique insofar as it sought to avoid the poverty, crime, inopportunity, and other problems of urban America proactively—through careful planning—rather than reactively, and insofar as these creative solutions would come from African Americans themselves. The key was black power, which provided the revolutionary impetus for economic development. "Power expresses wealth; in America money doesn't talk—it screams," he noted in *Three-Fifths of a Man*. "In their attempts to achieve Black ownership of business, Black participation in economic decisions, they [African Americans] are striving for nothing less than a Black 'nationalization' of American wealth and the means for producing it."[38]

Soul City may never have become the pulsing community that McKissick envisioned, but the tidy houses, the newly renovated HealthCo facility, and the Floyd B. McKissick, Sr. Assisted Living Center all testify that Soul City never "failed," as one article claimed. Soultech I may still stand empty with foreboding "State Property—No Trespassing" signs staked around its perimeter, but the Soul City Baptist Church, whitewashed and sturdy, stands as a testament of the faith of those who came here and who continue to raise their voices in praise. The juxtaposition of unused factory space and trim, tidy houses in Soul City's single neighborhood, Green Duke Village, captures the tension between what Soul City promised to become and what it became: a quiet, pleasant, predominately African American neighborhood on the edge of Norlina and Manson, North Carolina. And yet the mighty promise of McKissick's dream still lingers, haunting the rolling hills and woodlands. It was a compelling vision, and the strongest part of Soul City remains its power as a symbol, as a hopeful expression of community.[39]

NOTES

1. McKissick quoted in Roy Parker, Jr., "Negroes to Build Town in Warren," *Raleigh News and Observer*, January 14, 1969; Paul Jablow, "Soul City Has to Start With the Spirit Itself," *Charlotte Observer*, March 30, 1969. Both articles in North Carolina Collection Clippings File, Special Collections, Wilson Library, University of North Carolina at Chapel Hill (hereafter cited as "NCCCF").
2. McKissick quoted in Herman Mixon, Jr., *Soul City: The Genesis and First Two Years of the Soul City Project, With Questions for Its Future* (Chapel Hill: Center for Urban and Regional Studies, 1971) in North Carolina Collection, Special Collections, Wilson Library, University of North Carolina at Chapel Hill.
3. "Biographical Sketch," Floyd B. McKissick Papers, Manuscripts Department, Special Collections, Wilson Library, University of North Carolina at Chapel Hill (hereafter cited as "McKissick Papers"), "Press Kit Materials, 1970–1979" File, Folder 1752.

4. "Information on Soul City, North Carolina," McKissick Papers, "Press Kit Materials, 1970–1979" File, Folder 1752.
5. Carmichael quoted in Clayborne Carson, *In Struggle: SNCC and the Black Awakening of the 1960s* (Cambridge: Harvard University Press, 1981), 205; Stokely Carmichael and Charles V. Hamilton, *Black Power: The Politics of Liberation in America* (New York: Vintage Books, 1967); Floyd McKissick, *Three-Fifths of a Man* (New York: Macmillan, 1969), 140–42.
6. McKissick quoted in Herman Mixon, Jr., *Soul City: The Initial Stages* (Chapel Hill: Center for Urban and Regional Studies, University of North Carolina at Chapel Hill, February 1971), 11–13.
7. "Information on Soul City, North Carolina," McKissick Papers, "Press Kit Materials, 1970–1979" File, Folder 1752.
8. "Information on Soul City, North Carolina."
9. "Information on Soul City, North Carolina."
10. For more on Brooklyn, Illinois, see Juliet E.K. Walker, *Free Frank: A Black Pioneer on the Antebellum Frontier* (Lexington: University Press of Kentucky, 1983); Sundiata Keita Cha-Jua, *America's First Black Town: Brooklyn, Illinois, 1830–1915* (Champaign: University of Illinois Press, 2000). For more on Nashoba and Port Royal, see William and Jane Pease, *Black Utopia: Negro Communal Experiments in America* (Madison: State Historical Society of Wisconsin, 1963); Willie Lee Rose, *Rehearsal for Reconstruction: The Port Royal Experiment* (London: Oxford University Press, 1964). For information on the Exoduster movement, see Nell Painter, *Exodusters: Black Migration to Kansas after Reconstruction* (New York: Alfred A. Knopf, 1977). See also Normal L. Crockett, *The Black Towns* (Lawrence: The Regents Press of Kansas, 1979); Kenneth M. Hamilton, *Black Towns and Profit: Promotion and Development in the Trans-Appalachian West, 1877–1915* (Champaign: University of Illinois Press, 1991); Morris Turner, *America's Black Towns and Settlements* (Rohnert Park: Missing Pages, 1999); Hannibal Johnson, *Acres of Aspiration: The All-Black Towns in Oklahoma* (Austin: Eakin Press, 2003); Elizabeth R. Bethel, *Promiseland: A Century of Life in a Negro Community* (Columbia: University of South Carolina Press, 1981).
11. William L. Van Deburg, ed., *Modern Black Nationalism* (New York: NYU Press, 1997), 197–202; John H. Bracey, Jr., August Meier, and Elliot Rudwick, eds., *Black Nationalism in America* (Indianapolis: Bobbs-Merrill, 1970), 518–23. For more on the history of Columbia, MD, see http://www.columbia-md.com [accessed May 1, 2012].
12. U.S. Bureau of the Census, *County & City Data Book, 1972: A Statistical Analysis* (Washington, DC: Superintendent of Documents, U.S. Government Printing Office, 1973), 354–57; Manly Wade Wellman, *The County of Warren, North Carolina, 1586–1917* (Chapel Hill: University of North Carolina Press, 1959), v–viii.
13. U.S. Bureau of the Census, *Historical Statistics of the United States, Colonial Times to 1970, Part I* (Washington, DC: Superintendent of Documents, U.S. Government Printing Office, 1975), 32, 225, 244; U.S. Bureau of the Census, *County & City Data Book, 1972*, 354–57; Thompson quoted in Austin Scott, "U.S. Puts $14 Million Behind Black Capitalism Project," *Washington Post*, July 3, 1972; "Fact Sheet," McKissick Papers, "Press Kit Materials, 1970–1979" File, Folder 1752.
14. Wayne King, "Soul City, N.C. Is Moving From Dream Stage to Reality," *New York Times*, January 4, 1974.
15. Jim Smith, "Warren Officials Surprised by 'Soul City,'" *Raleigh News and Observer*, January 15, 1969 in NCCCF; McKissick and Capps quoted in "Soul City's Need Is Green Power," *Business Week*, January 17, 1970, 20.

16. McKissick quoted in "New towns need industry savvy to grow and survive," *Modern Manufacturing*, May 1970, 114; Joel Haswell, "Soul City Groundbreaking Seen in 2 Months," *Durham Morning Herald*, July 20, 1973.
17. Guy Olson, "McKissick Gaining Backing for Permanent 'Soul City,'" *Atlanta Journal*, January 11, 1973; McKissick quoted in Jack Scism, "Soul City: No Scoffers Heard Now," *Greensboro Daily News*, June 3, 1973.
18. Scism, "Soul City"; *Soul City News* 1:1 (August–September 1973), McKissick Papers, "Press Kit Materials, 1970–1979" File, Folder 1754.
19. Letter from Governor James E. Holhouser, State of North Carolina Governor's Office, to Floyd Hyde, April 16, 1973, McKissick Papers, Soul City Correspondence, "James E. Holhouser, 1973–1975" File, Folder 473; Speech by Governor James E. Holhouser, Groundbreaking for Soul City, North Carolina, November 9, 1973, McKissick Papers, Soul City Correspondence, "James E. Holhouser, 1973–1975" File, Folder 473.
20. King, "Soul City, N.C.,"; Remarks by Floyd McKissick, Press Conference, Ramada Inn Hotel, Thomas Circle, Washington, DC, March 19, 1974, McKissick Papers, "Press Kit Materials, 1970–1979" File, Folder 1752.
21. Crump quoted in Joanne Omang, "Fighting Still: Founder Won't Surrender His Hopes for Soul City," *Washington Post*, July 2, 1979.
22. McKissick Papers, "Street Names, 1977" File, Folder 2067.
23. Untitled brochure, [1973?], McKissick Papers, "Press Kit Materials, 1970–1979" File, Folder 1753; Letter from Rev. Jesse L. Jackson to McKissick, August 12, 1974, McKissick Papers, Soul City Correspondence, "Rev. Jesse L. Jackson" File, Folder 480; Letter from McKissick to Muhammad Ali, February 27, 1975, McKissick Papers, Soul City Correspondence, Muhammad Ali File, Folder 215c.
24. *Soul City: The Bold Alternative*, undated pamphlet, NCCCF.
25. Jack Anderson, "Thick FBI Dossiers on Black Leaders," *Raleigh News and Observer*, May 16, 1972; McKissick quoted in Mike McGrady, "McKissick's Moderate Image Opens Up New Opportunities," *Durham Morning Herald*, August 6, 1972. Both articles in NCCCF.
26. Austin Scott, "U.S. Puts $14 Million Behind Black Capitalism Project," *Washington Post*, July 3, 1972; McKissick quoted in Lynne Harvel, "Economics Called Key to Black Liberation," *Durham Morning Herald*, February 24, 1972 in NCCCF; Scism, "Soul City".
27. Letter from McKissick to Senator Jesse Helms, November 10, 1972, McKissick Papers, Soul City Correspondence, "Senator Jesse Helms, 1972–1975" File, Folder 794; Letter from Helms to McKissick, November 27, 1972, McKissick Papers, Soul City Correspondence, "Senator Jesse Helms, 1972–1975" File, Folder 794; Letter from McKissick to Helms, November 30, 1972, McKissick Papers, Soul City Correspondence, "Senator Jesse Helms, 1972–1975" File, Folder 794. For other examples, see same file.
28. "2 in Congress Ask Inquiry on McKissick's Soul City," *New York Times*, March 9, 1975; Pat Stith, "Funding Extended—Soul City Unit Reprieved," *Raleigh News and Observer*, February 3, 1976; "Governor Plays Grantsmanship," *Raleigh News and Observer*, February 3, 1976.
29. *Information on the new community of Soul City, North Carolina: Report of the Comptroller General of the United States* (Washington, DC: General Accounting Office, 1975).
30. McKissick quoted in Neil Maxwell, "Mixed Fortunes: Black Leaders of the 1960s Have Come Out Better Than Segregationists," *Wall Street Journal*, March 12, 1979; McKissick quoted in Omang, "Fighting Still".
31. McKissick quoted in "North Carolina Gets a New Town—Soul City Underway," undated press release, McKissick Papers, "Press Kit Materials, 1970–1979" File, Folder 1752.

32. Eileen Keerdoja with Holly Morris, "Slow Progress for Soul City," *Newsweek*, June 4, 1979, 15; McKissick Papers, "Soul City Dream Seems to Have Faded," *Henderson Daily Dispatch*, July 6, 1979, "Decline of Soul City, 1979" File, Folder 1811; U.S. Department of Housing and Urban Development, HUD Resolution/Task Force Report and AVCO Report, McKissick Papers, "Acquisition of Soul City, 1979" File, Folder 1827; McKissick quoted in Omang, "Fighting Still".
33. Howard Troxler, "New Life in 'Black Belt,'" *Raleigh News and Observer*, February 14, 1979; Martha Quillin, "Dream community of Soul City has all but faded away," *Raleigh News and Observer*, June 26, 1988; Elvira J. Kirkland, "Soul City Thrives," *Raleigh News and Observer*, July 16, 1988. All three articles in NCCCF. McKissick Papers, "Campaign to Save Soul City, 1979" File, Folder 1815; U.S. Department of Housing and Urban Development, *Final environmental statement, proposed new community of Soul City, Warren County, North Carolina* (Washington, DC: HUD, 1972); Soul City Census Report, undated, McKissick Papers, "Soul City Census Report" File, Folder 2194a.
34. Foon Rhee, "Visions, Illusions, and Perceptions: The Story of Soul City," (Honors thesis, Duke University, 1984), 143–46.
35. McKissick quoted in "Floyd McKissick Reports Soul City is Faltering," *The Asheville Citizen*, May 29, 1979; Letter from Emsar Bradford, Jr. to Floyd McKissick, April 25, 1975, McKissick Papers, "Correspondence: Support for Soul City, 1975" File, Folder 1806; Anonymous note to McKissick, [July 1979?], McKissick Papers, "Decline of Soul City, 1979" File, Folder 1812. For more on the Carter administration's urban policy, see Michael A. Stegman, "National Urban Policy Revisited" in John Charles Boger and Judith Welch Wegner, eds., *Race, Poverty, and American Cities* (Chapel Hill: University of North Carolina Press, 1996), 239–41; Raymond A. Mohl, "The Transformation of Urban America since the Second World War" in Mohl, et al., *Essays on Sunbelt Cities and Recent Urban America* (College Station: Texas A&M University Press, 1990), 23.
36. McKissick quoted in "North Carolina Gets a New Town—Soul City Underway," undated press release, McKissick Papers, "Press Kit Materials, 1970–1979" File, Folder 1752; Leadbelly, quoted in *The Soul City Sounder* 2:2 (November 1975), McKissick Papers, "Newsletters, 1975" File, Folder 1772; see also McKissick, *Three-Fifths of a Man*, 21–22. For further discussion of Soul City's demise, see Timothy Minchin, "A Brand New Shining City: Floyd B. McKissick and the Struggle to Build Soul City," *North Carolina Historical Review* 82:2 (April 2005): 1–31; Roger Biles, "Rise and Fall of Soul City: Planning, Politics, and Race in Recent America," *Journal of Planning History* 4:1 (February 2005): 52–72; Devin Fergus, *Liberalism, Black Power, and the Making of American Politics, 1965–1980* (Athens: University of Georgia Press, 2009).
37. For more on New Urbanism, see Andres Duany, Elizabeth Plater-Zyberk, and Jeff Speck, *Suburban Nation: The Rise of Sprawl and the Decline of the American Dream* (New York: North Point Press, 2000). Also see Peter Calthorpe, *The Next American Metropolis: Ecology, Community, and the American Dream* (Princeton: Princeton Architectural Press, 1993); Peter Katz, *The New Urbanism: Toward an Architecture of Community* (New York: McGraw-Hill, 1994).
38. McKissick quoted in "Economics Called Key to Liberation," *Durham Morning Herald*, February 24, 1972 in NCCCF; McKissick, *Three-Fifths of a Man*, 43.
39. Allen VanNoppen, "Soul City: A Dream Dies," *Durham Sun*, November 30, 1987 in NCCCF.

Contributors

Enrico Beltramini is a faculty member in the department of religion and philosophy at Notre Dame de Namur University in Belmont, California, where he teaches the history of Christianity and other courses. He has previously held academic posts at the Università Cattolica in Milan, Italy and Santa Clara University (California) where he taught courses in business and management. He is the author of a book on Modern Catholicism and articles in anthologies and academic journals in business and church history.

J. Michael Butler is an associate professor of history at Flagler College in St. Augustine, Florida. Butler has authored *Victory After the Fall: The Memories of Civil Rights Activist H. K. Matthews* (NewSouth, 2009), published essays in the *Journal of Southern History*, *Florida Historical Quarterly*, *Southern Cultures*, *Popular Music and Society*, and the *Journal of Mississippi History*, and has written numerous book reviews and encyclopedia entries for various academic publications. He is currently working on a book that examines the aftermath of desegregation in Pensacola, Florida, which is tentatively titled *Beyond Integration: The Long Civil Rights Movement in Pensacola, 1950–2000.*

Derek Charles Catsam is an associate professor of history at the University of Texas of the Permian Basin. He is the author of *Freedom's Main Line: The Journey of Reconciliation and the Freedom Rides* (University Press of Kentucky, 2009) and *Bleeding Red: A Red Sox Fan's Diary of the 2004 Season* (New Academia, 2005). He writes about race and politics in the United States and South Africa and is currently working on a book on bus boycotts in those countries in the 1940s and 1950s. He writes about African affairs for the New York-based Foreign Policy Association.

Carla J. DuBose is a doctoral candidate in history at the Graduate Center of the City University of New York. She recently defended her dissertation entitled "The 'Silent Arrival': The Second Wave of the Great Migration and its Effect on Black New York, 1940–1950," which examines the effects of the World War II migration of African Americans to New York City. Her research interests include American, African American, New York City, and urban history. Carla has instructed courses at City, Hunter, and York Colleges in CUNY and served as a teaching assistant at Barnard College.

Stephanie Dyer is an associate professor of American history and political economy in the Hutchins School of Liberal Studies at Sonoma State University. Her research focuses on the role of retail spaces in local economies and communities.

Michael Ezra is a professor of American multicultural studies at Sonoma State University. His previous books are *Muhammad Ali: The Making of an Icon* (Temple University Press, 2009) and *Civil Rights Movement: People and Perspectives* (ABC-Clio, 2009). He has contributed essays and reviews to the *Journal of American History*, *American Studies*, and the *Journal of African American History*, among others.

gloria-yvonne is an independent scholar who earned her Ph.D. in History, Gender, and Women's Studies from the University of Illinois at Chicago. Her dissertation "A Passion for Social Equality: Mary McLeod Bethune's Race Woman Leadership and the New Deal" examines Bethune's political activism while director of a New Deal agency, her leadership of the National Council of Negro Women, and her political friendship with Eleanor Roosevelt. gloria-yvonne's research interests include gender and ethnicity during the trans-Atlantic slave trade, transnational abolitionism in the nineteenth century, women's social and political activism, and life-writing studies.

Rhonda Jones is an assistant professor and director of the graduate public history program at North Carolina Central University. Specializing in twentieth-century U.S. history and cultural resource management, she recently completed a manuscript on African American philanthropy and voluntarism during the civil rights movement. A recipient of several honors, awards, and fellowships, Jones earned her doctorate at Howard University.

Justin T. Lorts is the director of studies at Whitman College, Princeton University. His teaching and research centers on race, civil rights, and popular culture in modern America. He is currently completing a book-length study of the cultural politics of African American comedy during the civil rights era.

Ibram H. Rogers is an assistant professor of Africana Studies at the University at Albany, SUNY. He is the author of *The Black Campus Movement: Black Students and the Racial Reconstitution of Higher*

Education, 1965–1972 (Palgrave MacMillan, 2012), the first national study of black student activism in the late 1960s and early 1970s. He has published essays on the black campus movement in several journals, including the *Journal of Social History*, *Journal of African American Studies*, *Journal of African American History*, and *The Sixties: A Journal of History, Politics and Culture*.

Christopher B. Strain is a professor of American studies at the Harriet L. Wilkes Honors College of Florida Atlantic University. A historian whose research interests include civil rights, hate crime, and violence, he is the author of three books: *Pure Fire: Self-Defense as Activism in the Civil Rights Era* (University of Georgia Press, 2005), *Burning Faith: Church Arson in the American South* (University Press of Florida, 2008), and *Reload: Rethinking Violence in American Life* (Vanderbilt University Press, 2010).

Kieran W. Taylor is an assistant professor of American history at The Citadel: The Military College of South Carolina. He is co-editor of volumes three and four of *The Papers of Martin Luther King Jr.* (University of California Press), as well as *American Labor and the Cold War* (Rutgers University Press). He is presently at work on a book about labor radicalism in the 1970s.

Orion A. Teal is a specialist in twentieth-century American political culture. He earned a Ph.D. in history from Duke University. His dissertation, titled "Building a Better World: Youth, Radicalism, and the Politics of Space in New York, 1945–1965," examines the importance of social space and intergenerational exchange in the American Left during the early Cold War.

Index

A

Abernathy, Ralph, 99
Ali, Muhammad, 3–4, asked to endorse Soul City, 195; bout with Chuvalo, 109–112; draft resistance of, 106–108; fights in Europe, 113–114; formation of Main Bout, Inc., 104–106; opens up hamburger restaurant, 176; title defenses in United States, 114–117
American Camping Association (ACA), 63, 66
American Civil Liberties Union (ACLU), 83, 94
American Federation of Labor (AFL), 41
American Jewish Committee (AJC), 82–83
American Legion, 65, 66, 110
Amos 'n' Andy Show, The, 3, 75–84
A&P supermarkets, 47, 128, 141, 142, 145, 146, 149, 150
Arum, Bob, 105, 108, 117

B

Baker, Ella, 11
Baker, General, 158, 160–164, 167
Barry, Marion, 177
Berkley, Charles, 39
Bethune, Mary McLeod, 2, helps NCNW build coalitions, 26–32; overview of career, 22–23; pressures Roosevelt for black representation in U.S. Armed Forces, 23–25, 38; speaks to Interracial Workshop, 53
Black capitalism movement: decline of, 182–183; increasing popularity of, 174–176; Nixon Administration support of, 176–182; origins of, 172–174
Black Economic Union (BEU), 173–174
Black Expo, 132, 133
Black Panther Party: as anti-colonialist vanguard, 137, 140, 151; battles with cultural nationalists, 161; London-based movement, 162–163; partnerships with Detroit auto workers, 155; rifts within, 159, 165; working relationship with Operation Breadbasket, 132
Black Workers Congress, 164–167
Blatz Beer, 75–76, 78–80, 81, 83
Brimmer, Andrew, 178, 179, 182
Brooklyn Navy Yard, 3, 37, 40–41
Brooklyn Urban League (BKUL), 3, 39–41, 43
Brotherhood of Sleeping Car Porters (BSCP), 2, C.L. Dellums representation of, 78; founding of by Randolph, 9; role in New Negro Congress, 10–14; support for March on Washington, 15–20, 24, 38, 48
Brown, Jim, 105–106, 111, 116–117
Brown v. Board of Education, 1, 55, 66, 77, 92
Build, Brother, Build, 138
Bunche, Ralph, 11

C

Camp Kinderland, 61
Camp Midvale, 60, 61, 68–70
Camp Wo-Chi-Ca: commitment to interracialism, 63–65, 67; pressure from authorities during Red Scare, 58–61

Camp Woodland, 60–61, 65–68
Charleston Hospital Strike, 155–158
Chuvalo, George, 109–115
Clark, Kenneth and Mamie, 66
Communist Party (CP), 14, 58–62, 64, 159
Conference on National Defense, 26, 31
Congress of Industrial Organizations (CIO), 13, 41, 42, 80
Congress of Racial Equality (CORE), 5, 94, embrace of black capitalism, 174–176; involvement in *Amos 'n' Andy Show* boycott, 80; as mainstream civil rights organization, 62, 70; McKissick's involvement with, 188–190; partnerships with auto workers, 155; rifts within, 159; sponsorship of Interracial Workshop, 52

D
Daley, Richard, 107, 108
Davis, Lorenzo, 41
Dobbins, William Curtis (W.C.), 93–100
Dodge Revolutionary Union Movement (DRUM), 159, 163–165, 167
"Don't Buy Where You Can't Work" campaigns, 35, 47, 48, 80
Drug and Hospital Workers Local 1199, 67, 157–158

E
Eisenhower, Dwight, 81
Elebash, Eugene, 100
Economic Opportunity Loan (EOL), 173, 183
Eurquhart, Raymond, 158, 162–63, 167
Executive Order (EO) 8802, 16, 17, 29, 39, 48

F
Fair Employment Practices Commission (FEPC), 16, 17, 19, 39–43
Federal Bureau of Investigation (FBI), 60, 62, 112, 120–22n22
Forman, James, 158–159, 164, 165, 166–167, 177
Fountain, L.H., 188, 197, 199

G
Garvey, Marcus, 12, 160, 173
Granger, Lester, 11, 16, 29, 38
Greyhound Lines, 46, 94–95

H
Haddock, Wilbur, 154–155, 159, 164
Hamlin, Mike, 164–165, 167
Hampton Institute, 13, 36, 166
Harvey, Raymon, 93–95, 97–98
Hastie, William, 25, 46, 49
HealthCo, 190, 197, 201
Helms, Jesse, 188, 196, 197, 199
Hill, T. Arnold, 24, 48
Hillman, Sidney, 25, 29
Holhouser, James E., 194
House Un-American Activities Committee (HUAC), 14, 60, 83
Howard University, 3, 46, faculty engagement with Interracial Workshop, 53; Negro Women in National Defense conference at, 30; student movement, 49–52, 55
Humphrey, Hubert, 174, 175

I
Illinois State Athletic Commission (ISAC), 107–108
Innis, Roy, 174, 176, 177
International Workers Order (IWO), 60–61, 63–65
Interracial Workshop (IW), 52–54

J
Jackson, Jesse, 4, buy-black campaigns, 176; coordinates boycotts of stores, 128, 141; "economic bill of rights," 181; endorses Soul City, 195; formation of Operation Breadbasket, 125–126; leadership of Operation Breadbasket, 130–134
James, C.L.R., 162
Jenkins, Esau, 156
Johnson Administration, *See* Johnson, Lyndon
Johnson, Lyndon, 131, 147, 173, 175, 183

K
Kerner, Otto, 106, 107, 108
King, Martin Luther, Jr., 1, 2, assassination of, 159, 189; contrasted with Jesse Jackson, 130–134; invited to speak in Pensacola, 99;

leadership of Operation Breadbasket, 125–130; March on Washington speech, 20; praises labor unions, 67; use of Christianity to justify protest, 93
Kirschner, Carl, 70
Ku Klux Klan, 65, 67, 69, 95, 192, 193, 194

L
Larkin Committee, 61, 66–67
League of Revolutionary Black Workers, 163–164
Lewis, John, 2, 46
Lipsyte, Robert, 112, 113
Liston, Sonny, 105, 109, 110, 116
Local 1199 Drug and Hospital Workers Union, 67, 157–158
Louisville Sponsoring Group, 104, 111

M
Madison Square Garden, 17, 18, 109, 115, 121
Matthews, H.K., 96, 100
Main Bout, Inc., 3–4, formation of, 104–106; initial resistance to, 106–109; promotion of fights outside the United States, 109–114; run out of business, 116–117
Malitz, Mike, 105, 111, 116–117
March on Washington for Jobs and Freedom (1963), 2, 20, 56, 70
Matthew, Dr. Thomas W., 173, 176
McGee, Willie, 58, 63, 73n14
McKissick Enterprises, Inc., 176, 189, 190
McKissick, Floyd, 5, battles resistance to Soul City, 196–201; building and formation of Soul City, 189–196; goals for Soul City, 176, 188
March on Washington proposed by A. Philip Randolph during 1940s, *see* March on Washington Movement
March on Washington Movement (MOWM), 2, 9, 14–20, 29–30, 39, 47–49
Minority Enterprise Small Business Investment Company (MESBIC), 179
Montgomery Bus Boycott, 1, 47, 84, 92
Moultrie, Mary, 155–59, 167–68

N
Nation of Islam, 104–106, 110, 117, 132, 160, 173
National Association for the Advancement of Colored People (NAACP), 3, 62, 162, anti-communism of, 59; at Howard University, 50–51; leads boycott of *Amos 'n' Andy Show*, 75–84; limited stance on economic issues criticized, 11, 12; national office relationship with Pensacola branch, 91–93, 100–101; push for economic inclusion of blacks in war industries, 36–39, 43; support of labor unions, 67; support for March on Washington Movement, 14–18, 24, 48; Washington, DC branch, 55
National Association of Colored Women (NACW), 22, 27, 30
National Bankers Association, 175, 179
National Council of Negro Women (NCNW), 2–3, 22–32, 38, 53
National Negro Congress (NNC), 2, 3, 9, rise and fall of, 10–14, 17, 19; pressure on government to integrate war industries, 36, 39, 41–43
National Negro Industrial and Economic Union (NIEU), 106, 173–174
National Urban League (NUL), 11, 15, 18–19, 24, 29, 36, 39
National Youth Administration (NYA), 22, 26, 38
Negro Labor Victory Committee (NLVC), 41–42
New Deal, 11, 12, 22, 23, 32, 134
New Negro Alliance (NNA), 3, 46–48, 53, 55
New York State War Council Committee on Discrimination (COD), 37–40, 43
1964 Civil Rights Act, 154, 157, 173
Nixon Administration, *See* Nixon, Richard
Nixon, E.D., 16
Nixon, Richard, 4, 131, effect of resignation on black capitalism, 182–183; relationship with Floyd McKissick, 195–96;

support for black capitalism, 147, 172, 174–181

O

Office of Minority Business Enterprise (OMBE), 177, 179, 180–181, 182
Operation Breadbasket (OB), 4, 125–134, 141–142
Operation PUSH, 134
Opportunities Industrialization Center (OIC), 137, 139, 142, 147

P

Patterson, Floyd, 105, 109
Pensacola Council of Ministers (PCM), 93–96, 98–101
Pensacola NAACP, 91, 96, 99, 101
Pensacola NAACP Youth Council, 93–101
Poitier, Sidney, 81
Powell, Adam Clayton, Jr., 11, 16, 37, 112
Powell, Ruth, 50–51
Progress Development Services Corporation (PDSC), 147–149
Progress Plaza, 4, attempts to replicate its success, 147–151; as black power symbol, 176; early stages of, 138–143; importance to Philadelphia African Americans, 137–138; struggles over composition of, 143–147
Puerto Ricans, 37, 63, 67
Pullman Company, 9–10, 12, 13, 16

R

Randolph, A. Philip, 2, creation of Brotherhood of Sleeping Car Porters, 9–10; creation of March on Washington Movement and pressure on Roosevelt, 14–20, 24, 28–30, 38–39, 48–49; formation and split from National Negro Congress, 10–14
Ransom, Leon, 53, 55
Red Scare, 3, 54, 59, 60–61, 66, 70–71
Robeson, Paul, 63, 64–65, 66
Robinson, Jackie, 64, 76
Rockefeller, Nelson, 27–28, 75
Roosevelt Administration, *See* Roosevelt, Franklin
Roosevelt, Eleanor, 23, 26, 28, 29, 31
Roosevelt, Franklin: authorization of Fair Employment Practices Commission, 19; pressured by Bethune to open up war industries and U.S. Armed Forces to African Americans, 22–25, 27–31; pressured by Randolph to open up war industries and U.S. Armed Forces to African Americans, 14–17, 38–39, 48
Rustin, Bayard, 15, 53

S

Samuels, Howard J., 175, 176
Saunders, William, 155–158, 168
Schenley Industries, 78–80, 82–83
Sit-ins, 1, 2, 49–51, 55, 95–96, 97–100
Small Business Association (SBA), 140, 147, 148, 173–176, 178, 180, 182
Soul City, 5, 154, 176, 188–201
Southern Christian Leadership Conference (SCLC), 4, 125–128, 133, 156, 157
Stans, Maurice H., 177, 178–179, 180
Strawberry Square, 148–149
Student Nonviolent Coordinating Committee (SNCC), 2, affiliation with William Saunders, 156; James Forman as member of, 158–159, 177; as mainstream civil rights organization, 62; rifts in, 165
Students for a Democratic Society, 155
Studer, Norman, 65–68
Stimson, Henry L., 31, 49
Sullivan, Ed, 77, 78
Sullivan, Leon, 4, 176, attempts to replicate Progress Plaza model, 147–151; capitalization of Progress Plaza, 138–141; management decisions with ZIA about Progress Plaza, 141–147; overview of involvement with Progress Plaza, 137–138; selective patronage campaigns, 125

T

10–36 Plan, 139, 140, 143, 144, 145
Terrell, Ernie, 104–112, 115, 120–122
Three-Fifths of a Man, 189, 201
Truman, Harry, 77, 78
Tuskegee University, 36, 51

U

United Auto Workers (UAW), 161

United Black Brothers (UBB), 155
United Food and Commercial Workers Union, 146, 150
Urban League. *See* National Urban League
U.S. Armed Forces, 14, 16, 22, 24, 39, 48
U.S. Department of Housing and Urban Development (HUD), 154, 176, 190, 194, 196–199
U.S. Department of War. *See* War Department

V

Van Osten, Edmond, 36–37
Vietnam War: comparison between being a solider and a factory worker, 165–166; effects on black capitalism, 131; GI support for Leon Sullivan, 140; Muhammad Ali's draft resistance, 104, 106–107, 108, 110

W

War Department, 24, 25, 31
Washburn, Robert, 37
Washington, Mary Harrison, 94, 97–98
Watson, John, 164–165
Weaver, Robert, 25
Wechsler, Katy, 67, 68
Weston, M. Moran, 42
White Citizen's Council, 92
White, Walter: influence on NAACP boycott of *Amos 'n' Andy Show*, 78, 79, 82, 83; meeting with Roosevelt about desegregation of war industries and U.S. Armed Forces 24; support for Brooklyn NAACP, 37–38; support for March on Washington Movement, 14, 16, 29, 48
Whitfield, Ed, 158, 167
Wilkins, Roy, 59, 77, 79
Williams, Robert F., 160, 162
Woolworth's, 94–98
World War II, 1, 2, 3, 4, 47, 49, 56, 77, "Double V" campaign, 35; effect on economy, 63, 131, 138, 173; fear of black unemployment after, 42; influence on black freedom struggle, 22, 23, 32, 43, 92; influence on communists, 58, 59–60, 70–71

X

X, Malcolm, 160, 162, 173

Y

Young Men's Christian Association (YMCA), as integrated institution, 62, 70; as Jim Crow institution, 53–54; pressure on Roosevelt to desegregate war industries, 38; support for March on Washington Movement 15, 18
Young, Whitney, 125

Z

Zion Investment Associates (ZIA), 4, 137, 139–151

Made in United States
North Haven, CT
17 December 2022